Mother/Daughter Duets

Relationships in Counterpoint:
A Story and Workbook for
Adult Daughters and Older Mothers

Jennifer Rosvally and Shura Saul

PublishAmerica
Baltimore

First printing

ISBN: 1-4241-5973-3
PUBLISHED BY PUBLISHAMERICA, LLLP
www.publishamerica.com
Baltimore

Printed in the United States of America

This book is dedicated
to
Great Grandmother Bubby
and
to Nanny
on whose shoulders we stand
and who taught us about unconditional love
and to
all the woman of our family-
past…present…and future

Acknowledgments

Our profound thanks to the women who offered their stories with or without revealing their identities. Their courage, openness, and willingness to share these important and intimate experiences of their lives lie at the heart of this book. The honesty and sincerity of their offerings authenticate its usefulness and fulfill the authors' purpose.

Contributors

Mollie Aarons, Leni Bonnevaux, Yvette Bonnevaux, Kristy Cadil, Danielle Constantine, Rosalie Cutting, Maxine Davis, Alicia Delzio, Antoinette Delzio, Lori De Paollo, Ann Danoff, Lani Donlon, Amy Eisenberg, Bonnie Eisenberg, Judy Feld, Carla Feinkind, Efriana Reyes-Figueroa, Beverly Feuer, Caryn Feig, Denise Frasca, Genevieve Gochuico, Sylvia Grobe, Hannah Jones, Judy Harris, Beryl Hoffman, Louise Kelsey, Charlotte Kamenir, Christine Kerr, Sara Kruzansky, Gitel Kuselewitz, Katherine Lacey, Mary Kay Lacey, Denise Lenchner, Celina Reyes-Levine, Jennifer Levison, Nina Lisenco, Wendy Lay, Barbara Loghry, Christine McDonald, Phyllis Mandel, Shirley Manknell, Blossom Neuschatz, Dorothy Perron, Wendy Perron, Judy Quist, Harriet Richards, Wendy Robinson, Arlyne Rochlin, Linda Marie Romeo, Peta Rowell, Edith Sarah, Edna Schneider, Jeanette Schneider, Shirley Schuster, Kathryn Stuckey, Faye Sultan, Carole Sussman, Bernice Trossman, Kathryn Wong, Suey Wong, Jocelyn Zartz.

Special thanks are due to William Rosvally and Jon Saul for their patient guidance through the mysteries of the computer; to Denise Lenchner and Mary Kay Lacey for their generous help in editing; and to Danielle, Matthew, and Amy Rosvally for their artistic and photographic talents. The authors owe a huge debt of gratitude to George Rosvally for his dedicated and creative expertise in formatting this massive manuscript in accord with the publisher's requirements. Finally, thanks to Publish America for recognizing the possibilities of our manuscript when many others did not.

—Jennifer Rosvally and Shura Saul

Table of Contents

Chapter One
Intermezzo

I'm not so fearful, dearest friends
Of growing old and juiceless
As I would find it tearful if
I just stayed young and useless!

—*Shura Saul*

"A woman isn't born a woman. One becomes one."
—*Simone de Beauvoir*

Please Read This First

About This Book

Duets examines a range of concerns in the relationships between mature daughters and their mothers growing old. We ourselves, the co-authors, are such a mother/daughter team. Shura is the older mother in her middle-eighties; Jennifer, the mature daughter in her early fifties. Both voices are represented in this book. Together, we address some of the concerns of this relationship and attempt to guide readers towards a heightened self-awareness of the individual and unique circumstances of their own relationships. The spotlight is focused on the dynamics of the adult mother/daughter interactions, highlighting the changes that occur during maturation.

To deepen and authenticate the perspectives of *Duets*, we have sought the views of women of both ages. Some have been interviewed. Some have written their own stories in their own words. Still others preferred to talk with us and allow us to tell their stories as they dictated them. We have checked our presentations with them to be sure we heard them as they wanted to be heard. Sixty women are presented here; twenty of them are the older mothers, a group whose voices are rarely heard.

Our respondents live in various parts of the planet. They come from many areas of the United States, New York, California, Florida, the Midwest and others. There are also stories from women in England, Scotland, South Africa, Puerto Rico, China, and New Zealand to name a few. These women are ethnically diverse as well; they include Caucasian American and Europeans, Hispanic, African-American, Hawaiian, Chinese, and Japanese. We believe their contributions validate the basic approach of this book, namely, that the mother/ daughter bond is never dissolved regardless of the impact, positive or negative, of life situations.

The women represented here are neither stars nor headliners. Essentially they come from middle-class and working class families. Some, not all, are professionally trained or educated.

Some are in a fairly high economic bracket, most are in the middle-economic bracket, and some are indeed in a very poor economic situation. They are quite different, yet the commonality of this bond becomes clear as we read their stories and understand their viewpoints against our own backdrop of experiences.

Every individual has a story to tell. Every person is unique and so is every story. We, the authors, feel privileged to have been permitted to know the experiences shared with us here. Sad, glad, funny, angry— the whole gamut of human emotions is filtered through these tales.

We have combined the first-person presentations with our commentaries and workbook exercises. Non-judgmental and descriptive, we offer these stories, presenting the teller's views blended with our own. The universality of the mother/daughter experience speaks for itself.

How We Hope This Book Will Be Used

This book is fun to work with as well as to read. We have employed various art forms hoping to reach you, our readers, through whatever media work best for you. We expect that the poetry, journaling, story telling, anecdotes, illustrations, and cartoons as well as the exercises, will be avenues through which you may explore your own views and perspectives toward deepening your insights and self-understanding. You are encouraged to use your own style and creativity for problem solving, coping with life's challenges, and furthering your inner peace.

Each chapter is concerned with a significant dimension of this multi-faceted exploration. Every chapter offers stories and interviews followed by authors' comments. You are encouraged to write your comments in the space provided. Each chapter includes exercises related to the theme of the chapter. These are intended as experiences through which the reader may extend her view. Every chapter also includes "guideposts for thought." These are offered to motivate the flow of your own ideas after reading the chapter.

Chapter One is essentially introductory, a sampling of the modes of expression that will be encountered throughout the book. Some attention is given to the earlier developmental stages, which are of course, critical to each person's maturation. The focus however is upon the two specific maturational stages, mid-life and aging, which are scrutinized throughout the book, always against the backdrop of each individual's circumstances and growth.

Chapter Two identifies some of the building blocks of relationships namely, love, trust, commitment and intimacy. These are discussed within the context of the mother/daughter relationship. This chapter suggests that for each woman of the dyad, her own maturation has offered new and added perspectives about her altered behavior, emotions, attitudes and thoughts as well as those of the other woman in the relationship. These are explored within the context of the storied experiences.

Chapter Three explores some issues of mothers and daughters living in proximity during their adult years. A range of possible scenarios is presented with thought provoking commentary and relevant exercises through which readers may relate to implications of the particular story.

Chapter Four similarly explores issues that arise for mothers and daughters living at a distance from each other during their adult years. Distance is considered in several different dimensions such as, geographic, ideological, emotional, etc.

Chapter Five considers the lifetime concerns of care giving and both physical and emotional nourishing. We discuss some issues of dependence/independence, changes in role and self-image, filial and maternal responsibility and their emotional accompaniments. These and other such concerns are viewed through a range of scenarios. The reader may begin to explore her own experiences against the backdrops offered by others.

Chapter Six looks at loss, death, and bereavement, and how these may affect the balance of existing relationships between mother and daughter, as well as within the family as a whole.

Chapter Seven is the final chapter offering a range of situations. Human beings being what we are, there is, of course, no recipe for "what works." The stories here are about "working it out" and/ or "making it work or not work." The stories in this chapter support the two basic premises of this book: one, that this unique relationship is a lifelong bond that requires understanding and nurturing as a vital dimension of the quality of each woman's life, and two, that this relationship can change and mature as the women themselves change and mature.

Prelude

We human beings are complex creatures and, like snowflakes, no two alike.

We are not perfect. With this as premise, we are perfectly imperfect. This world is one of duality. Two sides of the coin exist simultaneously. There is the glass half full and half empty. Both true, but we seem to focus on one half at a time.

It seems to be part of the human condition to want to go toward pleasure. Self-discovery is required if pleasure is to be achieved. The journey of self-discovery requires each of us to develop a non-judgmental, honest, self-accepting observer within ourselves, who is self-loving and caring. This observer can be helpful by pointing out her observations in a loving, accepting manner. The observer may often observe the person obsessing over a thought and will point out, "There you go, being human again!" Unfortunately, due to the nature of the human condition, we each seem also to have a saboteur within. This is a result of early conditioning and an imperfect world. Self-awareness can help to recondition and ultimately dissolve the saboteur.

Maturation is the growth and development of each person as life's path is traversed. Although the process is different for each person, there are some universal developmental stages of life. Viewed from the mother/daughter perspective, the infant is part of the mother and cannot survive without nurturing. The toddler begins to separate and becomes more of an individual personality. The stage known as latency, roughly four to eleven years of age, afford the child the opportunity to develop further as a separate being by exploring the world in a contained, safe environment. Pre-puberty prepares the child for the storm of adolescence through which the child becomes an adult.

The task of adolescence is for the child to find herself as an individual separate from her parents.

Early adulthood offers the canvas of life ahead into which the individual mixes and paints her own colors.

This book begins at the mid-life stage, when the spectrum of colors becomes deepened and diversified. For our variations, we say, "Vive la difference!" for we fill each other's lives with medleys of music, and we fill the world with radiant color.

In presenting thoughts about mid-life and aging, we realize that we can only touch on some of the contours of the process and present only some of the available images. Like the diversity of snowflakes, each of us must fill in our own designs and weave our own patterns as we live them.

However, being members of the same species, we also seek similarities which enable us to understand one another and with such understanding, to help each other as well as ourselves.

Toward achieving mutual understanding, as well as in appreciation of our diversity, we offer the range of thoughts and experiences in the ensuing chapters.

This book may be read forwards or backwards or portions selected randomly. We hope you find something with which you can identify, and which will give you pleasure, satisfaction and insight.

We ask each reader to use what is relevant, adapt what is suitable, and identify those individual differences, which make you the unique person you are.

"Why should we all dress after the same fashion? The frost never paints my windows twice alike!"
—Lydia Maria Child

The Woman at Mid-life
Jennifer's Voice

With Each Stroke of the Brush,
an Original New Shade of Color Is Invented.

As we move into the mid-life stage, perspective becomes redefined…as we ourselves become redefined. Just as the move from childhood to adolescence "shape shifted," so too, does the sense of self change at this time. We recognize that we are not our parents.

The mid-life shift teaches us that we are mortal. A woman with graying hair is reminded of her body's aging process. Some women accept this change and wear it like a trophy…others color the gray trying to deny destiny. Acts, like plastic surgery and face-lifts, are attempts to hold on to the "self identity" with which the woman has grown comfortable, the body recognition she has known. But even as she goes for that face-lift, on some level, she knows that her body is changing and that it needs to be cared for differently. There is no denying nature!

With Aging Comes Wisdom

What does that cliché mean? Well, wisdom at this time of life involves the ability to make effective choices among alternatives and existing conditions that present themselves.

Our perceptions of time shifts as we begin to perceive the road ahead as being shorter than the one that lies behind. The upside is that we have developed a collection of original shades that offer a greater repertoire of life skills and strategies. The wisdom lies in how we use those skills.

We seem to be more introspective and self-understanding at this point in life. This ability allows us to see our own boundaries and thus we are able to accept others and their limitations. In fact, such acceptance can offer great peace.

The Dramas of Life Weave a
Complicated Pattern for Mid-life Women

We are busy with our families and their growing members.

We are busy with careers in a culture where "seasoned and mature" are not as valued as "young and fresh."

We are busy with aging parents who are facing their own mortality, legal, financial and medical issues. Our views of our moms are changing to become more understanding and compassionate. The relationship develops a sweeter flavor as daughters celebrate moms' birthdays at seventy-five, eighty, and up.

We are busy reshaping our relationships with others around us…with our world.

We are busy creating and re-creating our friendships, our hobbies and interests.

We are busy redesigning our egos—and their relationships with the outside world. A perspective emerges…we are each not separate but rather part of a universal whole.

There is a great need to become more agile and flexible so that we can take in, absorb, and process these whirlwinds of change.

The Drama Also Includes Enormous Loss

Our children are separating and individuating.

Our parents are dying, becoming ill, or otherwise more dependent than before this.

Circles and patterns are altered or broken through these changes and losses.

With the Closing of Some Doors, Others May Open

Losses sometimes provide openings for new gains.

We may, perhaps, discover latent talents.

New roads may lead us to new interests.

We may become pregnant with new potentials...new expertise.

Sometimes the old takes on new shape and transforms itself into opportunities that only dreams could offer before.

Our careers are peaking as we become more competent.

Opportunities to advance become more available. New doors open.

The shades of invented colors become more vivid, deeper in quality because of our deepening understanding of ourselves.

So—although mid-life is a time of great change and some loss, it is also a time of great excitement for new potentials to take form.

As We Can Change and Accept Re-Shaping—Energies Shift and New Colors Appear

"The way I see it, if you want the rainbow, you got to put up with the rain."
—Dolly Parton

The Rear-View Mirror

by Suey Wong

Daughter of Ngai Ying Wong

My mother was born in 1926 in a poor village of about fifty families in the Pearl River delta region where the men had left home, being part of the Chinese Diaspora that found their way to the Americas. She lived in the house of her paternal grandmother, who had bound feet. She shared the house with the wives of two of Grandmother's sons. They drew water from the well. They used outhouses. Her grandmother wove her own linen cloth. They spent their days in physical labor in some activity or another related to food production, preparation, or preservation. They were considered fortunate because they had better than a dirt floor, and they had one of four looms in that village. Her mother was educated and could read and write and thus was a teacher to the village children. She lived in a matriarchal society of women who were unrelated to each other except by marriage and who were bound together only by filial duty and a general sense of responsibility to maintain the family social structure.

The years in between her birth and now have been difficult. She survived the Japanese invasion of China and the ensuing Second World War. She managed to survive the forced labor camp where she was beaten when the Communists took control of China. She dealt with the sadness from the death of the baby son lost to malnutrition. She managed to integrate into life in the United States after she immigrated. She labored with my father in the laundry. She is now often lonely as she misses her husband and sister who have predeceased her. She is remarkably upbeat and adaptive in dealing with her non-Chinese in-laws, managing modern electronic conveniences, making new acquaintances, and navigating life in the 21st century.

She is in the rear-view mirror stage of her life and is appreciative for all her good fortune, which she deems considerable. Her life is defined by her family and as her family is well, she is well. This core value, in elegant simplicity, is her lodestar. She is now in her late seventies and lives modestly in her debt-free condominium with enough of an investment portfolio to support herself for the remainder of her years. Her four children are educated, have families, and are prospering. She joyously counts seven healthy grandchildren as part of her great wealth.

Born in 1949, I am in the middle of my life, looking forward still but having an appreciation of the road already traveled. My road has been trying at times but far less arduous than that of my mother. Do I have the flexibility of my parents to accept future difficulties? Can I ever achieve her level of satisfaction and serenity? Will I look back at seventy-seven and be able to say I have accomplished as much as my mother? From my viewpoint, she's climbed a mountain. To date, I have managed a gentle slope. Has my Americanization polluted those early values and clouded my vision? Have feminism, consumerism, material comfort corrupted my sensibilities? Will my daughter appreciate my lifework as I appreciate my mother's?

I don't know. Ask her when I'm seventy-seven.

"Age is totally unimportant. The years are really irrelevant. It's how you cope with them."
—Shirley Lord

What We Think
Jennifer's Voice

Sometimes a voice with a strong Russian/Yiddish accent will speak to me about events in my life. It's my grandmother's voice. My grandmother was well known in our family for wisely summing up situations in one "saying." I can hear her advise me, "Jennifer dear, this too shall pass" or "Anything that tastes good tastes better on bread." She talks to me although she has been deceased for almost fifteen years.

We are close. She and grandpa told me many stories about our family. When I was twelve years old, grandpa took my entire family to Russia to visit the towns in which he and my grandmother had grown up. We visited the homes they lived in, schools they attended, and some of their friends there who were left behind. This gave me a deep appreciation of my Russian heritage. I understand, in a very profound way, whence I came. These experiences and stories give me a clear view of the ingredients of which I am made.

Like Suey Wong, I have a clear view of the core values that have been passed on to me like a burning torch down through the generations…family…health…education…the welfare of the community in which we live. Regardless of our ethnic differences, I, like her, am clearly able to define myself according to my role models. I too derive from a matriarchal family that practices loyalty, devotion, and dedication.

Such an awareness of history offers us an opportunity in the present to think of the past with the hope of improving the future. I refer to this as "mindful time travel."

Through "mindful time travel" I can be aware of what I pass down to my children. Cultivating this awareness is possible, and if I use the opportunity, I can be more able to work in the direction of shifting forward and backward, integrating my awareness with my behavior with that of other people. Then I can open the possibility of working towards sorting through and choosing behaviors that work for me in my current situations and, potentially, can leave behind bad habits that don't work.

When we are mindful of our differences, we can be respectful of them as well. For example, what may have worked for Suey's mom through her adversities may not be needed for Suey. Sometimes, the equipment needed to climb a mountain is not necessary for ascending a gentle slope. Perhaps Suey has climbed other mountains that allow her daughter to stand on her shoulders in order to reach a new peak.

I stand on my mother's shoulders, her mother's shoulders and her mother's mother's shoulders to reach my peak. I encourage my daughters regularly to stand on my shoulders.

> *"In search of my mother's garden, I found my own."*
> *—Alice Walker*

What Do You Think?

Write your response to "The Rear View Mirror." Do you "stand on your mother's shoulders?" In what ways? What do you know about your roots? What is the essence of your "mindful time travel"?

Looking Forward

Judy Harris

Here I am at the age of fifty and my mother in her seventy-sixth year. Even at this age, I think that my relationship with my mother is still evolving, and changing as the years continue. On my part this has much to do with my evolution as a changing and evolving woman. Much also has to do with the changes that my mother goes through as she evolves through her various life changes; care taker, widow, aging woman.

Watching my mom be a devoted care giver to my very ill father for many years, has often time propelled me to contemplate how I would handle that same role in my relationship with my husband if the time should ever come. It has actually made me think about whether I would have the stamina, mentally and physically, that she had in order to do all that she did for my father. I hope that I am not confronted with this reality, but observing her did give me pause for contemplation of my own potential.

My mother and I are very close, which in our case means being very open with our feelings. Sometimes this leads to friction, as I find that my mother has less ability to be selective about what she chooses to verbalize and I have less patience with some of my mother's behaviors. This seems to be intensified as the years go on. The good news is that I am trying to take stock of what is worthy of making issues of at this point in life, and so, for myself, I am learning to be more tolerant of certain behaviors that would have caused me to be reactive in the past.

"You just wake up one morning and you got it!"
—Moms Mabley (on old age)

At my age it feels like I'll never get to your age!

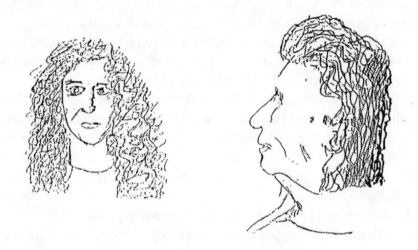

At your age I never thought I'd make it to my age!

What We Think

Shura's Voice

"Looking forward" to anticipate our behavior in the future is an almost impossible challenge. We can plan and hope, but we cannot foresee the turns in the road or the curves that life will pitch to us. As we make our way through the demands of daily living, we try to develop skills of adaptation and coping that will see us through the immediate problems and help prepare us for the oncoming unknowns.

Judy's realization about her "own evolution as a changing and evolving woman" is an important one. Actually, mother and daughter are changing as individuals as well as in their relationship. A woman's older years are a time of considerable challenge to adapt to enormous and difficult changes within herself and in her family constellation, to new developments in her personal circumstances, and to the times which may be confusing as they are changing rapidly for everyone.

Specifically, the older mother must recognize that her former "little girl child" has evolved through youth and adulthood and is now also coping with the complexities of her own life. The thoughtful mother recognizes and values her daughter's maturation and learns to accept its effect upon her and upon their ongoing relationship.

In her late teens, my daughter, active, busy teenager that she was, once told me, "Mom, don't think that, when I grow up, I'll be the kind of daughter to you that you are to your mother. For one thing, I won't phone you every day!"

I was deeply hurt by this unexpected remark. I repeated it to my husband and wept in anticipation of my lovely child becoming an uncaring adult. My husband comforted me saying, "Don't worry, dear. She doesn't know this now, but she won't be like that when she grows up. You'll see." He was right!

Willy-nilly, Mother is her daughter's role model. Whether her daughter behaves like her or in very different ways, her actions are guided, consciously and unconsciously, by her experiences as daughter to this very mother. Consciously or unconsciously, judgments about her mother have been made, approval and/or disapproval determined, while the girl matures into the woman and makes her own decisions. The relationship between the two women in their older years grows out of these experiences and reflects the wisdom each has developed in her own journey.

Judy's "good news" is an expression of this wisdom. It grows out of her sensitivity to the relationship and awareness of her responsibility toward maintaining it as the loving, positive one that it is. Learning to be more tolerant is evidence of a deepened understanding of her mother and a willingness to accept "certain behaviors" rather than quarrel with them. This altered perspective and new judgment reflects her own ability to grow and to change.

What Do You Think?

Write your response to "Looking Forward." Every woman is a daughter. As you have matured, how has your behavior been guided by conscious or unconscious judgments about your mother role model? Does your mother/daughter relationship reflect the wisdom you have each developed? In what ways?

Womansong

Shura's Voice

When the day is ended
And the moon glows gold
And all my chores are tended
Then my hands may fold
I grow open-ended
I grow bold

My mind opens wide
To the dreams deep inside
The poems I must write
And the music and songs

I lie there at night
And I right every wrong
I paint and I dance
My life's a romance
And I'm wild…

The night sings itself through
And the day dawns anew
Back to the tasks
And the chores I must do
For my world…
For my man…
For my child.

Too Many Shirts

Jennifer's Voice

Got too many shirts to fold
And there's too much on your plate
Don't got nobody's hand to hold
Yet you believe it's fate
And you cry at night
You simply cry yourself to sleep
Hard to believe that this is "right"
'Cause you're kind, you're smart
You're deep…really deep

The Older Woman Speaks

The Matriarchs

"There is a fountain of youth. It is your mind, your talents, the creativity you bring to your life and the lives of the people you love."
—Sophia Loren

The Older Woman

Shura's Voice

The journey continues. It has been long and is still ongoing. Sometimes arduous, sometimes sad.

Sometimes even unwilling. Often joyous, often fulfilling.

Always interesting. Always challenging. Always worthwhile!

Now, I face new territories. Life, it seems, is lived in layers. I am in a different place—living on a new level—facing new challenges. What are they? How shall I meet them? I am the same person who has been taking this journey—yet, in some important ways, I am different.

One, it seems, is always *"becoming,"* and so, as I am *coming* into this new place, how shall I now be?

My body is different…less graceful…less flexible…sometimes painful.

I Must Learn About This

My pace is different…uneven. My walk is slower…my thoughts are not. My mind is, therefore, in an altered state of homeostasis.

I Must Adapt to This

My memory is different. Memories of the past are rich, replete with emotion and detail, not always accurate. My immediate memory is sometimes faulty, erratic.

I Must Remember This

My self-image is different. Inwardly, I am vibrant, productive, competent, filled with ideas and desires. The mirror shows me a different face and form. Hardly inspiring.

I Must Accept This

My roles are different. At earlier points I was daughter, wife, mother, even grandmother, worker, leader, achiever, etcetera, and etcetera. There are fewer of these now—and the content and tasks of each role are different.

I Must Understand This

My social image is different. Those around me, even close family and friends, see an old woman whose shadowed image reflects a myriad of social stereotypes against which I am perceived and even, perhaps judged.

I Must Be Aware of This

My capacities are different. I can accomplish less in more time than it has ever taken before. Therefore, my plans must be different.

I Must Be Wise About This

My future is different. At earlier times I could envision endless time into which I could cram endless visions of experiences and achievements. Now, there is a foreshortened reality, and I must limit my expectations.

I Must Be Realistic About This

These are only a few of the differences. Actually, my life is in a state of flux which requires my constant awareness, learning, understanding, coping with new experiences—both within and outside of myself. I am required to rethink ideas about life and living that had not challenged me in the same ways before.

Is anything the same? I am challenged to dig deep into my consciousness to understand what of myself remains with me. I recognize that throughout my life, there have been numerous changes as I have grown and developed.

It has taken me decades to know, deep down within myself, what I believe and what I believe in. Everyone is different in the specific details, but we are all human in the generalities.

Therefore, I look back to learn…to understand.

What has worked for me? In what ways have I succeeded in earning my own approval?

What have I done well? Wherein have I failed?

What new skills must I develop to cope with the new challenges?

What can I continue to do? What must I cease doing?

What new things must I learn to do?

The answers to similar questions have guided my development throughout my life. I must ask them again within the present context of living as an old woman.

Was I always confident? No—but I was vested in certain behaviors, perspectives and ideas.

Was I always successful? Of course not, but when I slipped or fell, I picked myself up, dusted myself off and kept going.

These I must do again now. But within all the differences, I must find new ways of being and behaving.

I Have Been Working at This Task, Slowly, with Much Thought and Uncertainty

My new, but not totally different, identity is emerging. Now I must evaluate and shape this new identity so that it conforms to my basic notions of who I am and want to be.

And with it all, I must retain my humor, my love, my sense of beauty and duty, my dreams. These, one must keep as long as one lives.

I must retain whole portions of my old self, while growing new dimensions.

Yes, there is much work to be done when one is an old woman!

"The great thing about getting older is that you don't lose all the other ages you've been living."
—Madeline L'Engle

We Old Women

Shura's Voice

We old woman are considered unglamorous
Stereotyped, not pretty and surely not amorous
In short, maligned…and though sound of mind
We find we're unheeded, most often not needed

When a woman grows old she's to do as she's told
The greater her age, the less "center stage"
She's surely no centerfold!

The butt of jokes by many folks
Skin wrinkled, hair white—no pretty sight
Believed un-astute…yet often called "cute"
Or "dearie" or "honey"…think we are funny

And, as if hexed, considered de-sexed
Neutered, invisible, old women are risible
Most certainly deemed with little esteem

Yet we're greater in number of the old population
Three old gals to one old guy in the graying nation
We were the mothers
Of sisters and brothers and even of others

We raised you, we worked and we fed
Taught you and bred, and we even led
Made the coffee, washed the clothes
Cleaned the house, wiped your nose
And all else, goodness knows!

Now we're the grammas, still going strong
In spite of our losses, we have our own song
Learning the business of how to grow old
The tasks for which we've never been told

If you watch us with empathy, perhaps you'll learn how
To cope with your aging, as we're doing now
Struggling to realize how aging has changed me
Altered me, challenged me, it has not deranged me!

"If you want a thing done well, get a couple of old broads to do it !"
                              —Bette Davis

What Do You Think?

Write your response to "The Older Woman Speaks" and "We Older Women." What thoughts, images, or emotions have these pieces evoked?

Not Anyone's Number One

Interview with Sarah

Sarah is an attractive, vibrant, aging mother of three grown children—two daughters and a son—and seven grandchildren. Her husband of 51 years, Max, died one and a half years ago, and she is struggling with the loss.

Tell me what it is like for you to grow old?

I never thought of myself as getting old when my husband was alive. After Max died I said somebody forgot to tell us we were getting old. We both enjoyed good health. We did a lot of traveling and enjoyed ourselves. I liked getting older—it was the best time. Our kids were grown, married to wonderful people, and were involved with their own families. We felt so blessed, couldn't believe how happy we were. My husband and I were very close but had our own lives too. Now I am alone. Alone, you feel vulnerable.

How do you experience being an aging mother?

Again, everything changed when Max died. When the children were young, I stayed home with them. I only went to college after they were grown and in college. I went to graduate school in New York to get a master's degree in Modern Jewish History. I ended up teaching Jewish History at a local college. My husband was a tremendous support. He gave me the gift of time. He took over many tasks so that I would have more time to study and establish a part-time career. He adored me. No one can care for me like that anymore. I have family and good friends, but I'm not a "special someone" anymore, not anyone's "number one." I need to depend on my children for emotional support now. This is very hard. I am a relatively independent woman.

All of my children are devoted and caring. I don't spend a lot of time thinking about my relationship with my daughters simply because I am lucky to have an easy and good relationship with them. I consider them my loving friends as well as my daughters. Because I am unhappy, I think I am more needy now. I hear from them every day. If they happen to miss a day for one reason or another, I really notice it. I expect more now. They have had to learn to tolerate my neediness of them. I know they are busy women with their own families.

It is easier when I am teaching. The teaching and lecturing is not only a source of enjoyment. It keeps me from feeling old.

Max was my best friend. He was my safe harbor, and now I don't have one. When you have safe harbor, it doesn't matter what happens to you. There is always some comfort there. I don't have that safe harbor anymore. I may be lonely, but I am not alone. I am close to my children and my grandchildren, and that is my greatest comfort and security.

What We Think

Sarah's comments are particularly poignant as she tells of her aloneness. This came about with the loss of her husband and life partner. The awareness that she had entered the stage of life we call "old age" came upon her suddenly when the continuity of her life's journey was interrupted by his death. The abrupt changes wrought by this loss require major adaptations to the challenges of this new time of life. The emotional impact of the loss is immeasurable and has a profound effect on all aspects of a person's outlook, perspectives, and expectations. Sarah is in the throes of this process that is both painful and demanding. She tells us that she has lost her safe harbor. According to Maslow, safety is a basic human need, second only to the primary human need for physical survival. We see then, how deeply Sarah's life has been altered.

She recognizes the importance of her family's love and support during this time in which she must establish a new balance in her life. She recognizes that she must reevaluate her personal definitions of such basic life values as independence and happiness. Sarah has turned a corner in the journey of her life and must redefine its route. We can see that she is already working on a new map and that she will make the necessary adaptations to go on with her life, different and difficult though it certainly will be.

What Do You Think?

Have you experienced a profound change in your perspective? Have you had to find new and different ways to go on with your life? What has caused it? How did/do you cope with it?

Regarding My Aging
Interview with Shura

Shura is the eighty-five-year-old co-author of this book. Her daughter, Jennifer, interviews her about growing old.

Tell me what it is like for you to grow old?

I never thought about my age. I always thought about how I wanted to live and what I wanted to do with my life. Even then, since no one has complete control of her life, I had to learn to adapt to change. I think it has become one of my important skills of living.

When I turned forty a friend telephoned me to say "happy birthday" and to reassure me that life continues even after you turn the corner that is marked by this year's number. I was mystified. It had never occurred to me that forty was anything but a number! Ten years later, on my fiftieth birthday, my family took me out to celebrate with a special dinner. I appreciated their kindness, but it seemed to me that they were making a big fuss over nothing important.

Even when my husband and I retired in our late sixties, I really didn't think about growing old myself!

Now, in my eighties, I feel that I have had to experience many changes actually associated with the process of aging. Yet, I've tried to maintain some continuity in my life because I want to feel that I'm still the same person, though now grown old. So I maintain the interests of a lifetime, although the expressions of these interests may be somewhat different.

How do you experience being an aging mother?

That's a good question. Somehow, when I was young, it just seemed the most natural, unquestioned route of my life to have children. By and large, I enjoyed being a mother. At the same time, I managed to continue activities in some of my interests other than motherhood. Both aspects of my life were fulfilling to me.

Life was not easy. My husband and I both worked hard—at our professions and at parenting. We knew we were fortunate in having healthy children who were able to pursue their interests as well. I liked being their mother. I feel extremely fortunate to be a grandmother. Again, it is continuity for me to be involved with family members of a generation other than mine.

I've always felt that my kids enriched my life. Now that I am a grandmother, I find that being involved with my grandchildren enhances my older years.

Is it different being a mother of your mature "children?"

It is and it isn't. Life is a series of changes, and so is parenthood. As parents, we always tried to support our children's struggles to find themselves—to let them learn to be who they are as unique individuals. In that respect it is the same now. I accept and respect each of my grown children in his or her own right. When they were growing up, I didn't expect them to see me in my right as a person other than their mother. Now, in my older years, I hope that they do. I'm fortunate in having a relationship with my daughter who sees me for the woman I am, outside of my role as her mother. I believe my sons do too.

What are the down sides of your aging, as they pertain to your relationship with your daughter?

I think the biggest down sides are the physical changes and the new dependency needs that develop because of them. We have dependency needs of one kind or another throughout our lives, especially emotional ones. We each find our ways of coping with them. I was fortunate in having a lifetime partner, my husband, with whom I was able to share every aspect of life and we met each other's needs very appropriately in most ways.

Now, widowed, I try to be careful not to impose emotional dependencies on my daughter. This is one of the challenges of growing old—to recognize what kinds of help I can accept, perhaps must accept, and what other kinds I should not expect.

What Do You Think?

For the aging mother: What is it like for you to grow old? How do you see yourself as an old woman—an aging mother? How does it affect your relationship with your mature daughter?

For the mature daughter: How do you envision your own aging process? How do you view your aging mother? How does your view affect your relationship with her?

Musings About Aging

By Older Women

Here I am at seventy-five, and I'm barely beginning to learn what it means to be smart. I'm only now learning to assess what's important. I've begun to seek byways to happiness—how to let go so that happiness can arrive. I see many cohorts who realize they are getting smarter as they reach into their seventies and eighties. What a long journey—and why?

I ask that and these are the sounds that come back.

Let go...let it flow...be at peace...let it unfold...sing a song...do a dance...hear another's voice, let it all be...

The time for reflection has arrived, offering insight—the by-product of quiet thought. How do we push back old behaviors? How do we allow ourselves to enter into the maturing panorama? How can we let it happen? The old years arrive—seventy, seventy-five, eighty, something new afoot, what can it be?

From "It takes a Long Time to Get Smart"
By Edith Sarah

"Numbers don't matter. If there is no suffering, age doesn't matter."
Angie Hojos

From "Songs of Ourselves" by the Poetry Group of the Kings Bridge Heights Nursing Home, The Bronx, New York

Getting Older...Older...Old

By Rose Rudin

You don't get old all at once. You notice the first wrinkle, the first gray hair—but you are too busy living to really think of "when you'll be old."

Then, one day, you are "over seventy-five." Out of habit you continue doing all the things you did with your life.

You take care of your husband with constant concern for his health and well being. (I am fortunate to have a husband who is a great comfort and help to me in all ways, even in the process of becoming, and being old.)

You keep house—with more effort, of course.

You still do little things for those around you.

You also do your small share toward peace and a better world.

You anxiously watch the progress of your children and grandchildren—and hope that they will have a better life in a world at peace and real brotherhood.

You think of the past, and you are sorry for all the wrong things you did. You regret not having done more of the right things.

You long for all the dear ones who have gone. You cherish the ones still around and want to see more often.

You try not to "push time" unless a dear one is ill or you have a sleepless night.

You plan for tomorrow...next year...and next. And you know that there are not many of those left for you at your age so you feel a little sad.

From *Aging: An Album of People Growing Old,* by Shura Saul

To My Daughter
by Caryn Feig

As the time draws near for you to move on
To the next exciting stage of your life
I want you to know that wherever you go
You will always be close to my heart.

For there is a bond between you and me
That has always been and will always be

It stretched at first as baby fingers and toes,
Learned to creep, crawl and walk
And little voices turned into gurgles and talk.

It stretched again as a curly-haired tot
You played and you drew
Beginning to see all the things you could do.

It stretched even more as you discovered
Books, nature and art
And you pursued that which was dear to your heart.

It stretched further still as the teen age years
Thundered by
Bringing along many lows and highs

And though it is time for you to embark
On a most thrilling ride of your life
I hope that you know
Despite where you go
You hold a place deep in my heart
For the bond that stretches
Between you and me
Continues to grow
But always will be.

Do you see the young woman?
  Do you see the old woman?
    Can your vision encompass both?

Exercise...Growth and Development
What Changes...What Remains the Same?

Here is a series of questions relevant to the three stages of life identified below.

Select the stage you are at now and respond to the questions. Then re-wind or fast forward, however the case may be, to the other stages in life. If you haven't yet reached the stage to which you "fast-forwarded," try to envision your answers, or think about someone you know, or ask someone to join you who is in that stage.

How to Use the Chart

In the top boxes, write your answers as they relate to the external world: identify what you do, how you behave, what you say, what your responsibilities are, what you plan, etc.

In the boxes below, identify your inner world: how you feel about the above activities, what are your struggles, your fears, your conflicts, your challenges, your dreams, your wishes.

The Questions (for each stage of life)

What is your life like now, at this particular stage in which you are working on the chart?

What is your focus in the external world, e.g., your job, your relationships, your goal, your plan?

How do you spend your time, talents, money?

What is your social life at this point in time?

What are your goals/expectations at this point in your life? What are your future goals?

What satisfies, or doesn't satisfy you?
Who are your friends? What are your family relationships?
How do you feel about yourself at this point?
What, if any changes, do you want, or hope to make?

The Assessment (Study your answers; how do they compare stage for stage?)

In what ways have you changed? In what ways have you remained the same?
What inner conflicts have persisted? Which resolved?
What are your current struggles…conflicts?
What themes do you notice are recurrent?
What have been, or are, your chief concerns?
Have they changed? At all? Much? How?
What underlying moods, thoughts, ideas, hopes, dreams have prevailed through most of your life?
What has been your world view—your outlook—your point of view about living?
What are you learning about yourself?
What do you conclude from this exercise?

"Life is change. Growth is optional. Choose wisely."
—Karen Kaiser Clark

Growth and Development: Your Chart

ADOLESCENCE	MIDLIFE	OLD AGE
(Your outer world)	(Your outer world)	(Your outer world)
ex. My body is changing	my appearance is changing	my body and my appearance are changing

ADOLESCENCE	MIDLIFE	OLD AGE
(your inner world)	(your inner world)	(your inner world)
ex. These changes confuse me I am experiencing all sorts of new thoughts and feelings	How do I really look now? In what other ways am I these changes?	What must I do to adapt to all

Guideposts for Thought

Perspective

Recently at the home of a dear friend, the phone rang. I picked it up. It was another old friend. She said, "Just tell her, her oldest friend called."

I responded, "I thought I was her oldest friend." Then I turned the kaleidoscope a bit and realized that this old friend was a good 20 years our elder. I wondered to myself, "Did she mean the friend she had had the longest or the oldest person among all her friends?

1. Change is the only constant in life.
2. Strands and shades of similar themes color all of one's life.
3. Wisdom involves the ability to make effective choices among alternatives amid existing conditions.
4. Surround yourself with a range of opinions, ideas, techniques to give yourself a broad outlook on life.
5. Flexibility enables versatility and the ability to cope with change.
6. Be open to meet each different challenge, flexing a different "muscle" and using an appropriate coping skill.
7. Adaptation is the skill to create shock absorbers for processing the whirlwinds of change.
8. When the unexpected happens, consider new ways of responding.
9. Accept life as a drama replete with conflict and duality.
10. When something upsets you, consider both sides, pleasant and unpleasant.
11. Each of us is the sum of all we have experienced: the whole is greater than the sum of its parts.

12. Try to understand all that the other person has experienced in her life.

13. A healthy relationship seeks points of similarity that can unite rather than differences that may separate.

Chapter Two
Building Blocks of Relationships

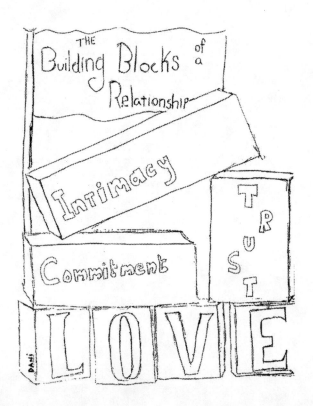

MOTHER

Always mother first
Regretting lost yesterdays
Attached with a thread
  Of separateness
Nurturing the mouth
Of creation
  I am the creator
    Always the mother first

DAUGHTER

Always daughter first
The curtain lifts...Act One
Disappointment
Spinning hurt and anger
Whirling...isolation...sadness
Act Two...Alone...Center Stage
  My arms open wide
    Always a daughter first

The Definitions

Love...Trust...Intimacy...Commitment

Intimidating words—what do they mean? Perhaps different things to each of us. The dictionary definitions are flat and one-dimensional. As integral qualities of our lives, these words are multi-faceted.

Nevertheless, we may still find commonalities of meanings, even though we act on them in different ways. Each of us chooses a range of behaviors to demonstrate the unique meanings of these words for us. When these behaviors fulfill our purpose, we believe we have expressed our sincere feelings.

What are the communication patterns between mothers and daughters? Do we accept each other's acts and words in the spirit in which they've been offered? Is there a special reciprocity between these two people that is perhaps different from other relationships?

Are there special "vibes?" Is there a secret, unspoken language between mothers and daughters that somehow expresses the love, trust, intimacy, and commitment that might seem to be inevitable between them?

What do expectations have to do with all this? What do we expect of each other? Do we understand our own expectations and how do we express them? What are the expectations of the other? Are we aware of them?

What is the "should" factor?" Is it always the same for mother and daughter?

What might make it different for each? What is shared by both?

Are these, the building blocks of any human relationship, inevitably in place for the mature mother-daughter dyad?

LOVE: *"A strong affection for another arising out of kinship or personal ties. Warm attachment, enthusiasm or devotion. The object of attachment, enthusiasm, or devotion; a beloved person. Unselfish, loyal, and benevolent concern for the good of another."*
—Webster's Ninth New Collegiate Dictionary

Love has many faces, many colors. Love sings many songs. It is experienced in a variety of contexts—each special, each with different meanings, different expressions. In all cases, love within a relationship encompasses the acceptance of some responsibility between or among those who share it. This responsibility derives from mutual expectation and hopes.

The love between mother and daughter is one of those special contexts. It is the child's first relationship. The physical connection of conception is followed by a long process of nurturing and caring. These develop into a lifetime habit of shared experiences as women.

In a healthy relationship, love between mother and daughter is unconditional. This does not suggest expectations of giving or receiving uncritical support or even acceptance for all words or behaviors. Rather, such love offers a stance of compassion and understanding for the other person's point of view regardless of disagreement.

Beneath heated differences of opinion, and even angry behaviors, there is recognition of this unique bond. Unspoken and perhaps even unacknowledged, unconditional love suggests that, "This too shall pass," and that the bond will remain unbroken. It may even be strengthened through honest expressions of differences.

When problems, issues, and life circumstances have intervened during the lifelong development of their love, the unconditional acceptance may be limited, narrowed, or otherwise affected.

Being human, we are full of surprises…some frightening, some confusing, some terrible, some wonderful. Being somewhat less than perfect, our unconditional status is likewise diverse.

This relationship does not dissolve as others might. It is a lifelong attachment, like it or not. Whether friendly or not, wanted or unwanted, the mother's voice always sounds over daughter's shoulder, a shout or a whisper, a shadow or a song. Similarly, the daughter is always a presence on the mother's horizon. Distant or close, viewed or ignored, she is always there. Like it or not, the attachment between these two women is always there.

Whether recognized or not, there is a special joy in the relationship when it is positive and a unique pain when it is not.

Love is the cornerstone of all aspects of the mother/daughter connection. Trust, commitment, and intimacy, spring from the first and basic love bond. Despite all changes in the flow of life, despite all efforts to the contrary, the bond remains permanent.

Love can be a tool for creative change.

TRUST: *"Assured reliance on the character, ability, strength or truth of someone or something. One in which confidence is placed: to commit or place in one's care or keeping. To rely on the truthfulness of accuracy of; to believe."*
—Webster's Ninth New Collegiate Dictionary

Trust Is the Key to a Functional Relationship

The first bonds of love and trust are born in the womb where the mother/daughter relationship begins. As the girl-child grows, mom builds a track record of trustworthiness (or not). As daughter develops, she also separates. Even under healthy conditions, the separation is slow, steady, difficult and painful for both mother and child.

When there has been trust between them during their earliest moments, the growing daughter builds upon this foundation and learns to trust herself and her own development.

Despite the rough spots and the "ditches and glitches" of life and growth, the relationship remains trusting and supportive.

Mom, also, must believe that the early years of love and trust offer the foundation for retaining their positive, if altered, connection.

The ripple effects that ensue in this process may last a lifetime. Aware of this life development, both must learn to survive. The young daughter learns to trust others as well. As she matures, she becomes her own person, free to create a strong sense of who she is and what she can do.

At times, conditions of living and growing are less than healthy—as when a mother may abandon the child physically or emotionally. Mother and daughter both feel the effects of this betrayal. Both are required to cope with the consequences and somehow to survive. The quality of trust in this bond is affected.

By the time mother and daughter have matured to a new level in their development, their boundaries are more clearly defined. The level and quality of conflict may or may not diminish. Expectations and trust are based on their track record and the coping skills learned by each woman in her own journey. We build a track record with each other for safety.

Trust can be a tool for creative change.

COMMITMENT: *"To put into charge or trust, to carry into action deliberately. To obligate or pledge oneself; may express the general idea of delivering into another's charge or the special sense of transferring to a superior power or to a special place."*
—Webster's Ninth New Collegiate Dictionary

Just as trust is the key, commitment is the structural foundation for all relationships, holding together the various segments of the life journey.

Bonding takes time, energy, love, and a strong commitment to weather the storms that occur through lifetimes. Commitment and trust develop hand in hand. They build upon each other, creating the framework within which the relationship develops. "I count on you, you count on me. Each time we fulfill this promise, our trust in each other is strengthened."

Mother/daughter commitment is a special bond, usually unspoken. When love and trust dominate the relationship, their mutual commitment may be taken for granted by both.

The bond of commitment underpins certain mutual expectations. Even when the relationship does not adequately meet the expectations of either or both of the women, the bond of their commitment is implicit in their attachment. The specific expectations will take different forms at different points in their lives, but the general theme is, "When you need me, I am there."

The child knows the parent is there—with no discussion

Commitment can be a tool for creative change.

INTIMACY: *"Belonging to or characterizing one's deepest nature. Marked by a very close association, contact, or familiarity. Marked by a warm friendship developing through long association of a very personal or private nature."*
—Webster's Ninth New Collegiate Dictionary

The only way anyone knows who you really are is through deep understanding and a communicated insight. This is called intimacy.

The only way anyone can communicate this deep understanding and insight is by knowing oneself in that same way. This requires an honest self-appraisal and a willingness to accept our less-than-perfect human selves.

Often, human beings don't understand themselves. This lack of self-understanding is a very common problem in relationships. When people lack insight about themselves, their ability to share with others is limited. This affects their capacity for true intimacy and the quality of any intimate relationship to which they may aspire.

Understanding oneself is a skill that can be acquired. When parents share some aspects of their own self-awareness, children can learn the skill and use it for themselves. When mother shows and expresses self-awareness, daughter understands mother more clearly, and also learns to understand herself as well. This is how capacity for intimacy develops and matures appropriately.

Intimacy is non-judgmental. The bond grows in a relationship of respect, trust, love, and commitment.

Within this milieu of caring and acceptance, each person recognizes the true nature of the other and communicates deep understanding and compassionate insight.

Intimacy can be a tool for creative change.

Intimacy

Shura's Voice

Oh, let it go, my dear
Love's on either side
Who wins, the other's gain is
And the loss...for both

We have merged ourselves
Each into one self
From the same cup, we drink
The thought you think...is mine
Mine...yours...your grief
Mine...who steals your joy
The thief of mine

Let it go, my darling
Smiles are sweet
And tears are but their counterpart

Come...Better let us dance
Our love makes light our hearts
Let us dance with our hearts

Always

Jennifer's Voice

Love is what you see
In someone else's face
No vision can be clearer
The reflection in your eyes
Tells me you know
    And so do I

Love is what you see
In the mirror
No vision should be clearer
My reflection shows me
Who they see
    Can you see me?

Love has no bounds
It breathes
It flows
No vision is clearer
Its changes are constant
    And so is my love

The Dialogue

Shura: From the beginning of my life, I was a daughter first...a daughter of two parents, a father and a mother.

Jennifer: It is a unique relationship. As a mother, I experience a powerful impulse to nurture and to care.

Shura: For a long time, I felt as if I was part of my mom, and she was part of me. Eventually I grew up and separated from her and became my own person. It was sometimes difficult and painful for both of us.

Jennifer: Nothing happens before its time. That separation is inevitable and healthy. "Once a daughter, always a daughter."

Shura: Similarly, "Once a mother, always a mother."

Jennifer: The daughter gives birth to the mother. I grew up. And at the same time, you were growing up too.

Shura: So much happens in life that may interfere with the healthy unfolding of this love.

Jennifer: Mom, you mean, "shit happens"!

Shura: Yes. People may get angry with each other, become impatient and frustrated. Changes in circumstances affect feelings and behavior, and people may be different afterward.

Jennifer: It takes time, energy, love, and a strong commitment to weather these heavy storms.

Shura: This mother/daughter feeling is that no matter what, we belong to each other. It is intangible.

Jennifer: That is intimacy!

Shura: Let's tell the stories of some women we know.

"The universe is made up of stories, not atoms."
—Muriel Rukeyser

71

Mother's Ambivalent Love
Jeanie's Story

Jeanie is a sixty-five-year-old daughter of Mary, who had just died at the age of ninety. Jeanie herself has two adult children, and three grandchildren. She met her friend Sarah at college, and they have been very good friends ever since. Sarah tells the following story:

"We met as previously planned, at a concert, which turned out to take place the evening after the very private funeral service that had been held for Jeanie's mother. At the intermission, Jeanie left her seat in the concert hall and went out to the lobby. I followed her, just to be with her, just to comfort her."

Jeanie: (*looking at Sarah's sympathetic face*): I'm standing here, trying to recall one incident of warmth between her and myself. I cannot remember a single time.

Sarah: But Jeanie, you know she cared about you.

Jeanie: Well, she took care of me when I depended on her. She did the things that, as a mother, she was supposed to do.

Sarah: I guess that was the way she showed her love.

Jeanie: She didn't know, really, who I was…what I was. She never thought I amounted to anything. When she realized that I was a professor at a city college and you were at Columbia, she told me she always knew you were better than me. She thought you were teaching at a more prestigious school than the one where I was teaching. That made you better than me, in her opinion.

Sarah: Oh, Jeanie, you and I never had any such thought!

Jeanie: Of course not. You and I are truly friends. We don't measure things, not in the way she did. But my mother thought about it.

Sarah: I know that made you feel terrible.

Jeanie: Of course. I never felt I was good enough for her.

Sarah: I don't think she realized that.

Jeanie: Probably not. I think she felt she was never good enough for her parents. She was such a wonderful pianist, yet she didn't have the support she would have needed to become a concert pianist. She should have. Nobody played Chopin the way she did.

Sarah: I guess she was disappointed in herself…and in her life.

Jeanie: Oh, yes, that she was. And she made me feel disappointed in myself.

Sarah: She did try to help you. She took care of your children when you had to go to work.

Jeanie: Yes, I hated that! I didn't want her to make my children feel the way she made me feel about myself.

Sarah: I think she thought she was fulfilling her maternal commitment to you.

Jeanie: I think she was judgmental about our marriage, and that my husband didn't earn enough so I had to go to work.

Sarah: Did she actually say that?

Jeanie: No, we never talked about such things. We were never that close, you know. But I felt it.

Sarah: Yet, she appreciated his work as an artist. Remember how willing she was to display his paintings in the living room?

Jeanie: Yes. That's what was important to her.

Sarah: You don't think it was a gesture of her love for you both?

Jeanie: No—I really don't. It was her artistic judgment, and I don't think she would have allowed me to do it if she hadn't judged them as being worthy of display. I did trust her artistic judgment, but never her feelings for either him or me.

The gong sounds for the intermission to be over. Jeanie continues to talk as we return to our seats.

Jeanie: I guess that was about all the love for me she could muster to show. I guess she showed it in those small ways. I wish I could believe that she really loved me.

I feel so bad for her
because she felt deprived
of her mother's love that
she wanted all her life.

Her mother's harshness obscured
her love for Jeanie and
got in the way of
developing a
warm relationship.

What We Think

Jennifer: I feel so bad for Jeanie. It seems she never had what she really wanted from her mom.

Shura: She always suffered from her mother's disappointment in her own life.

Jennifer: Often, there are themes that get passed on through the generations. Disappointment seems to be the theme in Jeanie's family.

Shura: Disappointment develops from unrealistic expectations of life; or because hopes, dreams, wishes remain unfulfilled.

Jennifer: There is an expectation of what should be…rather than an acceptance of what is.

Shura: And perhaps a lack of acceptance.

Jennifer: This interferes with the development of a healthy relationship.

Shura: In the face of so much disappointment, a person feels that life has let her down. She feels abandoned by hope. Certainly, it is difficult to learn to trust.

Jennifer: Criticism and harsh judgment seem to stifle relationships especially the one between mother and daughter.

Shura: Sometimes such harsh judgments seem to obscure the real love between the two.

Jennifer: Jeanie questioned her mother's love for her to the very end of her mother's life.

"No one can make you feel inferior without your consent."
—Eleanor Roosevelt

What Do You Think?

When mother or daughter is harshly critical, it may feel as if she doesn't love you. Have you ever experienced this feeling?

The Daughter's Commitment
Hilda's Story

Hilda is a youthful, active woman who has passed her seventieth birthday. Her mother, Roslyn, died some years ago. Personally and professionally, Hilda is well known as a woman of profound integrity. She never lies or pretends. She always means what she says and says what she means.

My mother and father were divorced when I was 12 years old. My mother, Roslyn, had custody of my older sister and me. She was always very angry with our father, as she was "the woman scorned" in their scenario. She directed many invectives against him and always told us to convey her unfriendly remarks to him when we saw him. We saw our father weekly. He was very friendly, and, of course, we never repeated her angry words to him.

I was often alone in the house. My mother would leave food for me and tell me to drink my milk. I never obeyed. I would pour the milk down the drain. When she came home, she'd ask me whether I had eaten and whether I drank my milk. I would look right into her eyes and tell her I did. I always lied.

I lied because it was the easiest way to get along with her. I knew what I was doing, and I hated doing it. But she was so volatile and excitable when she was disobeyed, and I couldn't cope with it. She was difficult with us, and her behavior with other people was often odd. She always made me uncomfortable. I swore that when I'd go out on my own, I'd be different. I knew I didn't want to be like her and, as you know, I am not!

Post Script (Shura's Voice): When Hilda was 18, she did go out on her own. She married a young man, Jim, much against her mother's will. They developed a good family life and parented two sons and two daughters. As Roslyn grew older, Hilda and Jim, as well as their children, maintained supportive relationships with her. They met her growing dependency needs, treated her with respect, and saw to it that she had good care until she died.

"We can only learn to love by loving."
—Iris Murdock

What We Think

Shura: This story illustrates how complex and diverse these building blocks can be.

Jennifer: This has got to be a limited relationship. Hilda describes how she needed to walk on eggshells when, as a young person, she was with Mom. Mom was so excitable and explosive; Hilda needed to find ways to survive in her own home.

Shura: Even as a young person, somewhere within herself, Hilda must have felt the strong commitment to her mother who was a single mom with many issues.

Jennifer: She did what she thought she had to do to survive growing up with that kind of a mom—but also, "Once a daughter, always a daughter"—she understood her commitment in that relationship.

Shura: In spite of the obvious problems they had with each other, Hilda found ways to maintain a positive relationship with her mother through the years.

Jennifer: Do you think there was love?

Shura: Do we think there was trust…or intimacy?

Jennifer: It is hard to experience intimacy when you are afraid of Mom and her reactions.

Shura: It's hard to really know how these qualities develop in such a conflicted relationship. There had to be a conflict within the young Hilda. Yet, we know that there was caring in this situation which prevailed to the end of her mother's life.

Jennifer: There's got to be so much conflict about love, trust, and intimacy for the child who grows up with such a mom.

Shura: Hilda's mom continued to act in the same difficult ways.
           As Hilda matured, she began to sort through her own values
           and made her own judgments and decisions.

Jennifer: As an adult she maintained commitment and responsibility
           to her mother as she herself lived true to her own values. I
           can respect that!

The daughter had so
much conflict in the relationship.

She still respected the relationship

What Do You Think?

Hilda, the daughter, felt that she could tell her mother only what she knew her mother wanted to hear, thus limiting the honesty of their relationship. Have you experienced anything like this in your mother/daughter relationship? How did it make you feel?

The Ripple Effect
Isabel's Story

Isabel is a 54-year-old woman married to John. This is her second marriage. She has a daughter, Janet, age 24. Her own mother, Mary, age 85, has long been emotionally abusive toward Isabel.

Isabel matured into a very independent adult, able to take care of her own needs—financial, emotional, and otherwise. She was even able to buy her own house at the age of 20, while she was still in college.

Over the years, she shied away from intimate relationships. She married an alcoholic and gave birth to Janet. Isabel divorced and raised Janet by herself. At age twenty-two, Janet became a drug addict and suffered from an eating disorder. Isabel did everything she could to assist her daughter in getting professional help. The disease of addiction had Janet in a very strong grip, and she struggled with it on a daily basis.

Through all of this, Isabel's efforts to offer her own daughter healthy boundaries have been sabotaged by the interventions of Grandmother Mary.

In the guise of helping, Grandmother Mary has undermined Isabel's support of her daughter by getting in the middle and offering opposing advice. Isabel finds that this raises significant conflict, as she wants to run her own life and deal with her own daughter's issues without the interference from her mother. Gramma has her own agenda, however, and is not honoring Isabel's boundaries or her role as the young daughter's guiding star.

After a lifetime of her conflicted issues with Mary, both in her earlier life and in the current crisis with Janet, Isabel realizes that she cannot have a trusting, loving relationship with her mother. Mary shows no self-awareness and rationalizes her destructive behaviors as loving ones.

Isabel has wondered whether there is anything she can ever do to alter this relationship. After many attempts to talk with Mary about all these issues, she sees no light on that horizon. Sadly, she begins to close the door of hope that she will ever achieve a healthy relationship with her mom.

"Most of us become parents long before we have stopped being children."
—Mignon McLaughlin

What We Think

Jennifer: Isabel believes she is alone in the world. She cannot trust that she will be supported. She tends to feel ineffective and inadequate.

Shura: There seems to be a continuity of interactions through the three generations in this family: continuity of harsh judgments, lack of support and trust, so that it is impossible for these women to achieve any level of intimacy.

Jennifer: I see continuity of isolation, emotional abuse and neglect, alcoholism, addiction, and other self-destructive behavior.

Shura: Still, one does expect that the mother, Isabel, is trying to express a love for her daughter.

Jennifer: The grandmother is very self-absorbed and incapable of seeing anything beyond herself. So her advice to her daughter and granddaughter is fueled by her own limitation.

Shura: So—Isabel tries to avoid Mom, and hopes then, to avoid conflict. As a result she betrays herself by not facing and accepting the truth, that her own mom is not loving towards her.

Jennifer: This is beyond hurtful. The daughters are feeling the absence of the kind of relationship they would have wanted…the absence of the basic bond of love. It has affected their own behavior throughout their lives.

Shura: The mother/daughter bond is so basic.

A self-absorbed mother is limited in ability to express love.

When daughter feels the
absence of this basic bond,
it is very difficult to trust
oneself and develop
intimacy in life

Mom never took the time to
build the framework for
a home of trust and commitment.

Each time she undermined Isabel,
she undid a brick in the
wall of their home.
Isabel then had trouble
trusting the world to
be a safe place.

What Do You Think?

Do you feel that there is a basic bond of love in your mother/daughter relationship? How does it express itself?

The Tentative Ones

Dorothy's Story

Dorothy, a woman in her eighties has had a long, creative and interesting life. She is now retired.

I am an eighty-four-year-old mother of three daughters and two sons. I have nine grandchildren. My daughters and I are all mature, intelligent, educated women. We've had many years of relating to each other, they as mature offspring and mature siblings.

One weekend, after no word from them for two weeks, we touched base. I was picked up (I no longer drive,) and taken to my middle daughter's suburban home. Her family consists of herself, her husband, and three little ones. My youngest daughter and her two children joined us the next day. We shared pleasant, simple, direct talks for a finite number of hours and days in their large, comfortable home. We made certain not to discuss anything controversial, like politics, religion, or the best way to bring up children today.

When I returned home, my oldest daughter called to tell me about her most recent publication and to invite me to go with her to the theatre next week. Theatre is our common denominator.

I think we all appreciate each other and are proud of our accomplishments and each others' accomplishments. However, occasionally I can't help pressing one of their buttons. But no strong rifts develop. All of them are parents themselves and hold down demanding, rewarding, and full-time jobs.

In one sense, our roles have reversed. Each of them takes turns going to my doctors with me. My retention of what the doctor or I said is untrustworthy.

Obviously, my three daughters are in constant communication, keeping my mental and physical health status on their front burners. This affords me a great sense of security.

They constantly ask me to tell stories to their children about my/ their early adventures. All the little children are trained to be absolutely polite to Grandmother.

I'm not sure what "love" or "codependence" or any other "close relationships" are, but I am certain that decades of struggle and respectful appreciation are the webs that bind us, mother and daughters.

What We Think

Jennifer: It seems to me that these daughters and their mother are trying very hard to do the right thing by each other.

Shura: Why does Dorothy have such a feeling of insecurity?

Jennifer: It seems they all walk on eggshells around each other. I wonder if that is a theme in the family's relationship.

Shura: Some families seem to feel the need to avoid controversial issues. Apparently they feel that controversy may interfere with good relationships.

Jennifer: The controversy in this family may stem from their difference in style and values, which they don't want to address with each other. What do you think Dorothy means by, "I can't help pushing their buttons?"

Shura: I think she realizes that there are some important differences of opinion. Perhaps Dorothy is wise to be sensitive to them. She feels she must exercise some self-control, but sometimes isn't completely successful.

Jennifer: Her daughters do care for her, and Dorothy really feels and appreciates their concern.

Shura: Yes. Love has many faces. The same words have different meanings to different people. Dorothy is trying to maintain their commitment in the relationship—looking to enjoy their mutual interests.

Jennifer: There seems to be a large measure of restraint in the way they behave together.

Shura: Are they afraid that the relationship will be harmed if they get too close…afraid of being hurt…of somehow hurting one another?

Jennifer: Of daughters hurting mother? Of mother hurting daughter? Of hurting their relationship?

Shura: Dorothy explains that she's not sure what close relationships are. It has taken her many years of struggle and mutual appreciation to develop the webs that bind them.

They are all afraid of being hurt.
They are very careful with each other.

They are looking for ways
to express love and
compassion instead of fear.

What Do You Think?

Are you afraid of being hurtful in your mother/daughter interaction? Are you afraid of being hurt?

Continuity
Carla's Story

Carla, herself a mother of three, is the oldest of three sisters. She writes of her own mother:

My mother had always been the glue of the family, the literal center. Each of us thought and felt ourselves to be her favorite child. She was the fun and vision, and although we felt very free to argue and disagree, even loudly and forcibly at times, we always felt she knew stuff. She knew mothering, how to welcome friends and family, about cooking, art, and decorating. She was a teacher at home and in school, and later in her community. She was a wonderful, supportive, and accepting wife. We saw what it took to make a marriage. Also, although Mom always treated each of us with respect, and we were listened to all of our lives and our opinions counted, Mom was still MOM. She was a powerhouse and every bit in command. We had opinions about everything. ALWAYS. Nevertheless, Mom still did what, and as, she felt was right. The hard part for me was watching and being part of the power shift.

When Dad first got sick, Mom was very secretive about it with their friends. She didn't want anyone to know how bad Dad really was…Things were tense but fairly status quo until her health greatly weakened also, and we were making the trek south every few weeks in groups or singly. Very suddenly, she began to relinquish control of her decisions and life-style. There were skirmishes and flare-ups. What would she take and leave and/or give away? With the move to Chicago, Mom had really let it all go. It was a surprise. The final surprise came when Mom asked me to do her banking. For me, this symbolized our entire change in roles. Pay the ladies, deal with the movers, ask the doctors, protect me, take care of me! It was surprising and horrifying. We still fought over things, but always, in the end, I won. I see now that was a function of her trust and love and respect and special closeness that we shared. It was exhausting for me and, I am sure, for her at the time.

I also see more clearly now, though I saw it at the time, that this final move was the most selfless and generous thing that she could have ever done for us, her daughters. I think the move may have hastened her death, though she certainly didn't have that much longer (to live). The last year of her life was filled with much love from us and all of her friends and also a terrible kind of frenzy. We all fought to maintain control, get control, and give it back because of what gaining it meant!

She was and remains my true hero, and I know we all wish that we could be half the person and mother that she was. I hope I make the sacrifices for my kids that she always made for us and with as much love, dignity, and optimism as she did.

> *"Love is a fruit in season at all times and within reach of every hand."*
> *—Mother Teresa*

The pattern of love, trust and
commitment went throughout
the daughter's life.

They could even disagree
and argue and still
retain their closeness.

What We Think

Jennifer: Carla speaks of her appreciation of her mother's role in her life…even the sacrifices.

Shura: She also makes judgments about her mother's behavior in a stressful situation, but because of their loving connection, she is able to understand and cope with it. And because she understands, it does not diminish their love.

Jennifer: When the basic love is expressed, one person is more open to the duality of the behavior of the other.

Shura: Carla sees that throughout the years, despite various conflicts, her mother was still a mother first.

Jennifer: The reason she could see that is because it had been ongoing throughout life. She could recognize the pattern and trust her mother's commitment to her.

Shura: They could reach true intimacy in spite of their differences— even conflict. Mother and daughter could disagree, argue, and still retain their strong, healthy bond.

Jennifer: This bond enabled the smooth power shift when Mom needed Carla's help in all sorts of activities and decision making. In contrast to Isabel, Jeanie, and Hilda's stories, this daughter felt cared for and loved throughout her life. The changes in the way they filled each other's needs evolved more naturally.

Shura: Even though the tasks became difficult for the daughter, there is no resentment.

What Do You Think?

Can you argue and disagree with your mother/daughter without fear of hurting the relationship?

Affirmation
Edith's Story

Edith, mother, grandmother and great-grandmother writes:

I must admit that I haven't read too much on this subject, having always thought I would do the best I could under any circumstances. Now, in my 82nd year, I wonder occasionally if I had inherited a bit of the cheerful, ego-driven optimism I shared with my mother.

My first husband, who died at the tender age of 39, and I, were not only good parents but very conscious of our responsibility. We were also aware of all we had undertaken when we decided to have two children. We had put a small number on that project—only two! We expected to enjoy being parents if we didn't overwhelm ourselves. Gene (his name) was such an unusual dad! He was magnificent, and I guess I was pretty good myself. No problems of who was who—who governed this issue or who was in charge. We tried to create understanding between all four of us, and most of the time it worked.

I wanted to have a life of my own as well and, of course, a life of our own with my unusual and loving husband. I do believe the ground of the children—Joan, now 60 and Marlene, now 57—evolved to be firm, reliable, and creative. Our lives were altered quite dramatically when Gene died, and I was thrown into depression—an "I can't do it alone" kind of feeling.

My daughters helped me—no question. We were each concerned for the other; that just happened because of the loss we shared, but I must add that we had learned the beauty of "trust" many times via the manner we used in dealing with issues that arose from time to time. We had come to know that if we pulled together we might make it. We each became conscious of the other as never before.

As I write these words for the first time, I am sort of strangely aware that they are so very true. In fact, I have become aware of so much in the process of writing this—yes—confession.

I feel that my daughters are both chips off the old blocks. It takes guts, we all know, to move in new directions, and I believe that was a major element in our relationship. We did believe we could change and move on—when I say "we," I mean myself and my two daughters. It takes courage also to select a new path and give it your all, but without courage, nothing changes!

One other factor is essential—or was for me—and that was, of course, "The truth can set you free." Simple—then we know what in hell we are dealing with.

"One generation plants the trees—another gets the shade."
—Chinese Proverb

It takes courage to select a new path.

Without courage nothing changes.

What We Think

Jennifer: These women don't seem to be afraid that anything might hurt their relationship.

Shura: To cope with their tragedy they created a bond which kept them committed to each other.

Jennifer: In spite of the terrible loss of the father, the connection and strong commitment carried them through. Their bond of love was strengthened through the years. They are like war buddies.

Shura: As I read Edith's story it is clear that she had a very strong, positive idea of how she wanted to build her family life.

Jennifer: Sometimes what makes the relationship work are strong boundaries and a desire to pull together through adversity.

Shura: Edith has a strong sense and trust in herself, so she can trust others. Her daughters have learned the beauty of trust through her.

Jennifer: She is honest with herself and others.

Shura: She calls it like she sees it.

Jennifer: She also talks about courage and truth. Truth sets you free and no change happens without courage. She seems to have lived these concepts, and it worked for her.

What Do You Think?

Have you had to call upon your courage in your mother/daughter relationship? What did you do or say?

The Blocks in Place
Louise's Story

Louise writes: "I have recorded for you how my relationship with my daughter Meg has been affected by our life experiences (often shared), enriched through our growing understanding about one another's needs, and our mutual concern for each other's challenges and well-being."

Meg, fifty-two, and I, eighty-five, live about five miles apart. Meg at her home with her husband Jonathan and their three children, extremely busy, each of them, in school, or at work, and as participants in their community, with their various gifts, friendships, and contributions to organizations and programs. I have lived in a retirement community for the last 10 years and have been fortunate to be among people still very active and interested in community and cultural events, and most are able to take part in them. This is true of me—still driving and living my own life independently. The wonderful thing for me is that, because of Meg's love and kindness, and Jonathan's as well, I am included in much of their lives. Earlier, I could go sailing with them, and I could help out with the kids while still in my 70s till I could no longer keep up!

What has been remarkable has been Meg's generosity in understanding and respecting my limitations while encouraging me to come with them to the club to swim, for example, and even planning to swim at the Y with me, and going for coffee and a bagel nearby before we went home. We go to concerts together, and I've gone to numerous Suzuki concerts for over more than 10 years.

I have tried to be aware of how Meg has been coping with times of stress when she feels she must respond not only to the unrelenting demands of home and family but also to the challenges of her musical life. This is her joy and her "work," and she has been insistent about keeping up that nourishing aspect of her life. So one hears the stress in her voice, and she is always pressing herself to keep up. In more recent years, my energy and problems walking won't permit me to step in and substitute for her. That's a hard discipline for me—to accept the realities of aging—and I despair that I don't grow old gracefully. Instead, I'm apt to promise more than I can deliver, which just causes Meg to have to be understanding and me to feel guilty. I do tend to be critical of Meg for not allowing herself more rest or free time. She just doesn't have any in that household! This is why she really loves to come over here for lunch or a brief visit—and I love it when she can.

There have been crucial times when I have gone in to take over for her so that she can and does rest. This happened when Amy was born, and I realized she was not strong enough, so I'd just show up and be there, and she began to be comfortable about letting me take over a little. Of course, me being there for the children has allowed her to practice and teach.

For the future, I pray to be able to go on to the larger life soon after ninety. I DO NOT want her life to be tied to the necessity of visiting me when I can no longer be alert and appropriate!

> *"People living deeply have no fear of death."*
> *—Anais Nin*

In this important relationship
it is not enough to give "fifty-fifty."

Each one must make the
needs of the other a
priority but it must be mutual!

What We Think

Jennifer: I'm impressed with Louise's selfless consideration and understanding of her daughter's perspectives.

Shura: There's a deep-seated, mutual love and respect and appreciation between these two.

Jennifer: There is also a mutual understanding. For example, the mother's love is reflected in her concern about her daughter's stressful times. The daughter is concerned about her mother's need for independence.

Shura: There is generosity as each gives to the other.

Jennifer: I'm impressed with the daughter's sensitivity to her mom's needs through her aging process.

Shura: This may seem like role reversal, but I don't think there is such a thing. It's simply a continuation of a relationship in which two women who love each other can understand what the other needs.

Jennifer: If you think of aging as a process—you can release yourself from the guilt of feeling you are not doing enough. It just changes.

Shura: Guilt doesn't even enter into this relationship. There's been a profound loving and caring through a lifetime of trust, intimacy and commitment.

Jennifer: In this relationship all the building blocks are in place.

What Do You Think?

In your mother/daughter relationship, are you each sensitive to the needs of the other?

What We Think
Concluding Dialogue

**Jennifer and Shura share concluding
comments on the stories in this chapter**

Shura: So much can interfere with the development of a healthy mother/daughter relationship.

Jennifer: In my practice, I come across many casualties resulting from the behavior of the narcissistic mom. She's the person who is concerned only with herself and her needs and leaves no room for her daughter.

Shura: This is a form of betrayal. The expectation of the child is that the mother will take care of her.

Jennifer: Such a mother leaves everlasting scars that affect the relationship in their mature years.

Shura: This is also one face of abandonment. There are many other ways in which a mother can fail the child.

Jennifer: The daughter can also fail the mother. Expectations are mutual.

Shura: All kinds of traumatic situations may arise.

Jennifer: Illness, death, loss, divorce, a reverse in finances—all these life realities can detour healthy development.

Shura: That depends on how extreme they are.

Jennifer: And how the mother and daughter deal with them.

Shura: They need healthy, open communication, an exchange of thoughts, a willingness to be honest and to accept some pain.

Jennifer: They both need to have some hope that things can be cleared up between them.

Shura: Often the situations are so threatening, frightening, and unacceptable that they are repressed.

Jennifer: They are expressed in other ways, through behavior, anger, cynicism, avoidance.

Shura: Some people separate completely because they can't cope with such intensity of feeling. The separation can be geographic, intellectual, or emotional.

Jennifer: Either way, it just doesn't work. Mother and daughter inevitably act out those unexpressed thoughts and feelings somehow. If they are not resolved, they are passed on to the next generation.

What Do You Think?
Write Your Own Story...

I Always Hear My Mother's Voice Over My Shoulder

This?

I'm not smart enough to be successful.

You were never as smart as your sister

OR

I'm not smart enough to be successful.

You're smarter than you think.
You can do anything you set your mind to.

I Always Hear My Mother's Voice
Over My Shoulder

This?

This is a real rough time.
I don't see the light.

You always get yourself
into these situations.

OR

This is a real rough time.
I don't see the light.

This too shall pass.

I Always Hear My Mother's Voice Over My Shoulder

This?

I'm so worried
I don't know what to do.

I told you this would happen.

OR

I'm so worried I don't know what to do.

We'll get through this together.

The Body-Mind Connection

Exercises

You may not be aware, but everyone, at sometime or other, has experienced a first hand demonstration of how our bodies (some bodily functions) are actually an expression of our minds. This is mostly true in those parts of the mind/body of which we are generally unaware, referred to as the "unconscious mind."

Headaches due to stress, diarrhea due to anxiety, are both clear examples of this mind/body connection. Sometimes the sensations in the body may be so uncomfortable that we behave with the intent of relieving the unusual sensation.

Exercise 1: The Body Scan

• Close your eyes…take three breaths slowly.
• With each breath, pay attention to the birth of the breath and follow it through.
• Observe it as its every moment of being fades into the next one.
• Notice, as you do this, what your mind is thinking.
• Refocus on the breath.
• Now, pay close attention to any sensation in the bottom of your feet, your toes, your ankles, calves, legs, thighs, hips, lower back, abdomen.
• Take your time and notice the sensations in your upper back and shoulders, stomach, chest, your neck, arms, hands, fingers.
• Now move on to your head, jaw, mouth, eyes, and crown of your head.

Exercise 2: Listen to Your Body

• Pick one sensation from those above…Pay attention to the size, intensity, and color shape
• Allow the sensation to speak to you. If you could put words to it, what would it be saying?
• Pay attention to the message—honor it. What is your body telling you about what you need?
• Pay attention to your thoughts related to the sensation. What are your thoughts commenting on?
• What patterns do you see in your thoughts?
• Are you judging your body? Are you criticizing yourself for these thoughts and/or sensations?

Message: *I feel my eyelids are heavy and my eyes hurt. They are telling me how tired I am. And I need to close them.*

Critical thought: *You've already slept 9 hours. You shouldn't need more sleep. Keep going!*

The critical thought is sabotaging my best interest if I truly need more rest.

Sometimes what's in the mind
is so uncontrollable, we try to
relieve it by putting it into our bodies.

Exercise: Inventing the Myth

Human beings are the myth makers. We create inner stories based on our experiences and our emotional reactions. This combination has a lasting impact and becomes a belief.

Experience (leads to) behavioral reaction (leads to)
Thought (leads to) belief.

Example: Positive Experience

Memory: When we went to the park, Mom always had a treat for me.
    Reaction: I felt warm and happy.
        Belief: Mom likes to treat me and make me happy.
            Myth: I feel safe with Mom. I know she'll make me happy.

Negative Experience

Memory: Mom scolded me in front of my friends.
    Reaction : I was ashamed.
        Belief : Mom puts me down
            Myth: It's dangerous to have Mom around When I'm
with my friends.

Exercise: Now You Try It

Think back to an experience with a member of your family of origin.
What was your reaction?
What conclusion did you draw from this?
What did you continue to believe?
What lasting myth has resulted?
Memory:
   Reaction:
      Belief:
            Myth:

Exercise: Love, Trust, Commitment, Intimacy

How is your relationship built? Do you want to rebuild some of it?

Love
1. *What I was missing most was…*
2. *My body reminds me by…*
3. *My plan of action for change is ….*

INTIMACY
1. *What I was missing most was….*
2. *My body reminds me by…*
3. *My plan of action for change is…*

COMMITMENT
1. *What I was missing most was…*
2. *My body reminds me by…*
3. *My plan of action for change is ….*

Trust
1. *What I was missing most was….*
2. *My body reminds me by…*
3. *My plan of action for change is…*

Musings

What are the atoms that create these blocks? How do they grow into healthy cells? What might render them less healthy?

Relationships offer a playground for projection of the internal experience. The internal experience is the drama of life. We humans love drama. The world is our stage. The characters are the people in our lives. Each individual is the author, director, producer, and star of her own daytime dramas.

Because of the profound, intense connection, the mother/daughter relationships are a vital part of character development for each.

Let's talk about the script of the daytime drama. The unconscious mind qualifies as the most creative of authors. It has its own agenda, its inner stories which direct our behavior.

Our conditioning, expectations, perceptions, and projections all contribute to the story line. Then the inner actor within us takes to the stage and breathes life into the story as it gets played out in the external world.

Human beings tend to see the world through only one narrow point of view. Opening the lens cap to a broader view reveals more angles and provides a greater in-depth view.

***

About trust: I offer my trust to those I love in the hope that they will not let me down by betraying me. My experience with you shapes the depth of my trust in you. The degree to which I am able to risk being vulnerable is in direct proportion to the degree that I can trust you. We base our trust on what we believe is the truth. Truth is not absolute and is often a matter of perception. Many truths are painful. What I think is true for me may not be true for you.

We can trust others when we trust ourselves.

***

Despite underlying heated differences of the unique bond between mother and daughter, unspoken and perhaps unconditional love suggests that, "This too shall pass," and that the bond will remain unbroken. It may even be strengthened through honest expressions of difference.

However, unexpressed anger often becomes transformed into other emotions and is expressed indirectly. These indirect expressions are not always healthy for growth.

***

It's not for me to forgive you, nor you to forgive me. Rather, it is for us to respect the other's existence and celebrate the importance of the relationship. In accord with this perspective, apologies are obsolete. Acknowledgments are more relevant. "I know you exist. I know you are important to me. I have hurt you. I was acting from a place of 'self.' I did not intend to hurt you."

"Loving is not just caring deeply. It is, above all, understanding."
—Francoise Sagan

Guideposts for Thought

1. Whether acknowledged or not, the mother/daughter relationship is a lifetime connection.
2. Building the relationship begins with nurturing at the start of life. It is the mother who initiates or does not initiate the building blocks of love, trust, commitment, and intimacy.
3. In the healthy course of events, the daughter needs the space and opportunity to become her own person.
4. New boundaries begin to separate them, and each must let go of the other.
5. Angry words and insensitive behavior are often normal, healthy expressions of emotions. They need not be feared but do require afterthoughts and acknowledgment.
6. As each matures, mother and daughter must trust their early love and commitment to reach a new level of intimacy.
7. Needs change with maturity. Both women are required to make adaptations and changes.
8. True intimacy is mutual recognition of each other's growth and changing needs and behavior.
9. This healthy process requires courage and integrity to cope with life's challenges.
10. We must be prepared to open our hearts to the voices within our minds that may sabotage our happiness.
11. We must develop an internal, non-judgmental, accepting observer who is willing to point out our humanness, and we must be willing to listen openly to that observer.
12. We must be willing to change some conditioning that may be sabotaging our healthy maturation.

Chapter Three
The Family Village: Living in Proximity

The Family Village

A family is a unique blend of people who live and function within their own complex system of values, circumstances, relationships, expectations, and goals. It is a veritable village, replete with a philosophy, a world view, and a history all its own. This community has a tremendous influence on the lives of its members. The people who marry into this community, and their children, are also shaped by it. The children, especially, are remarkably able to learn and cope within this system. They develop many life skills of relationships, commitment, and human interaction, that they are taught within the total environment of their family village.

In the United States today, the women of the family are squarely at the center of family activities. For the most part, it is the mother who orchestrates most of the many daily tasks performed in the home. The familiar presence of a nearby grandmother, and the way in which she cooperates with the mother, are extremely important.

The details of their interaction are less important than the principles that guide their actions. Implicitly or explicitly, there must be understanding of some of the basic ideas that guide them. Children are aware of the behavior of their adults, even when situations are not discussed explicitly. When mother and grandmother live close to each other, or when they live together, the delicate balance of the family system is affected by the manner in which they deal with each other about these important daily concerns.

Even when mother and grandmother do not agree completely, the children can learn to respect differences of opinion, especially within the larger context of love, trust, and commitment.

Not all family villages live in such harmony. Many families struggle with the multidimensional problems of family life and communal living. The pressures of life and the difficulties of the external world can and do affect the family climate and the behavior of family members. The anger and conflicts of the external world may and do affect the family village.

Individual personalities influence family dynamics. Parents may repeat dysfunctional patterns of their own earlier life, thus contributing to an unhealthy climate within the family. Such unhealthy behavior as scapegoating, fostering competitiveness among family members, neglect, abuse, abandonment, a lack of nurturing—all such conduct, and similar others, contribute to an undesirable family climate.

Within the family village we may find all manner of situations— nurturing and non-nurturing; more often than not, quite mixed.

Yet it is here that the mother/daughter bond is born.

Living Together...A Family Tale
Shura's View

"Let's give her a chance to follow her dream," I said when my daughter told me that my granddaughter, Danielle, had been admitted to the high school of her choice. "It's time for me to make some kind of change myself. I'll move into the city with her, your family can move in here, and we'll give it a whirl." The whirl turned out to be a tornado!

It was possible for me to make room in my large home for Jennifer and family to move in. But the move required much rearranging of rooms, furniture, and possessions. The family homestead housed many items cherished by other family members. My husband and I, two aging adults, had lived in the house for a number of years by ourselves, and we had occupied every nook and cranny.

The moving process was monumental, and I was required to make radical changes. For example, my plant room/greenhouse became granddaughter Amy's bedroom. The attic, furnished as a guest suite became the master bedroom for Jennifer and her husband. Closets were rearranged and many things packed up and put away for some unknown later time.

Once again my house became home to a family with growing children. While our basic values were much the same, our foci in housekeeping were different. If we were to get along, I needed to cede control over what had been solely my domain for some years. My daughter faced the same challenge. She too had had control over her own domain for many years. We two housekeepers had to accommodate to one another, or the entire plan would become a fiasco.

Also, I realized that having turned eighty, I would not be able to maintain the big house alone much longer. I knew that sooner or later,

I'd require some help. My daughter and her husband, who lived geographically closer to me than my other grown children, would probably be called upon for this help. Looking ahead, we all realized I would require increasing assistance in managing the complexities of my big house. And so, their moving in seemed a good plan all around.

Despite these obvious issues, we made a good thing of it all. The little apartment in the city suited Dani and me, and we settled down to what I termed comfortable "dorm life." It was much like camping out with bare necessities and few frills. Despite its small size, we were able to give each other the space and privacy we each required.

Dani had spent many days and nights with me in our Westchester home so we knew and respected each other's patterns. Despite our age differences, they were quite similar. We both spent time reading and writing. For phone calls, we gave each other privacy. I enjoyed Dani's young friends when they came around. Life here was compatible.

Time schedules required communicative sharing among the adults. Children's needs had to be accommodated, as did job emergencies. Activities, recreation, and visitors had to meet a variety of tastes and interests.

Jennifer's View

When my daughter Danielle was fifteen years old, our entire family made monumental change that caused a tidal wave in our family structure for years to come. Being an aspiring actress, Dani auditioned for and was accepted to a public performing-arts high school in New York City.

This required that my family move out of our small humble home in Westchester and into a family homestead where my 82-year-old mother lived. Mother planned to divide her time between living with us in her house and a small apartment in Manhattan that we bought in order to support Dani's career choice.

As a result, the entire family structure changed. My mom became an integral part of my immediate family to a new and different degree. All decisions and plans included consideration of her needs as well as those of myself, my husband, and my children. The mutual expectation was that Mom would be a steady presence during Danielle's acclimatization, providing her with the safety, security, and adult supervision that we all felt was still required for her. In exchange, Mom was closer to her working obligations in Manhattan, more mobile and socially accessible to her city friends. She expected some joy from this change, so it seemed like a win-win situation. Dani was flourishing in the new school, getting actual acting jobs, and seeming to respond well to her new living situation away from her immediate family.

For the most part, Mom seemed to adjust remarkably well to her new apartment, comfortable with the neighborhood, making friends with neighbors and enjoying her mobility. The hardest part for her seemed to be the problem of living in two places at the same time, dividing her stuff, planning for her week, where she'd land on Thursday and what books she'd need for the weekend.

The hardest for all was the task of defining our boundaries and our expectations in our newfound roles. As we began this defining process, we realized that the details of daily living kept changing. For example, on Sunday I might expect that Mom and Danielle would be spending the next Friday and Saturday at home. Then Danielle would be called on Wednesday for a job, or an audition on Saturday. Something similar might happen for the other children at school in Westchester. Consequently we all needed to learn to be very flexible and fluid while, at the same time, not ignoring the needs of the other family members or our own. We learned to focus on what we weren't willing to compromise, and to let everything else flow as best it could. For example, Dani might be performing on the evening that her younger sister Amy, an aspiring musician, was to play in the band concert. My husband might go to the band concert while I attended Dani's performance.

It became important for us that all family members knew that we were there for each other, including Mom. Everyone's needs were to be met whenever possible. No one was greedy or demanding. Each respected the demands of the situation.

In Summary

Again, we made it! We learned to lead our lives separately as well as together. We made room for each other's different needs and tastes. We coordinated plans, helped each other with our skills, and respected privacy needs. Fluid in expectations and boundaries, we learned to function interdependently. As a family group, we shared common values and accepted the ever-changing assignments as they arose.

Some of the times were more difficult than others. For example, a handicapped nephew had a serious medical emergency. The entire family dropped every ball to provide aid. Each of us assumed appropriate roles to meet the emergency. There were no obstacles that could not be overcome. The love and commitment went hand in hand, taken as a given. The trust for future crises was being built on the foundation of the track record. This type of crisis management occurred many times within our lives and the procedure has been the same each time.

If the house full of action and joys
For Grandma seems just too much noise
She'll not listen nor look
She'll find a good book
And she'll just keep her cool and her poise.
—Shura Saul

Proximity

PROXIMITY: *"Closeness, nearness, next to or nearest the point of attachment or origin."*
—Webster's Ninth New Collegiate Dictionary

The bonds between mothers and daughters extend through a lifetime and beyond—even "unto the third generation," as it were. Family patterns, themes, traditions, behaviors, idiosyncrasies, and biological and genetic attributes prevail for generations. Through the twists and turns of time and place, they may assume a range of different forms in the thoughts and actions of individuals. So, too, the idea of proximity offers many variations on its central theme.

From my house to your house
　　From my time to your time
　　　　From my way to your way
　　　　　　From my thought to your thought
　　　　　　　From my heart to your heart

As we begin to translate these idealistic and emotional reflections into our daily lives and interactions, other rhythms and melodies begin to invade our consciousness.

"So Close and Yet So Far Away"
　　"Free to Be Me"
　　　　"No One Is an Island"
　　　　　　"Love Is a Many-Splendored Thing"
　　　　　　　"You Say Toe-may-toe and I Say Toe-mah-toe"

The songs outline and summarize the twin concepts of proximity and distance, similarities and differences, isolation and sociality, privacy and comradeship, boundaries and bondings, the yin and yang of our humanness.

Our lives are a jigsaw of pieces whose forms and colors we strive to blend into one acceptable creation uniquely our own.

We puzzle over the seeming contradictions as we struggle to resolve them.

The endless creativity of the human spirit results in as many variations as there are human beings—each different and somehow, in some ways, all the same.

Proximity's joys don't belabor
You may live right next door to your neighbor
Their noise may be heard
You may say not a word
And still feel like rattling your saber!
—Shura Saul

Exercise: Proximity

How has close proximity to your family members affected you in your life? With whom are you most close? With whom are you least close? With whom are you not close at all?

In what ways is proximity a benefit to you?

In what ways is proximity a hindrance?

What are the pros and cons as you see them?

Is this closeness a burden? If so in what ways?

Would you like to change anything in this situation? What and how would you do it?

Interdependence

Webster's Unabridged Dictionary defines this simply as *"mutual dependence."*

This definition suggests a state of being in which individuals rely on each other. The people involved may be two or more individuals, for example a couple, a group, a family, or a larger collective as a community, or even an entire nation.

There is no escape from the fact that, in existence, we are all interdependent upon each other in some way.

A number of related concerns suggest themselves. Our culture strongly promotes the idea that we are each a separate entity. The concept of a separate and independent self is highly regarded. The suggestion is that being separate includes being self-reliant and, therefore, needing no one else to depend on.

Consider the extreme of this notion; that is, isolation. Consider the isolation in our society—the isolation of alcohol, drugs, nicotine, and other addictions. Is this the healthiest style of being?

The idea that anyone can be totally independent and self-reliant is an illusion.

Can we consider remodeling our idea of the relationships among family, friends, and community to include the concept of interdependence?

What do we risk? Some say we risk individuality. Does this need be so? Is it possible to develop a respect for individuality while practicing interdependence?

Some say an individual's boundaries would be threatened if one were to allow oneself to be dependent. But dependence is an inherent part of our existence.

What about the threat of being selfish, that is, totally focused on the individual self with minimum regard for the input of others? Don't we expect others to contribute in some ways to our well being?

What about allowing for a healthy dose of neediness? What's wrong with neediness? We tend to become so critical as if, once I tune into my neediness, I will abandon my independence and impose on your boundaries.

We folks are imperfect, and that makes us perfect human beings. No need for fear, self-doubt, self-criticism. We can learn to "just be," to accept who we are in a pure natural form, to allow for our vulnerabilities. We can share our true selves. We can give and take simultaneously.

This is interdependence. A strong sense of self includes the whole self, which is both weak and strong, needy and self-reliant.

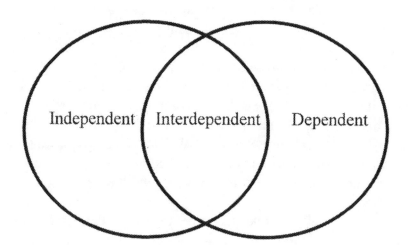

Note: All variations on the root word "dependence." Dependency is an important ingredient of the human condition.

Interdependence: Inter-generational Living

Jennifer's Voice

When I was a child, my mom worked full time. I hated this because I wanted to spend more time with her. I was rewarded with the best of all possible substitutes for her. My grandmother and grandfather became my fairy grandparents. They took turns coming to my home and taking care of me in my mom's absence.

Sometimes I'd go to their house. We had special games and activities that were reserved for those times. For example, my grandma ("Nanny," I called her) was an amazing cook and would make me blintzes for lunch. (This is a Jewish crepe filled with cheese or potato.) She taught me how to make this delicacy her special way. Of course, when I grew older and made them, they never tasted the same as hers. (I think it had to do with the lack of her unique finger flavor!) Grandpa would play educational games with me. They always involved either spelling or making change of a dollar. We would also go for walks and make up stories about people we would see along the way. Or we would buy fresh bread at the bakery and walk around the Bronx Zoo eating bits of bread.

I think we are all better people for having shared these experiences. We all relate easily within the multi-generational model and are able to experience mentors within the family.

An additional postscript to this story involves another facet of the interdependence theme. My grandparents, by enabling my mother to go to work, made it possible for her to repay the loans she had had to accept while my dad, newly returned from overseas during World War II, was completing his education. My own parents were thus enabled by their parents to purchase a house for our family so that we could have stability in our home life.

Five Generations of Mothers and Daughters
Rose's Story

When Rose left her home, and left her husband, Frank, and their baby daughter, Sue, to marry another man, they had all been living together with her widowed mother, Sarah. Grandmother Sarah was an active, caring member of this three-generation family. Rose vowed that she would never allow her mother or her daughter to suffer because of the divorce. She began a life-long pattern of caring and devotion to her mother and daughter.

Through the years, she visited her mother every day. She shopped for her, took her visiting, to the doctor, and fulfilled other filial responsibilities. Sue grew up, went to college, married, and learned to drive. She would drive Rose almost daily to maintain their longtime visiting schedule with Sarah. This routine continued even after Sue's own daughter, Jenny, was born. All three of them visited Great-grandma Sarah daily.

When Jenny was old enough to be left with Nanny Rose (as they now called her), Sue went to work at her chosen profession. Rose continued to visit Great-grandma taking Jenny with her, even using public transportation. Whenever possible, Sue would drive Nanny Rose and baby Jenny to visit their beloved Sarah. They would all go shopping and perform other errands together. Sarah died at the ripe old age of 89. Her granddaughter, Sue, was the last person to visit her in the hospital and to feed her the last bit of food she would taste.

But the chain of the mother/daughter/grandmother relationship was maintained. As Nanny Rose grew older, Sue, now aging herself, and Jenny, now a mother herself, continued the pattern of caring and visiting Nanny Rose, who was now the family matriarch.

Although they never lived together, they lived close enough to each other to continue frequent interaction. Shopping, cooking together, caring for the smaller children in the family—all these feminine tasks were shared with pleasure.

Nanny Rose lived long enough to see her daughter Sue become a grandmother. When Jenny's babies were born, Sue adjusted her work schedule to care for them one day a week in Nanny Rose's home. This enabled the working mother, Jenny, to have a bit of special time for herself.

Sue, now the grandmother, lives with Jenny and her family very much the way she, as the baby, had lived with her own grandma Sarah before her parents had divorced. Now Jenny, and her daughters of high school age, share daily tasks, problems, and pleasures of womanhood with their grandmother, Sue. The inter-generational chain has continued to add new links.

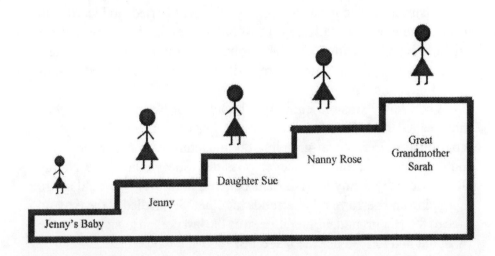

Throughout five generations
there was a continuity of
care and values.

In this story we see the
repeated pattern of
mother/daughter relationships.

For Mother's Day

by Denise Frasca

Mother
Your womb created mine
and there I am
infant
molded to your breast
your confident hands
holding me high above your head
tickling
laughing
Tucking me safely into bed
Growing up
with homemade cookies
and stories on your lap
teaching
preaching
singing silly songs in the bath
Trudging through
the dark times
guiding
praying
doing the best that you can do
Watching me
become a woman
connecting
holding
your hand upon my bulging belly

waiting
knowing
the life inside will create another
Mother

What We Think

In this family, the threads of support and mutual need meeting are clearly woven through the generations. The value system of mutual assistance, protection, and concern for each other became the essence of the mother/daughter relationships. These values were expressed in the activities of daily living and extended beyond them to affect other aspects of the family dynamics. This story demonstrates how the power of the value system is carried through role modeling to have an important impact on the lives, attitudes, and behavior of family members. In this story the building blocks of love, trust, and commitment culminated in an intimacy of respect and caring.

What Do You Think?

Can you trace similar patterns through the generations of your family? How have they affected your life, your activities, your feelings, attitudes, and relationships?

Co-Dependence

Co-dependence may be described as a relationship of two (or more) people in which each one's identity and sense of self derives from the perception of others. Each one's feelings and behaviors are reactive to the moods of others. Each is enmeshed in a dance of intimacy in which there is little or no self-awareness and beyond which there can be little or no growth.

A daughter who lives and grows in close proximity to her family may or may not become co-dependent upon her parents. Lillian matured in a co-dependent relationship with her mother and grandmother. Here is her story.

Lillian's Story

Lillian's family lived in a small private house in a large city in Ohio. She lived there with her parents, Ed and Grace Brown, and her grandmother, Mrs. Brown. Bright and pretty and the only child, she was cared for with love by the three adults. She graduated from high school with excellent grades, but elected not to attend college. Even though her parents would have done their best to send her to college, Lillian made this decision because she felt they would be financially taxed. Instead, she went to a Beauty School, and upon completion of the course, she took a job as a hairdresser. Although she was pretty, pleasant, and intelligent, she never made many friends. For socializing, she preferred to attend extended family events.

Soon after Grandma Brown's seventy-fifth birthday, Grandma developed a terminal illness. Lillian helped her parents care for their mother and enabled her to die at home, surrounded by her loving family. Lillian continued to live with her parents. Shortly thereafter, her father became terminally ill and died. Again, Lillian remained living in the same house in which she was born, this time only with her widowed mom. They took care of each other, and as Mother Grace aged, Lillian, of course, took care of her. After a long and difficult illness, Grace died.

Lillian remained alone, mourning the loss of her mother. Now a mature woman in her sixties, she lives alone, sequestered in the house in which she has lived all her life. Some of her few friends have died or moved away. She is quite alone. It is difficult to predict how her later years will be lived. Any change will be a difficult decision for her to make and maintain.

This is a three-generation story.
The third generation chose to
care for mother and grandmother.

She remained living in
the same house
and quite alone.

What We Think

Where do we draw the line between interdependence and co-dependence?

When each member of the relationship can pursue individual as well as interdependent activities, then we can say that this is not a co-dependent situation. When their lives are limited to the boundaries of the dependent relationship, we may think of it as co-dependency.

Until her mother died, Lillian was co-dependent on her mother. She never grew beyond these boundaries. Her loss never seemed to have affected her to the point where her world seemed to collapse. She remained fixed in her lifelong pattern of living, except that she now remained alone. She made no change in her life. She was left empty.

What Do You Think?

Do you find elements of co-dependency in your mother/daughter relationship? In what ways do you notice these? In what ways do these elements affect your life activities?

Typical Thoughts in Co-Dependence

What the daughter thinks

What the mother thinks

I am my mother's possession. She
expects me to act the way she
wants me to.

If she behaves a certain way, what
will everyone think of me?

I'm not good enough for her.
She's always critical of me.

I'm not good enough for her.
She's always critical of me.

Typical Thoughts in Co-Dependence

What the daughter thinks

What the mother thinks

What I do depends on how she feels.

What did I do wrong so that she isn't what I hoped for?

I feel my anger when she speaks. I can't stop myself from reacting.

I feel my anger when she speaks. I can't stop myself from reacting.

If I know mom won't approve, I won't tell her.

I wish she'd talk to me, I feel abandoned.

Exercise

Dependence...Interdependence...
Independence...Co-dependence

Identify the relationships in your life, as you perceive them to be. With whom and in what ways are you:

Interdependent (give-and-take)

Independent (what I do on my own)

Dependent (what I need from another or others)

Co-dependent (when my self-image is based on how others perceive me)

What of the above is satisfying?

What would you like to change? How will you do it?

Daughter and Mother, Both Changing

Where Is Each at This Point in Their Lives?

The Daughter: Jennifer's Voice

I couldn't believe I wasn't pregnant. I have always been reliably regular. My conditioned mind told me not to worry. The pregnancy test that I took told me I didn't have to worry. I wasn't pregnant.

As I begin to consider my middle-age status, my body reminds me that I must attend to it differently from when I was younger. My energy level needs more replenishing. I must recharge my daily battery with a siesta. I've developed arthritis in my hip and can tell you when it is going to rain. I discovered that I've inherited glaucoma from my grandmother. (You couldn't have passed on your talent for cooking instead?) My gums are particularly needy of professional cleaning. All of these issues developed during the years of my forties.

The upside of my middle age is that the changes which my body and mind are experiencing offer me an opportunity for rebirth of another sort. Of course, it is with a reconditioned engine rather than the new one I acquired at birth. But there is more wisdom this time around. I consider death a real potential any time now. My paternal grandmother died at the age of sixty-two. That is only twelve years away from my closest birthday. This could be a depressing thought. However, I consider each day as a gift.

Relationships are a priority for me. My older daughter starts college this year. Leaving the family nest, she announced to us very recently, "I'm not going on any more family vacations." This could leave me feeling empty, lonely, devalued. But, I figure, it is just for now. Maybe for her this opens the door to have new experiences, but my family life must take a new shape. My relationships must be re-knitted into this new shape.

Menopause is often seen as a time when many women feel empty and abandoned with no more reproductive potentials. I say, "Not necessarily so." The reproductive activity becomes less biological, more intuitive, more spiritual, and more abstract. I don't know what lies ahead for me, my family, my friends, but I need to feel purposeful and live as close as possible to the core of who I am. And, at this point, I know what that is.

"It doesn't happen all at once. You become. It takes a long time."
—Margery Williams

HOUSEWIFE'S LAMENT

(Song: music and Lyrics by Jennifer Rosvally)

Listen to me, honey
Tell me, baby, that you want me
And I'll tell you that I'm not around to have
You won't catch me cooking, cleaning, washing dishes, doing housework
While you sit around the house....

Chorus

I need to breathe, I'm gonna fly
And...don't ever think you own me
Don't you even try!

Cause I'm trading in my pots and pans
Saying I've got better plans
Maybe I'll just write myself a book
I have a PhD in mind
Or better yet some peace I'll find
In traveling the world just to take a look...

Chorus

From *Harmonies* by Jennifer Rosvally
and Shura Saul

156

The Mother
Shura's Voice

I am well past eighty years old. My future is limited. My plans and hopes unlimited. I know that I cannot cram them all into the few years of activity I still may have before me. What to do? What to plan?

Like my mature daughter, I know that my body's demands take precedence. I've learned to eat differently...less at one time. I get hungry at odd times of the day. My sleep patterns are often broken. I awake frequently during the night to check the time. How long have I been asleep? How long until morning? I need to rest during the day.

Why do my bones ache? Is it weather, arthritis, something else? At different times, all of the above. I hate to take unnecessary medications, so I tolerate the pains and wait to see whether they will vanish of their own accord. Most of the time they do.

In this altered physical state, my body is a harsh dictator. My thoughts and desires are in constant rebellion against its tyranny. I must constantly find a way to establish a balance.

This struggle has yielded new insights about myself and also about my important others. I've learned to recognize and respect the limitations of these changes. I also seek constantly for ways to extend the horizons of my ideas and the love I feel for my family and friends.

I have let go of unrealistic expectations for myself and even found some peace in the struggle. I have developed new understanding of my daughter's struggles, her concerns about herself and her relationships, especially with her growing children. I've been there, at that point in life where she is now. My experiences have paralleled hers, but no two lives are ever the same. I cannot wave a magic wand and make all her problems, normal as they are, go away. I can offer reassurance. Mostly, I can support her and help where I can.

For myself, I cannot control the future. I cannot submit to fears about what may happen. I can only cope with present challenges, understand my limitations, and do what I can for my loved ones. To some extent, I have become less grandiose in my expectations, more realistic, and a bit more at peace.

I haven't changed very much. My value system holds firm.

We all grapple with new
complexities of our modern times.

While each generation must
deal with differences,
we all face similar challenges.

*"In youth we learn how little we can do for ourselves; in age how little
we can do for others. The wisdom of experience is incommunicable."*
—Isabel Patterson

At My Time of Life

Shura's voice

It isn't enough to have loving friends
Who visit and dine at my home
Nor even these wonderful children of mine
Loving and kind
I still need a life of my own

It isn't enough to visit
Sip coffee, drink wine, and chat
With a roof overhead
Four walls and a bed
What sort of life is that?

       I need to plant seeds
            To watch them grow
       To expand the horizons
            Of all I know
       To study my mind
            And all humankind
       Unleash the dammed waters
            And feel their swift flow

       I need my own kind of spirit
       To explore its merit
       To know myself better
       Through music and letter
       To learn about freedom
            And being unfettered…

For you see, I'm still yearning
Still burning
Still churning
Yes, I'm still learning
How to be me!

Role-Modeling

What Mom Did to or for Me, I Pass on to My Daughter

So many times a young woman may say, "I'll never do that to my child." Yet, it may be *exactly* what she does to her child—without being aware that she is doing that! In this way, she passes the torch of a given behavior while thinking that she is fixing it.

On the other hand, when she is aware, she may truly be fixing it and correcting her mother's mistakes. The story of Karen is illustrative.

Karen's Story

Karen is a 50-year-old woman whose mother is bi-polar. Suffering from this mental illness over which she had no control, the mother would exhibit manic behavior randomly or become very depressed for extended periods of time. This behavior was never explained to Karen in any way. Therefore, to Karen, growing up, her mother's behavior always seemed very irrational. Not understanding it, she would explain it to herself by thinking or saying, "Mom's crazy."

Now a mother herself, she tries to avoid inflicting on her children the same behavior she had suffered with her mother. Yet, without the awareness and understanding of her mother's mental illness, this adult daughter also behaves inappropriately with her children. Her chief symptoms are rage, temper tantrums, lack of boundaries, inappropriate responses, and unexpected demands.

Her twenty-year-old daughter, Jane, recounts a typical example. She says, "I'll never forget the day when Mom, my three siblings, and I had spent the morning getting ready for a family outing. Finally, we were all in the car with Mom at the wheel ready to go. Suddenly, she remembered something she had forgotten. She left us all sitting in the car and ran back to the kitchen. She returned in a few minutes saying, 'We can't go now, the refrigerator is dirty. Everybody come inside and help me clean it.' Without a word we all piled out of the car to help her. We left for the outing only after the fridge was cleaned to her satisfaction."

Karen was the casualty of her mother's irrational behavior patterns, and she visited them upon her own children. If confronted about such an incident, she would have found what she considered an important explanation. Not having been able to develop a close bond with her mother, she remained emotionally empty and needy. Because this primary, basic bond never matured, all her subsequent relationships were superficial and image conscious. She was always concerned with how something looked, not with its substance or content. She was totally unaware that she was actually repeating her mother's irrational behavior.

We each do the best we
can but we are handicapped
by our own limitations.

Awareness is the key to
easing our limitations.

When There Is No Role Model

Maggie is a forty-seven-year-old mother of five teenagers. Her mother died after her younger sister was born brain damaged. Maggie is the middle child of nine children. The family was very poor with few resources. Her father's sister moved in with the family, but found the responsibilities too much to take on alone. It was necessary for the older children to become involved in caring for the younger ones. Father began to drink alcohol heavily. He became less and less involved with his family.

Maggie was very precocious and a "good girl." She saw the need for a family leader and she became the self-assigned leader. She was only sixteen years old when her mother died. She had no one to tell her how to deal with any life or parenting issues that arose.

Maggie lost her childhood to this job. She could not have a normal, healthy social life like most teenagers. She did not date until she was twenty-five years old. She married at the age of twenty-nine to a man who always told her she was never good enough. They had five children.

Maggie's lifelong aloneness continued even while she was a mother. She never knew whether she was handling her children appropriately. She created her own model of mothering based on what she saw around her. Having had very limited experiences, these observations were derived from her creative imagination, her strong common sense, the media, and her earlier experiences with her family of origin.

Maggie continues to struggle with her feelings of emptiness, lack of support, and no role model from whom to learn. What a lonely and unfulfilling way to live one's life!

Maggie undertook so much
responsibility with no help
and no one to teach her.

What a lonely and
unfulfilling way
to live her life!

When There Is a Poor Role Model

Donna is a forty-three-year-old mother of three who was raised in the Midwest. Her father was sexually abusive. Her mother was a compulsive woman who acted out by overeating and pill popping while denying what was going on in her home. Donna grew up watching her Mom's ways and suffering the effects of her father's abuse.

She married at a young age and found herself following her mom's behaviors, denying her pain and compulsively acting out her avoidance. She became a drug user and abuser. She ran away from everything that disturbed her until she found herself driving four hours daily to keep a part time job. She realized she was exhausted and became depressed. Her depression was the signal to her that something was wrong.

Her struggle culminated in two hospitalizations. As a result, she sought psychotherapeutic help. She worked hard to fight her avoidance. She joined AA and began a committed routine of self-care. This self-searching program was a very painful but enlightening time during which she uncovered layers of awareness.

The process led her along a path of huge change. She became more accessible to her children, always aware of and tending to their emotional needs even while she continued to suffer through becoming drug free. Even after she achieved the drug-free and sober state, she has continued to struggle through her ongoing maturation.

Donna has been on a
roller-coaster of
experiences in her life.

No one is ever finished coping
with the impact of such
serious circumstances.
She must continue
to cope and grow.

The Tornado

By Denise Frasca

Whirling
She pulls you
Into her eye

Quiet pressure lulls you

Has it passed?
You step forward

Smacked
With familiar force
Round and round

At dizzying speed
Confusing your senses
Into believing

Her eye is the only safe place

Step into her eye, step into the spin
Step into her eye, step into the spin

Look back
In the wake of her path

Step aside
And find shelter

When There Is a Positive Role Model

Beryl is the middle of three sisters, all of whom lived with or near their mother, now deceased. Beryl writes of role-modeling:

My sisters and I always appreciated all of Mom's greatness. However, we've discovered that her impact—and our full appreciation of all that she was to our family and to others—continues to grow even after she's gone. There are many times I want to call her now and tell her about how I'm recreating the home in which we grew up—or doing things with my kids that she did with us—or doing things she'd be proud of as a woman, wife, and mother myself. The moments are big and small. One small example is that now I take my kids with me when I go to the Red Cross to donate blood. I vividly remember when Mom took me to the B'nai Brith blood drives in Queens, and I smile as my kids talk about how they'll donate blood when they grow up.

There is also the tug of war between viewing Mom as the expert and wanting to assert my own expertise! Mom really was an expert in so many things, from political insights to home cooking, to parenting, to the arts, and arts and crafts. She was a Renaissance woman! Somewhere along our journey together, however, I started feeling more confident in my abilities. I preferred steaming my vegetables till they were a bright green, even though Mom thought they were too *al dente*. I knew I was right about certain parenting decisions—even if they differed from how Mom would have handled a situation. You must understand that my sisters and I believe that Mom was perfect. We use her parenting as a standard and only try to improve on that high standard. It was sometimes frustrating that Mom continued to offer her opinions about everything. She would share those opinions, and if we didn't agree, she would shrug her shoulders and look somewhat hurt or maybe even disappointed.

In her maturity, Beryl
appreciated the differences
between herself and her mother.

She learned from her mother
as a role model and
added her own ways.

Exercise: Role Modeling

This is a self-awareness exercise. Sometimes it's difficult to be honest with oneself about our own behavior. So much of it is unconscious. Although we can't always see ourselves clearly, while doing this exercise, try to tune into your body's signals to become as aware of yourself as you can in this moment in time.

Identify a behavior of Mom's that I notice and that has never worked for me.

Identify a behavior of Mom's that I find myself repeating in my behavior/actions/attitudes.

Identify a behavior of mine that I learned from Mom and find my children repeating.

What corrections, if any, have I made
For myself?

For my children?

What changes have I made in my relationship with my mother and/or daughter?

What different or additional changes would I like to make with my mother and/or daughter?

What It Takes to Live in the Family Village

The following journal entries record a range of episodes, insights, and techniques by daughters and mothers who live in close proximity to each other. Their brief notations illustrate their insights into their relationships.

Efraina's Journal—9/12/02

Before my daughter Celina was born, I had not planned to have a baby. The day she was born, I was an immature 17-year-old. My mom was unable to give me advice as she had had horrible experiences during childbirth in Puerto Rico. I had to go to work and painfully had to leave my baby with a babysitter. Luckily, my aunt volunteered to watch her. My aunt loved her so much and would bring her own 5-year-old daughter to play with her. The two cousins have maintained a lifelong connection.

I loved and protected my daughter from anyone who would hurt her. I wanted her to be loved and have everything great in life. At the age of 14, Celina began to gravitate away from me, as she wanted to be her own person. One day, when she went shopping with some of her friends, I wrote her a poignant letter that she read on the train. On her return home, she and I became closer, as we are still today. I have continued to remain Celina's mom and best friend.

During her junior year at college, Celina met and married a man and immediately became pregnant. Her marriage was turbulent, and I had to try so hard to help her to get through this because a baby was on the way. She took time off from her studies to have her baby, and then she returned to school.

I adore my grandson. However, my primary concern was my daughter. Celina developed multiple sclerosis a few months after her precious son was born. I hated to see her suffer emotionally in her marriage and now physically with this new diagnosis. It hurt my heart and the only thing I could think about was, "How can I make everything better for her?"

Celina was blessed with wisdom and the capacity to love everyone endlessly. I saw her begin to blossom and become quite independent. When her son was 4 months old, she returned to college despite all her obstacles, her pending divorce, caring for her infant, coping with her illness, and completing the work towards her graduate degree.

She has always been able to talk to me about everything. Sometimes it breaks my heart to see her going through her difficult times, but we always reassure each other that things will get better. We have been through many trying experiences together, such as my mother's stroke and placement in a nursing home, as well as the premature sudden death of my beloved husband, Celina's father.

Many people respect our love and close bonding. There are others who are jealous of our relationship. Celina and I do not care about the opinions of others either way because this is how "we grew together to be."

Next, Celina's writes in her journal about her mother's unconditional love, support and help, her respect for their privacy, sharing tasks, and other examples of her sensitivity in their beautiful relationship.

Celina's Journal—10/30/02

In my senior year I met and married the man with whom I had fallen in love. I became pregnant very soon after. I was in the midst of my graduate studies and my internship and had to take time off to have the baby. Mom immediately promised to stand by me all the way.

My marriage was not stable, as we were both young, and I was certainly inexperienced. My mom felt my torment but had the gift of not meddling in the marriage. However, she was very much on the side lines (to me they felt like the front lines). For example, she would buy giant boxes of Pampers, sneakers, shoes, and clothing. She never made me feel bad, as she was always spontaneously supportive in her most humble way. She knew that I had to suffer through the process of analyzing my tumultuous marriage on my own. It must have been one of the most frustrating times in her life, but she knew that I had to feel it for myself.

When I returned to my studies, Mom cared for my son all day so that I could attend class. This was difficult at times because of my very poor ambulation, as my legs would become badly uncoordinated and numb. Mom and my infant son would drive out to the school to meet me in the parking lot. Sometime later, I was divorced. During my days of illness, Mom helped me with the baby and all my chores, shopping, and laundry. I spent almost every weekend with Mom and Dad. Both of them gave me emotional support as well as concrete assistance.

Their unconditional love and support helped me to cope with the problems of those difficult days and has seen me through to the better times I now enjoy.

Efraina, Celina's mother, initiated the quality and substance of her relationship with Celina. In the next journal entry, Debby explains how she learned, through her own maturation to find ways to make changes she wanted in her relationship with her mother.

Debby's Journal—4/03/2003

I am realizing how much my relationship with my mom has changed. I guess, when I was younger, I had many expectations of her. She embarrassed me. She's so socially inappropriate. She speaks her mind and offends people. I didn't like that and had very little tolerance for it. She angered me because she thought very little about anyone other than herself. It was difficult for me to get past that.

But I think that since becoming a mother myself, and through my experiences as a teacher, I have learned patience and acceptance. I stopped expecting Mom to be someone she's not. Imagine that! We are actually friends now. She's even there for me, and I try hard to be there for her. When my husband and I plan a vacation, she offers to be available to my teenage children as needed. When I am ill, she is willing to accompany me to the doctor if I wish. I think she's more able to give to me in these ways because I need less from her than when I was younger. My expectations are less demanding, more realistic. But it sure is nice having what I always wanted, a decent relationship with Mom without anger and frustration! I think that my change in viewpoint was motivated by my forward-looking desire for my own maturing daughters to excuse my imperfections as we all age.

While Debby looked forward to healthy relationships in her own family, Anna, retrospective in her maturity, realized her need to "belong" as she grew older. She too had to find ways to connect with her mother

Anna's Journal—5/4/2003

My mom is dead one year now, and I can't believe time has gone so quickly. It's taken me so long to get over the pain of my childhood. She was so mean to me. She humiliated me all the time. She hated my friends and made fun of them when they were not around. She seemed to disapprove of me and of everything I liked. I could never do anything right in her eyes. I became angry with myself and stayed angry throughout my young adult life. It was so hard for me to see that I was tormenting myself. I couldn't find a way to make peace within myself or with her while living in her house. I realized I had to move far away and work out my issues, find my goals, make my life. I needed to feel that my life had some substantial meaning. I also needed to know that I was doing something to make a difference to someone.

Then, as I moved through adulthood, I realized that I needed to belong to a family group. I have realized that I need a mom. I had to find ways to let go of my hurt. Having developed some depth of understanding of myself, I knew that I had to develop some compassion for my mom and her past. She had a very abusive childhood and youth, during which she had been humiliated and devalued. She seemed not to have been aware of how these early experiences had shaped her behavior toward me. She had neither the knowledge nor the skills to grow beyond what had been given to her in her childhood.

Finally, I came to terms with this. I learned to channel my needs through my work, and this has brought meaning to my life. I began to believe that I'm making a difference in the world. My anger toward Mom seems to have dissolved with my more mature understanding. I can barely remember what it was like to live and behave out of anger toward her. I guess it's all water under the bridge now.

Debbie and Anna have both been able to mature into a satisfying relationship with their mothers. Julie is still "working on it"

Julie's Journal—5/12/04

I've tried so hard to please Mom. I've realized today that it is not only that I'm so different from my mother, but also, at this point in our lives, that we are not good for each other. She brought me up thinking that we are one person.

She led me to believe that I am responsible for her happiness.

I've begun to wonder, is it my job to rescue her from a bad marriage? As long as I am close by, she doesn't have to face my dad. I'm her best friend in the world, but I don't want her to be mine. I need a life of my own. I'm just beginning to understand who I am and how I am different from her. She's very materialistic. She wants me to go shopping with her to very expensive stores. Mom is from a very wealthy family and can afford this. I can't. She knows it, so she bribes me by buying me things—expensive, beautiful things. It's very seductive.

I realize that this compromises me. It's really all for her, not me. She doesn't see outside herself. Her boundaries are unclear. That makes me unclear about my own boundaries. I get worried that I won't be able to deal with the real world without her. I need some distance from her to find my own way. I feel like I need to go far away so as not to be intruded upon. I need to establish myself as a competent woman in the world without her constantly influencing me. I need to sleep on that thought.

Do proximity or distance play a role in clarifying self-doubts? Betty is a grandmother/mother who is seeking a stronger, more realistic relationship with her mature daughter. Her journal entry reflects her self-doubts along with her new found awareness.

Betty's Journal—5/20/03

These days, I am aware how much my life has changed in recent years. For most of my life, I suffered with what the doctors called a "clinical depression." For much of my life, I was in and out of the hospital, not functioning. I was aware only of myself and my pain. It felt like a dark cloud was hovering over me, following me everywhere I went. I was in treatment for many years, and now I have a healthier perspective of the world. This allows me to see other people's suffering, not just my own. I'm also more accepting of others and can better tolerate other situations that present themselves in life. I am no longer feeling like a victim. That black cloud no longer hangs over my head, no longer follows me.

I do, however, have many regrets. I know my children have suffered terribly while I was always ill with depression. I was not there for them while they were growing up. I can see the scars it has left on them, and it troubles me to know I was the cause. Now that I am out of the dark, I'd like to be more accessible to them, but it seems as though they don't want that at this point. Maybe they can't trust me, and I need to prove to them that I am trustworthy. This is the most important thing to me right now. I don't want to die and feel I could have made a difference for the better in their lives. I'm not sure how I can teach them to let go of the past, as I have finally done, but I'm going to try my best. God, give me strength to face their rejection of me.

While some mothers and daughters grapple with the very basis of their relationship, others realize that it is constantly developing. Their journal entries reflect some of their thoughts about specific issues, and some techniques they are both learning in the process of getting along within the proximity of the family village.

Jessie notes a mother's sensitivity to her mature daughter.

Jessie's Journal—6/21/04

As I search for a deeper understanding of my mother, I also begin to find evidence of her ability to understand me. I don't know why, but flying in an airplane really scares me. It seems so anti-intuitive for a big heavy machine like a plane to go up in the air and stay up there!

However, I love to travel. I want to go places whenever I can, and I don't want this fear to rule my life. My mom has been helping me to overcome my fear. In the last few years, she has made it possible for us to travel together once or twice a year. The more I fly, the easier it becomes. Her presence is reassuring. During take-off (the part I hate the most), she holds my hand. I'm actually learning to like the time in the sky and to appreciate the view from up there. I also appreciate the time away from my many responsibilities and the telephone!

Memo to self: "Thank Mom about this!"

Older mothers reflect on the challenges they face as their daughters mature. In the following two journal entries, Sheila and Sharon, grandmothers themselves, consider some ways that they found to maintain their ongoing relationships with their adult daughters.

Sheila's Journal—2/25/03

A short time ago, my daughter-in-law had a falling out with the rest of the family. By now, the crisis has passed and, in the interests of good relationships, I have long forgiven what there was to forgive. In the interests of family peace, I want to maintain friendly relationships and let go of past hurts. However, my own daughter does not feel this way. Even though the incident did not directly concern her, my daughter objects to my accepting attitude.

She and I have a very loving relationship. I've discussed my feelings with her and explained my reasons, hoping to minimize her continuing anger toward her sister-in-law. We didn't agree. Since then, having shared our differing views and respected each other's feelings, we leave the subject alone. So, I've learned how important it is to let go and to respect differences. I've also learned to compromise and still feel satisfied.

Here's an example. I love to buy gifts for all the members of my family, especially my daughters. It pleases me to please them. Once, however, I bought each of them the same expensive gift, and it was not well received by any one of them. For example, one of my daughters commented, "Can you get your money back?"

I was deeply hurt but said nothing. Since then, I either buy them their gifts when we are together on a shopping spree, or I give them gifts of money and suggest that they buy something they prefer. This way, they know I think of them, remember their important dates, and they realize that I want them to be pleased. The purposes of my gift giving are fulfilled. I don't have to control the gift itself. I am quite satisfied with this solution.

Sharon's Journal—2 /15/04

I have done some serious thinking about the ways in which I strive to maintain my good relationships with my daughters. I try to understand each one as an individual grown woman, each unique and special to me in different, if sometimes the same, ways. Although they are good friends with each other, each has developed her own lifestyle and world view. I relate to each within her frame of reference, finding my own points of commonality with each.

My older daughter is very successful in her profession. She is also a very creative and caring person and does many beautiful things for a number of people, including our family members. I am disappointed, however, that she is not married. I find myself worrying about her future and her older years. I'm concerned that she doesn't always take good care of herself. But I refrain from expressing my criticism or negative thoughts. I believe she has the right to live the life she has chosen.

Of course she knows what I think. I've had plenty of opportunity during her younger years to attempt to advise and guide her. But at this point in her maturity and our relationship, I relate only to her considerable interests. I appreciate her talents, support her numerous socially productive projects, and enjoy her remarkable intellect. Our relationship is wholesome and fruitful for both of us as we view each other as mature women.

Fortunately, I learned to be patient and sensitive with both my daughters. It was quite difficult for me when my younger daughter divorced her husband after some 18 years of marriage. She was left with her two young sons, who had enjoyed their family life and taken its stability for granted. The boys were confused and bewildered by this break in their lives.

Since it was their father who left the house, they blamed their mother bitterly for what had happened. I was distraught and tempted to intervene to set them straight on some of the facts. However, my daughter would not allow me to do this. She did not permit me to say anything negative about their father to the boys.

Much as I felt hurt, I realized that this was her life and her decision, and I respected her request. Time has proven her right. As the boys matured, they began to understand both their parents. They made peace with their mother and have come to terms with the divorce situations. I am satisfied now that, despite my misgivings during the crisis, I respected my daughter's wishes. She is happily reunited with her sons, and I am reunited with my grandsons. Thanks to the wisdom of her maturity, the family is healed!

What Do You Think?

Do you identify with or recognize anything about yourself or your relationship in any of these journal entries?

Now Write Your Own Journal Entry

Can you illustrate an insight, episode or technique in your experience that it takes to "make it work?"

Exercise: Expectation Inventory

Identify the important people in your life, e.g., mother, father, daughter, husband, children, friend.

1.

2.

3.

4.

5.

6.

7.

8.

9.

10.

What are your expectations of each?

How do you express your expectations of each?

How do they know, understand, accept and/or respond to your expectations? How do you know?

How does each measure up to your expectations?

How do you respond to the above? What do you feel, think, do, wish?

Exercise: Create a Collage

Make a collage about your family village. Look through magazine, newspapers, the internet and select words and pictures that reflect who you are and what your personal village includes. Be creative. There are no limits!

Musings

In these musings, women think about their time of life, their needs and desires, within the "family village." As children grow and the household changes, so do the women who keep things going within the village. How do they change? What are they thinking?

I'm discovering how to give up control of others, how to see and appreciate another's road, another's timid footsteps, to understand the impact of fears, the multiplicity of reckonings. How long does it take to comprehend another's style? How long does it take to tune into your grown sons or daughters and realize their experiences are different from your own? How long does it take to realize that what you know from your life and choices is different from others in your family and friends?

It takes a long time to get smart! The fear of age disappears—the power of age speaks up. We are free to give the lie of old age its burial and smile as we make ourselves known. Our new self-realization imparts a beauty that encourages everyone to make their own choices, take their chances.

From "It Takes a Long Time To Get Smart" by Edith Sarah

***

I've always been quick. Now I'm slow. As I've changed physically, I've felt some resentment. I look at the photos of my energetic, cheerful, outgoing self and realize how creative and positive I have always been. I can remember how hard I was working. I recall my multilevel living—doing so many different things all in the same time.

Observing mature women younger than myself, I see how they have matured into new levels of thought and behavior. Evidently, I too went through this same process.

Now as an older woman, I struggle with all kinds of physical challenges. I cope and overcome, but all the time I feel that these changes are invalid. This is not really who and what I am. The pain of this inner struggle is a form of depression and one cannot duck these feelings. However, facing daily challenges, I can continue learning, indulging my curiosity, and enjoying what changes may result. If some changes seem too hard, I hope to grasp the fear and make the best gist of it one can. *From conversations with "Kirsty."*

***

About forgiveness, acceptance, letting go…how do I do this? In my heart I feel, "You have done me wrong. You have betrayed me. You have hurt me." Am I supposed to forgive? I don't really know what that means. I'd rather think of it differently. I think about accepting you, as you are, whatever you may have done.

I need to be able to step outside myself, my hurt, my betrayal, and consider what may be my part in your behavior. Most of the time, each of us has a part in human dynamics. How can I step outside myself when I am hurt? Does acceptance mean that it was okay for you to do whatever you did? Oh no! Acceptance simply means I can see clearly how this incident or situation came to be. How it is. Now, it has occurred. Can we change it?

Free of wanting it to be different, I can see beyond my own hurt. How things "are" may be totally not okay but that's how they are. Sometimes we may be able to discuss the incident openly and honestly. But sometimes, for various reasons, that cannot be done. Alternatively then, perhaps given some space and time, I can let it go. Perhaps you too can let it go. I can move on. Perhaps we can both move on.
From conversations between Shura and Jennifer

Guideposts for Thought

1. The family village is the garden whose fruits bear the guiding principles for thought and action.
2. The culture of the family village extends through generations while shape-shifting beliefs and behaviors.
3. Proximity and distance are chosen circumstances that influence the individual's lifestyle.
4. There are always pros and cons.
5. Human beings are social folks. We are interdependent on one another.
6. Sometimes the interdependence can become unbalanced. Then we may become too dependent while losing our sense of adequacy. Or we become co-dependent, when our sense of self is only in response to another. Or we become too independent, when we refuse anyone else's input.
7. We may all experience this varied range of behavior. It is desirable to achieve a balance.
8. The aging process is pregnant with change, opportunity, and loss. The changes are both external and internal. We must remain open and aware of them and the new shapes that our lives can develop.
9. We all tend to respond to the role model provided by our mothers. Either we repeat their patterns in our own behavior or we react to them in an effort to change. Our role models are a part of ourselves.
10. Sometimes, our reactions are not in our best interest. Self-awareness, mindful speech, and mindful behavior are the keys to purposeful change.

11.   Sometimes, within the family village, we struggle to live in harmony with ourselves and each other. The clearer we can be about our own individuality, the better we can share unconditional love for one another.

12.   It takes a lifetime to achieve these skills. We can learn from each other if we stay open in the process.

Chapter Four
The Other Side of the Mountain:
The Village at a Distance

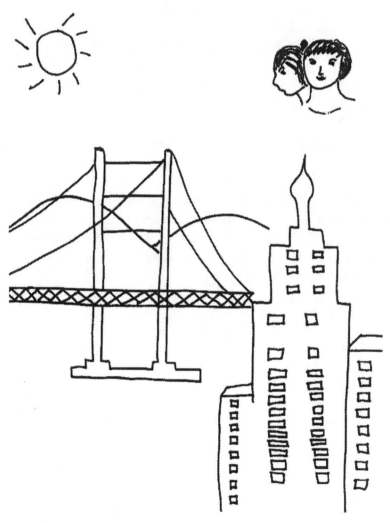

Letter from Judith

My Dear Shura and Jennifer,

It is a very interesting and delicate enterprise you are undertaking. It is quite difficult to express my feelings without resorting to self-pity! Let me say briefly, it is very difficult to live so far from one's daughters (one in Japan and one in the States). Without constant feedback the relationship suffers.

Also, due to the great expense of traveling, visits are not regular. I find that when we visit together the bonds are strengthened again. But after no contact for a considerable time, one loses touch—especially in regard to the everyday activities of the family that are so important to both mother and grandmother.

I feel very cut off from the lives of Bonnie and her family as well as from Deborah and her family. Take care and best wishes.

Fondly, Judith

This letter sums up in a
nutshell, the emotional
impact of distance.

No mother wants to feel
cut off from her children.

What We Think

Telephone conversation between Jennifer and Shura following receipt of this letter:

Jennifer: Hi, Mom, how are you? I just received the letter from Bonnie's mother that you forwarded to me.

Shura: Yes, I'm sure you feel as I do about it. I realize what a struggle it is for her to be alone and so far from her daughters and their families.

Jennifer: I imagine it is hard for her daughters to be away from her too.

Shura: She's really missing some of the important experiences of being a grandmother.

Jennifer: I feel sorry for her grandchildren who don't have her in their lives.

Shura: It's interesting that she says the relationships have new meaning whenever they get together. But money and energy are important issues for her. It's hard for an old woman to travel such long distances.

Jennifer: The extended distance between visits makes it doubly difficult to keep the bonds strong.

Shura: Grandmother doesn't see the kids growing and isn't in touch with their daily experiences. She doesn't see her own daughters maturing as women and mothers.

Jennifer: I know how much it meant to me to have my grandparents as part of my childhood. I have this memory from long ago that when I was very upset with you and dad I would run into the bathroom crying. I would chant, "I want my grandma…I want my grandpa!"

Shura: And my whole life has been beautifully colored by my relationship with my own grandmother. She was close to me in my adult years as well as she lived to be quite old. We were both very lucky.

Jennifer: I know you've been a major influence for my children as they grew so close and so involved with you and dad from the get go. I can see why she feels self-pity, being so cut off from her daughters and their families.

Shura: No mother wants to feel self-pity or any sort of pity, as she grows old. It feels as if your life was a failure.

Jennifer: No mother wants to feel so cut off from her children.

Shura: Yes. It's very sad for all the generations.

Jennifer: Let's begin Chapter Four, about the effects of distance, with this letter. It sums up, in a nutshell, the emotional impact of being far apart.

What Do You Think?

Do you experience distance of any kind in your mother/daughter relationship? What kind of distance is it? How do you maintain the mother/daughter bond despite such distance?

THE RELATIONSHIP SUFFERS

Jennifer's Voice

Distance dividing
We cannot speak now
I want to be part of your life
But I'm not sure quite how

I yearn for feedback
Too much I'm alone
We write, we e-mail,
We speak on the phone

When we do get together
Bonds strengthen again
Then long times of no contact
Lonely nights in my den

Cut off from family
Though distance divides
My heart always with you
My love always provides.

Global Closeness

There are new possibilities for the people living on earth at this point in time. For one, people of the world can communicate with each other through a range of media. We have ready access to information at our fingertips. We can connect with strangers anywhere on the globe. Our grandparents would have found all of this fascinating and fabulous. Yes, these are interesting times.

This chapter demonstrates and discusses some of these methods of communication that help to maintain bonds over distance.

Clearly, these thoughts are relevant to mother/daughter relationships at a distance. We are more accessible to each other. Some families who live far from each other e-mail each other daily. This may seem cold and distant, but e-mail does provide a framework for connecting that otherwise may not exist for shut-ins, handicapped or aging people. This is a doorway to the world, which transcends physical limitations.

People may be living at a distance from each other for many reasons. Geography is only one kind of distance through which people are able to communicate with relative ease. Other forms of separation, emotional, ideological, legal are more powerful and difficult barriers to overcome.

So we have come up with a phrase "global closeness" to suggest that we can remain close to each other despite the various distances. This open door view presents wonderful possibilities as well as challenges.

We can remain close
to each other despite the
various kinds of distances.

Geography is only one
kind of distance. There are
others even more
difficult to overcome.

We in the Universe

Shura's Voice

The world and universe are one
Endless sky and untold sun
Within its mystic unity

Creatures live and flowers bloom
Tides in rhythm with the moon
Ocean, clouds and wind and rain
Created in a magic chain
Thus the universe is wrought

       Separate is a human thought
       From this united majesty
       We alone are set apart
       To span such distance as divides
       To weld heart to heart
       And sundered soul to soul

Conquest of our human space
Challenges our human race
To blend within the universe
To complete the cosmic whole.

I Live in a Place Called "Far"

The title for this segment came to us during a discussion with a group of older mothers and mature daughters who were attending a national conference on aging. The following comments are excerpted from this session and others that related to "distance." They suggest a number of concerns expressed by mothers and daughters who live far apart...sometimes their remarks explain the reasons this is so...sometimes the feelings are voiced...sometimes they describe the dilemmas and conflicts they experience. All of these remarks are quoted almost verbatim from notes taken at the discussion.

"I live in a place called "far." Yes, I really mean it; it is far from everywhere and sometimes I feel very lonely and isolated. Sometimes I wonder why I'm here—but I guess the reasons for being here are stronger than the reasons for staying back home. So here I am and I put up with the loneliness!"

***

"When I was living near my mother, I found myself doing to my daughter what my mother had done to me. Much of that was negative. For example, my mother was compulsive about cleanliness—we needed to observe every strict rule of hers. I found myself doing that with my daughter and really didn't like it. That was only one of the things I couldn't bear. Now we're separated by distance, and I'm very satisfied with a relationship at a distance."

***

"Even though we lived near each other, we never did discuss important concerns. How I felt, or what I wanted or thought—these were never anything we talked about. It was always about what she wanted or needed or thought. It was often what she thought about me and what I was or wasn't doing. Or what I should be doing! Finally, as soon as I could, I moved as far away from her as I could, so that I could learn what I wanted for myself. Learn to be myself. I got a pretty late start on that process, but it worked. Now we can talk like two mature women, at least on the telephone. And she's not right there to tell me what to do all the time. I think my mother forgot I was no longer a teenager. Now she knows."

***

"Well, I've become the 'bad guy' with my daughter. I had always been a housewife and mother. When my husband died and I turned seventy, I decided to try a different life. I dyed my hair and went into business. I'm very successful.

"But I am disturbed about something. My daughter, who had been living near me with her family, moved far away. I don't understand. Just at the time of my life when I can be there more for her, she's leaving me. Maybe she doesn't approve of my new life.

"It makes me nervous to be alone at this time of my life. I am separated from her and my grandchildren. I really don't know what to do. I don't know why she suddenly moved away. It seems I have no choice."

***

"My mother hurt my feelings in many ways when I was younger. I moved far away because I couldn't take her insensitivity...her coldness. Now I am trying to forgive her, and perhaps myself, for the impatience we both showed to each other. I'm not sure I know how."

***

"I'm getting older and frailer. I can't really do everything the way I used to. I have been a very independent person all my life and hate to ask for help. My daughter lives quite far away. I haven't shared this with her. I don't want to be a burden to her—she's been so free herself all these years."

***

"My mother has remarried in her older years. I can't stand her new husband, and I don't see how she can. I stay as far away from them as I can. I don't know how else to handle it."

***

"I love my daughter very much, and I respect her too. She's very smart and capable. But she treats me like a teenager. She tries to tell me what to do all the time. She knows better than me about everything. She worries when I go out and come home late. She hovers over me. I can't take it! It's best that we don't live too close to each other."

***

"I moved away before I was married. Now I'm a mother myself, and realize that my children and I are missing the presence of my mother in our lives. It isn't easy to communicate at a distance. We cannot move. I don't think she should be uprooted. But I do believe we'd like to be closer than we are."

***

"Oh, dear. It is all so complicated!...Is it too late?"

> *"Just remember. We're in this all alone."*
> —Lily Tomlin

What Do You Think?

Do you experience distance of any kind in your mother/daughter relationship? What kind of distance is it? How do you maintain the mother/daughter bond despite such distance?

Far

Jennifer's Voice

I live in a place called "far"
Nobody knows my name
Alone in my room
I live
in a place called "far"
I traveled a lifetime to find
My heart sheltered from past hurts
Past life, memories painted with teardrops
So
I live in a place called "far"
Far from those who love me
I hide
I'm safe in a place called "far"

I've been told that the
further away you live
from your parents the better.

Yeah! Anywhere from
500 to 3,000 miles
is enough!

What We Think

Shura: The word "loneliness" comes up frequently in the remarks of these women. Yet, each speaker seems to feel that this is how things must be…either she sees no way out or doesn't want a way out.

Jennifer: Perhaps they have achieved a certain acceptance of their loneliness. Maybe that offers them some peace.

Shura: Some of the daughters suggest that many of their earlier feelings and ideas have become clarified because of the distance and that therefore they are able to maintain what they consider a reasonable relationship with mother.

Jennifer: As daughter grows up and becomes her own person, it is also her task of maturation to develop her own acceptable boundaries in relation to mother. She needs to implement these boundaries in whatever way she can be comfortable with their limitations and her relationship with her mother. I think that's what we are finding in these comments.

Shura: The issues of understanding and forgiveness seem to puzzle and disturb both the mother and the daughter. Some of the speakers cannot seem to find a way to get past these obstacles which are part of the process of healthy separation…part of the process of letting go and then coming together in more adult ways as each woman herself grows into new phases of her life.

Jennifer: Some daughters seem to find it difficult to remain clear about their own adult identity while they remain present in their mothers' energy field. This skill of "identity clarity" takes maturity and self-awareness. Establishing a firm and

207

comfortable sense of one's self takes time, thought and openness to learning and change.

Shura: Yes. The struggle for one's identity can be a lifelong process because while we know we change in some ways, in other important ways we remain the same. We must be aware of the specifics of this process as we mature. In other words, we must recognize for ourselves in what ways we change and in what ways we remain the same.

Jennifer: As we mature we learn to cope with what we know are our behavior patterns. This knowing both confirms identity and helps us learn ways of coping with those behavior patterns that don't work for us. This is an important aspect of maturity.

Shura: I suppose for some people "far" helps the process.

The skill of "identity clarity"
takes maturity and self awareness.

I suppose for some
people "far" helps
the process.

Celina and Efraina:
How They Manage Their Distance

Celina and her mother (Efraina) both write about how they manage their distance apart.

Celina Writes:

After my dad died, Mom married a wonderful man, Louis, and they built a beautiful home in Cape Coral, Florida. Steve and I will hopefully, one day, join them after we know that our son is fine and settled in his career endeavors.

I tell Mom I don't miss her because, "If I need to speak with you, I just pick up the phone or I can just book a flight with Jet Blue and be in Fort Myers in three hours." Last year, when I was not well I told her, "Mom, you don't have to worry because Steve is here." Mom, of course, was on the next plane to New York so that she could cook, clean, and support Steve, Alex, and me during the difficult time. She is too much!

I know that I will always be there for her.

I love you, Mom.

Celina

Mother Efraina Writes:

I now live in Florida with Louey my husband, and I was actually able to make a new life for myself after my husband Carlos' death…and after being certain that Celina and I had done a good job helping and loving her son. Louey adores Celina. He recognizes and respects the strong bond that I have with my daughter.

I was able to sustain this geographically distant decision because I know that Celina is blessed with an angel, her husband Steve, that her father sent her. I believe that Carlos sent Steve to care for and love my daughter. Steve is the best, and my daughter deserves only the best.

Separation is the worst time for me, but my daughter and I assure each other that we will see each other very soon. The airplane is just three hours away from each other. My thoughts make it possible to endure this separation.

Love you forever.
Mom

What We Think

Celina and her Mom clearly have a solid relationship. It is plain to see that the geographical distance is not an obstacle but a challenge. Both of them realize they can use the telephone to keep in touch and plan to be together. They do not use the expense as an excuse. Of course, in many cases, travel expense is a real problem. However, for some people it is used as an excuse and becomes a primary obstacle. For Celina and her Mom, the financial expense is part of their emotional budget. The cost of a telephone call is as important as milk in their budget.

It is a given that for many moms and daughters there will be emergencies. What constitutes an emergency? The answer is individual and personal. Even though Celina told her mother that her (chronic and debilitating) illness was under control, Mom was on the next plane to help.

What Do You Think?

What constitutes an emergency for you? What do you do in such times?

Letter from Lisa

Dear Jennifer and Shura,

We are blessed that our families have been able to visit often around special events and holidays. It delights me that we remain so close and supportive of one another's lives and work.

Ann L. is still in California, a family and child therapist, with many friends. Her daughters, Helen from New York and Mary with her husband Abe from Concord came to have a happy Thanksgiving dinner with the rest of us at Emily's in Northampton.

The big news in the family is that Mary and Abe are expecting their first child in April! Ann will be with them as that welcome child arrives. And I'll be thrilled to be a Great-granny!

I continue to be grateful for good health and for the wonderful love of family, and for friends. This brings my love and fervent prayers for Peace in the year ahead! We all send our best regards to you.

Lisa

In what way does your
extended family keep in touch?

Does Lisa's letter
give you any ideas?

What We Think
Jennifer's Voice

Lisa's family of grown sons and daughters is scattered with people living at distances from each other. They use special events and holidays during the year to maintain their relationships. During these times, they share viewed about each other's work and activities. (The good news as well as the difficult news.)

Clearly, mothers and daughters keep in touch in other ways as well, but these family gatherings become a time of replenishment. The rhythm of the development of the family is shared and they become involved with the growth and development of young and old wherever they may be.

What Do You Think?

In what ways does your extended family keep in touch? Does Lisa's letter give you any ideas?

Letter from Shirley

Dear Shura,

Your mother/daughter project gave me cause to think! Not very productively, I fear: some memories being pretty negative and not leading to much enlightenment.

Two scenarios stick with me. As my mother got frailer she gave up her house in the Lake District and, as so many do, took a flat near my older sister in the Midlands. When unable to drive, she would press my sister or anyone else into taking her on an urgent shopping quest for something, often electrical. Some two days after acquisition there would be another phone call to my sister to say she did not want whatever it was, "Would one of the girls want it?" Sadly, no, they didn't, so it had to go back to the store. As an occasional exercise this was amusing, but as it became a habit my sister got more and more irritated.

Since I lived some 400 miles away, this did not present a particular irritation to me. However, it did give me pause for thought. I realized that this was one of the few ways in which my mother could exercise any form of power or control—and thus a sense of identity. Because I did not bear the brunt of this, I think I was able to help my long-suffering sister to understand and therefore tolerate this identity-confirming behavior with more equanimity.

The other, a process rather than an event was at a later stage when Mum had to accept residential care. We were finally lucky in finding a residential home in which she was as contented as she had been for years. It was a place closer to where I live. Trying to settle her in, I was anxious to make it as much her "home" as possible. All of my suggestions had been vetoed. Photographs, no…souvenirs, no…Eventually I began to realize that she wanted to remember her lovely living room with its treasures as it was, and not dismembered for her small room. She needed the memories of her gracious living to remain intact.

Not easy to accept, because it made me feel helpless to make things good for her, but it made some sense and I had to accept it, and the change it represented in her.

I hope these notes are helpful to you and Jennifer.

Love, Shirley

What We Think

Shirley has given us two very sensitive thoughts. An older mother may well feel that she has lost her power to control many parts of her world, many aspects of her life. This loss may seem like a minor one, as it expresses itself through an effort to control what seems unimportant to others. The pattern of behavior that Shirley describes, as it is reported, could easily be interpreted in many other ways. Her mother could be seen as thoughtless, or heedless of the effort to which she pushes her daughter. She may be seen as "addled," that is, not knowing what she wants. She may be seen as annoying and ungrateful to those who are only trying to please her.

Again, in the second instance, the daughter is trying to please, and mother seems impossible to please. Shirley searches for a reason and finds one that helps her to understand and therefore, to cope with, what seems like her mother's unreasonable attitude.

It is difficult for those who still retain their life styles and most of these powers, minor as they seem, to understand how important they may have become to an older person. Daughters may become impatient and judgmental when they have to bear the brunt of such behavior. The sensitivity that Shirley displays goes a long way toward helping a daughter as well as a mother, to cope with this kind of behavior.

What Do You Think?

Do you observe or feel issues of control in your mother/daughter relationship? If so, how does it make you feel? What do you do with these feelings? What do you say or do in response?

Quirky behavior may
be expressing an important loss.

It's important to look
beyond the behavior
if you want to
understand the person.

What We Think

Shura's Voice

On the One Hand

There once were a daughter and mother
Who truly loved one another
Denying dependence
And also ascendance
They stayed close and yet far from each other.

On the Other Hand

There once was a daughter named Fay
Who wrangled with Mom night and day
So, she got in her car
To follow her star
And was friends with her Mom far away.

Now Think of This

Some families at distance were scattered
And feared their relationships shattered
Their values they shared
And for each other cared
The distance, they found, hardly mattered!

Sonia's Story

Modern Technology has affected family life in many ways. Some of our respondents have written about its effects on their opportunities to enable and enhance relationships.

Sonia is a 70-year-old woman with multiple sclerosis. She came from Puerto Rico. Her family was very nasty to her during her early years of growth and adolescence. She was physically abused as a child. Growing up, she became estranged from her mother who had continued to treat her abusively even as an adult.

Sonia married and then divorced an alcoholic husband who was also mentally abusive. She has three daughters now grown themselves. They try to be kind to her, but Sonia tends to push them away. In her older years, Sonia became cynical, angry, and depressed. She became more and more isolated as the years went on. Sonia had minimal financial resources and lived very frugally on the income from her disability. She had a few friends and remained distant from her daughters.

Someone gave her an old computer, and she suddenly discovered that she was able to use the Internet to open her world. She became computer wise and explored chat rooms, surfing the net for information about her medical problems. Her oldest daughter, who lived at a distance, started to e-mail her. This sparked a new type of relationship with others in her family. The privacy of her computer allowed her to communicate with family at a safe distance.

This communication offered an opportunity for her daughters to understand Sonia better. Having been the product of an abusive home, Sonia had learned to be abusive herself. She had always been difficult to deal with, especially as she had always exhibited mood swings. Her daughter had never understood how to deal with these mood swings. However, by communicating through the computer they were able to bypass the emotional consequences of Sonia's erratic behavior. Actually, they learned that their mother's irregular ups and downs of her emotional state had developed while she had been living alone. In her isolation, she had developed a state of mind that caused her to raise and lower her emotional state unpredictably. This had seemed to her daughters to be mood swings. They thought that she was irrational and crazy.

Today, Sonia continues to live an isolated life, quite distant from others. However, she is a little less lonely thanks to her computer and the opportunities it provides for safe communication with important people in her life.

What We Think

Jennifer's Voice

Sonia had been living in a lonely world, isolated from people and resources. Due to her unhappy childhood, early adulthood and marriage, she had sunk into a state of withdrawal and depression. She coped with her pain by becoming distant from normal social interaction. Her entire emotional map became distorted as she continued to live at this social and emotional distance from others.

At an earlier time in history, believing that she had no options, she might have remained this way until she died. However, through the opportunities afforded by modern technology, Sonia found ways to overcome some of her loneliness. The computer became a safety filter against the possible toxicity of the problems she had experienced in her younger years. The web and e-mail became lifelines for Sonia allowing her to socialize and communicate with her daughter. These were relationships she had been unable to maintain before learning to use the computer. Modern technology allowed her to develop safe connections with significant people.

What Do You Think?

Have you observed or experienced any ways in which technology has helped your relationship? Have you found it to act as a channel to safeguard family dynamics? Has it altered physical distance and/or brought relationships closer?

Sonia's daughter realized
that contact through the
computer assists her mother
to be more appropriate.

The computer allows Sonia
to keep connected while
maintaining boundaries.

Judy's Story

Judy moved to California shortly after she was married. Her mother, Dorothy, remained living in the East. Judy wrote us this letter some months after her mother died, when her adoptive father was reorganizing their home.

"Here, do you want these back?" he asked handing me a stack of videotapes, highlights of the last ten years—my California garden, grandchildren, great grandchildren, a wedding—that had been my connection with Mom across 3000 miles. She loved all of them and in our phone conversation we would chat about the details.

We connected through the tapes, phone calls, letters and visits. Me and "Mommy," the woman who sacrificed to make my life better than hers. For, in a strange twist of fate, I too (like herself) became a fatherless daughter and the focus of her life.

Dorothy was a selfless, protective mother. "Here, you have the sweater, jacket, largest bedroom, balanced meals, piano lessons, college, even an adoptive father…" knowing that these were all the things she never had. "No, we were sent to boarding school. I never had any of this," she would say. "I want you to have it. I want you to be happy."

Great happiness, embarrassment and rage would well up in me. I hated the obligation attached to all this. Pressure I couldn't live up to. I was ashamed of her love then.

Only in my adult years could I sort through these issues and make sense of our relationship. That she loved me deeply was evident. She eagerly, joyously shared my life through phone calls, visits and mail after I moved west. Who else would send her daughter autumn leaves?

Or be charmed by the antics of her grandchildren and great grandchildren?

As we aged we became closer. On my visits East, I sat long hours listening to and videotaping some stories of her girlhood and marriage to my father, mostly skirting around the occasion of his death when I was two and she just 28. It was the tragedy that bound us together, secretly, separately from all else until her death.

"No, Dad, [my adoptive father,] I guess I don't need the tapes anymore," I answered.

What We Think

In contrast to Sonia, Judy had had a warm loving relationship with her mother from her earliest days. They were able to maintain this relationship despite the distance that ultimately divided them.

Through creative use of various technological media they were able to share important and significant stories. The grandmother was enabled to develop a positive, relationship with her grandchildren. Videotapes, phone calls, e-mails—they used whatever media possible to keep in touch. This ongoing record across the miles and through a number of years allowed Judy to mature in her own role as mother and also as daughter to an aging mother.

Judy's growing understanding of their relationship also contributed to the healthy development of her insight into her own maturity and self-understanding.

What Do You Think?

Does this story trigger any ideas for you?

Rosalie's Letter

How many ways do we measure distance? Rosalie, incarcerated for many years, has used all possible media available to her to keep up with the lives of her daughters and grandchildren. Many families encounter unusual obstacles to separate their members. Rosalie's story is unique and exceptional.

The relationship between my six daughters and myself has been put to tremendous test over the past sixteen years. I should note that I have been incarcerated these sixteen years of which I speak. Five of my daughters live in the far south west. One daughter lives in New York State an hour and a half from this correctional facility.

Even though we have remained in touch through mailed packages, letters, cards, and phone calls, plus yearly visits, I have missed very significant happenings in their lives: pregnancies, births, holidays, birthdays and many other special occasions that have been celebrated.

My second oldest daughter, Wendy, was diagnosed in the year 2000. The worst, the most painful, news a mother could ever hear is that her child has cancer. I have experienced many painful, dark days throughout my life, but all have paled by comparison with my daughter's illness. Wendy cried for me every day. I was with her in every way possible. Phone calls were granted to me on a daily basis. I mailed cards and letters every day. Finally I was granted permission to make a video for my daughter to watch me and to hear my voice. Our relationship became more important than breathing for me.

I could not be transported to visit my daughter. She lived thousands of miles from where I live. In New York State there is no provision in place which would allow for family-illness visits. As my daughter

Wendy's time grew short, my daughter Michelle searched and found a foundation that would pay for a video conference. She contacted the Department for Correctional Services and the facility for permission for the video conference to take place. Once this was approved, she received confirmation from St. Mary's Hospital for the conference to take place. They readily embraced this request. On August 27, 2002, my daughter Wendy and I would visit for the last time. This was without question the darkest of my days. The distance between us was like the Great Divide.

I had mailed, at my daughter's request, a pair of my cotton pajamas. She did not want me to wash them, but rather to wear them and mail them to her. My son-in-law made another request some weeks later as Wendy hated to take the pajamas off and she did not want to wash my scent from them. I mailed another pair of pajamas. The first pair was mint green; the second pair was pale pink. Wendy lost her courageous battle on September 10, 2002. She was surrounded by her children, sisters, nieces and nephews. Her husband and I were on the phone nearby. The relationship between all my daughters and myself became intensified during those painful years. I was needed by everyone. The great distance was the geography. Our love survived the miles.

Recently, each of my daughters, in one fashion or another, have been identifying with me. There grew a strong desire to know what my childhood had been like. Their need to know me has become even more important since my daughter Wendy passed away. I understand their need to know, their positions and why they seek answers from me to be able to move forward with their lives.

They still need my support, guidance, and advice whether they listen or not. My love and hugs are of equal importance to each daughter. We continue on our journey through phone calls and visits at the facility when they can afford to travel and when they have vacation time. We send letters and cards keeping up on current events and special times.

When I was young my mother drifted in and out of my life. We had no special relationship. For years I had thought she was dead. I never knew her. It was because of this great distance between us, that I had no guide, no role model as I grew into womanhood. My self-esteem was shattered as I grew up. I felt abandoned and stuck with the fact that my mother did not love me. It was late in life when she wandered back from the past. As fate would have it, she lived two blocks from where I parked my vehicle at night where I worked for years. She had missed the important years that could not be repeated. She was a grandmother who had not yet met her grandchildren.

Children do grow up and relocate leaving what families they were with, what they had felt secure with. They leave the nest in search of their journey on their lives' paths. Relationships change between mothers and daughters, but not to the point of severing the relationship with their mothers. They find themselves years later with a reunion as a perpetual goal. A mother's place in her daughter's life is hardly the site she occupied years before. This relationship leads to a new bonding between a mother and a daughter. It is really like a tentative partner in a woman-to-woman camaraderie.

Being a mom who is incarcerated, I realize that while I still have a place at the family table, this place is different now. My daughters are grown, and they are like the great mythical bird, the Phoenix, who rises from the ashes of its own destruction. My beautiful daughters have flown the nest and have come full circle…with the ability to emerge from the tragedy of the past 17 years, and take flight.

> *"The giving of love is an education in itself."*
> —*Eleanor Roosevelt*

What Do You Think?

For this mother the separation from the daughter who needs her is due to her incarceration and geographic distance. Is there a type of geography other than physical distance?

Ideological Connections

A Conversation with Bernice

Bernice's daughter, Marian, and her husband left family and hometown to live at a distance for many years. Yet she took the essence of her family's values with her. Her mother tells how, "My heart always with you, my love always provides."

"My oldest daughter, Marian, moved to Arkansas. Her way of life was different, but her values were the same as our family's have always been."

"My Bubby always told me I should never say I have nothing to do. She would say, 'think of something else.'"

"I would ask, 'Bubby, what should I do?' And she would say, 'You know Mrs. G. upstairs? Bring her newspaper up the three flights of stairs.'"

Bernice said, "I did that for years. I've remembered that all of my life. Now, whenever I get up in the morning I think of whom I can help and how. I always do something like that first thing in the morning."

"I never wanted material things," Bernice continues. "Marian likes helping people. Material things never meant anything to her....

"We bought Marian's house for them when they got married. Her husband never wanted to own a home. They used that money to buy acreage in Arkansas. Her husband was also from a privileged home. Marian never got an engagement ring, but her husband, being an avid bicyclist, taught her to cycle and bought her a very, very good bicycle. But then they moved to Madison County, Arkansas. Why did they move so far away? Because her husband wanted to. They built their house themselves. Marian said, 'I've got to have the best bathroom and the best kitchen.'

"No heat," Bernice told us, "no air-conditioning; the walls didn't touch the ceiling. But there was a big stove in the main room. They had the money for anything they wanted. But this is what they chose to do. Her husband didn't want children. So she decided she would help other people's children.

"I once asked her, 'Marian, are you sure you don't want to have children?'

"Marian answered, 'Mom. Think of Henrietta Szold. She never had children of her own, but she saved thirty thousand children through Hadassah Youth Aliyah. Some people save children who are not their own.'

"Marian's neighbor's child was deaf. Marian asked her, 'Why doesn't she go to school?' She found out that there was no school for handicapped children. Marian rounded up 15 deaf, blind, retarded, epileptic, and other handicapped children in the area. She started a school for them. She called it, "School for Exceptional Children." She went to the local church, and they allowed her to use the basement.

"My father-in-law, her grandfather, sent mattresses down for the kids to rest on. I came down the first year to visit and see the school.

"When Clinton was Governor of Arkansas, Marian went down to Little Rock and petitioned for her kids to be admitted to the public school. They were all admitted. Every year, Marian took her kids to the Special Olympic Games run by Eunice Shriver."

Bernice looked over at us and said, "I was always a volunteer, you know. I worked with the Brownie troop. Marian does that too. She reads to blind people. Maybe she got this from me. I don't know. What do you think?"

We asked her how she felt when Marian moved away to live this different-from-her-family life.

Bernice said.,"I was very much against it when she moved down there. I was concerned about the different way of life she was choosing. I went down to visit the first year. I went to the Christmas Party. When

I saw all she was doing I thought, 'Who am I to criticize?' She made a life for herself, and I was very proud of it.

"At the party a woman came in looking like someone out of a Norman Rockwell painting. She was carrying a little girl whose eyes were like a frog. I said to the little girl, 'Why don't you go and play with the other children?' After hesitating, she did go off to play.

"The mother asked me, 'Which child is yours?'

"I answered, 'The teacher is my child.' The woman looked at me and began to weep. 'Your child,' she said, 'is truly the most exceptional child in the room.'"

We asked Bernice "How did you keep in touch?"

She told us they'd talk on the phone. "Not often," she said. " I didn't call her every day. They both knew we were there for them if they needed us. We also went down to Arkansas to visit a few times."

We asked "When you'd talk on the phone, did she tell you about her work?"

"Yes, she'd tell me what she was doing. There was one deaf boy who could hear the animals, yet his mother called him 'deaf.' She worked with him. She was so excited when he would start repeating to her what she was saying. Yes, I always followed what she was doing.

"Marian and her husband moved back to Chicago a few years ago. She lives near me. It was wonderful to have her home. She began to go to the library and help some non-English speaking people to read. The librarian suggested that she become a librarian, and so she did. She works in the children's section."

"It's easy to be friendly with my daughter. She doesn't ask for much. We are not materialistic people. We never belonged to country clubs, never had fancy cars, or anything like that.

"Yes, I consider myself close to her. She may even be closer to her father. As for taking care of me—I'm not one to run to doctors. She's so afraid that I'm not telling her everything about my health. She has my doctor make copies for her of his prescriptions for me.

"She was far away for a long time. But I knew she took so much of her early life with her…the giving…the helping…the teaching. She made a life for herself and I have always been proud of that.

"Now I'm happy to have her nearby."

"Life will be over sooner than we think. If we have bikes to ride and people to love, now is the time."
—Elizabeth Kubler-Ross

The daughter carried her
family values with her even at a distance.

Mother and daughter stayed
connected through their
shared values.

What We Think

Marian made a number of significant changes in her lifestyle from the privileged and traditional style of her mother and family, yet her mother was able to realize that she retained the values and principles she had learned in the family. Another mother might have felt abandoned and rejected by Marian. Bernice saw that Marian was making her own life in a positive way. Here were two amazing women living close to their mutual values. Geographic distance and lifestyle differences notwithstanding, they still remained true to the core meaning of their lives. The essence of their relationship remained very powerful.

What Do You Think?

Do you share mutual values in your relationship? In what ways are they experienced or expressed?

How Emotional Distance Comes About

Jennifer's Voice

My family has its own way to deal with anger. You swallow it. Some branches of the family try to eat it down. Some drink it down, and some smoke it down. It is a family tradition to avoid expressing anger overtly at any cost. Sometimes when I'm angry, I don't even realize it. I may project it out onto something or someone else and experience it as if someone is angry with me. Or else, I may see it head on and just sit with it, watch how it moves, dancing into different shapes in my mind and finally disappearing.

My experience has taught me that most people have some version of this issue in their lives. I have since learned to allow room for anger as a human experience and not dwell on the passion that could develop. I think, however, this is a skill that most people have not yet learned.

Many times, anger is a mask for other emotions. Professionally, I often see people who access anger easily, but really underneath this anger is a great deal of pain. For them, it is easier to feel anger than to acknowledge pain. When the pain derives from our families, it can be extremely, not a little, painful. When pain is unacknowledged, it can turn into anger or resentment.

Distance can be created by a belief that this anger is permanent. This thought derives from the idea that there can be no change, and that the only exit from pain is distance. However, to get beyond the anger may open channels toward getting beyond the distance. In this way, it is valuable to connect with the underlying emotions.

Awareness is the first baby step toward such change. Let's keep in mind that anger and pain, like happiness, are temporary states and will change in many ways, many times.

244

What Do You Think?

Emotional distance can take many forms, e.g., rejection, anger, withdrawal. What forms of emotional distance do you experience in your relationship? Are you aware of it? How do you handle it?

"Believe me, you can fret and fume all you want, but whoever it was that wronged you is not suffering from your anguish whatsoever."
—Della Reese

A Verse About Anger
Shura's Voice

How's your anger meter today?
Is it up? Is it down? Would you rather not say?

Is your anger sort of slow, that it may overflow
And you don't even know how to let go?

Or do you sweat it, fret it, then regret it?
Is it a fast boil and you recoil and your day is spoiled?

Does it give you a pain in your neck or your head
Or make you explode and then wish you were dead?

Well—I have a temper—oh yes I sure do
It's quite hard to swallow.
When I express it…it makes me feel hollow.

Was I wrong or right to engage in this fight?
Is there a right side or wrong?
That is a question that I've pondered long.
Did I derive satisfaction from anger and action
Or provoke a reaction? Change things a fraction?

Oh I have been angry and I have been burned
And after much scarring, this I have learned

Anger itself is neither bad nor good
Doesn't accomplish what you think it should
Of the human condition anger's a part
Raises blood pressure and quickens the heart

Like fire that burns, but also warms and gives life
Anger can harm or give meaning to strife
Sets feelings and thoughts a-whirling in motion
Anger's a genuine human emotion

I must understand it, nor be underhanded
Recognize…not repress it, learn wise ways to express it

Yes anger's a role in life's dramas to play
It has a message to bring in its own way

But if I let my anger rule
I realize soon that I'm the fool

And so I strive emphatically
To master my anger…it shan't master me!

Ideological Distance

A form of anger is illustrated in the terrible break that developed between Rebecca and her daughter Betty. Bernice and Marion maintained their closeness through continuity of values. In contrast, Betty, the mature daughter in this story, as well as her mother found herself unable to do this.

Rebecca and Betty
A Tale of Tragic Proportions

The great depression of the 1930s had been very hard on Bob and Rebecca. Although Bob held a graduate degree in engineering, he was forced to accept a job as an elevator operator. Rebecca supplemented the family income by working as a "practical nurse." In those days this was a health care job for a person who had some care giving experience but little or no education. The couple had lost two babies who had been born with spinabifida and died. They were finally able to rejoice in their third child, a healthy and pretty daughter whom they named Betty.

Life was a terrible economic struggle. Bob and Rebecca had to give up their small apartment and, with their daughter, boarded in two rooms. Despite the severe economic difficulties that they shared with most Americans, they both vowed that their daughter would be well educated and have every opportunity for a good life. Betty proved to be a bright and able student. By the time the depression had ended and the United States entered World War II, she had earned her graduate degree as a librarian. She landed a position in the Library of Congress in Washington D.C. Although this meant her leaving home and family, her parents were ecstatic. They felt that their goals for her were realized and that she would have the fulfilling life they had dreamed for her.

In due time, Betty met and married the love of her life. He too worked in Washington D.C. and they planned their home and future family there.

The aftermath of World War II brought a terrible political backlash to the United States. A Congressional committee (HUAC) headed by Senator McCarthy created a list of selected labor unions, organizations and individuals that were attacked and labeled as "un-American." People called before this committee to testify about their own activities were also pressured to identify friends, colleagues and family who might be "subversive." Refusal to "name names" could be and often was punished by legal action, imprisonment, or further persecution in the workplace. Non-citizens could be deported and many were.

Bob and Rebecca belonged to an ethnic, non-political fraternal group that offered health care, insurance and burial benefits. This was one of the organizations on the McCarthy list. Fearing for her husband's job in Washington, Betty asked her parents to withdraw their membership. Rebecca and Bob, like many resisters of the times, refused on two grounds. First, they saw this as a betrayal of their principles, and second, at their age, they knew they would not be able to duplicate the benefits of their membership.

Betty gave her parents an ultimatum. "If you don't publicly denounce your membership I will have nothing to do with you."

Bob and Rebecca's expectation was that this was a temporary situation in the entire nation. They had experienced periods of violence and unrest before and they had survived until normalcy was restored.

And so, the parents "stuck to their guns." Betty, also, kept her word. She cut off all communication with her parents. Rebecca was distraught. Her daughter refused phone calls, letters, and gifts for the grandchildren. There were several cousins who also lived in Washington D.C. and who, despite threats and fears, maintained their relationship with Bob and Rebecca.

They also remained friendly with Betty. Hoping to ease the pain of this sharp family break, they would share news of Betty with Rebecca. Also, they attempted to bring news of her parents to Betty. When she realized that they were intervening in this way, Betty cut off communications with them too.

Throughout these bitter years, Rebecca looked forward to the day when the persecution would come to an end. Eventually the furor did abate and its accompanying fears were dissipated. Some jobs were restored and even some public accolades were offered. But Rebecca's anticipated day of renewal never dawned. Betty's hurt and anger prevailed. She refused to reconnect with her parents. She never spoke to them again. They were never permitted to know anything about her children.

Years later, after a debilitating illness, Bob died. The cousins came from Washington to attend his funeral. Everyone asked Rebecca, "Did you notify Betty about her dad's death? Did you tell her about the funeral?"

Frail, old and needing care herself, Rebecca replied sadly, "If she didn't want to know about him while he was alive, why should she be told about his death?"

Mother and daughter never reconciled. The other family members never knew anything more about Betty either. Rebecca died without ever seeing or hearing from her daughter.

"Selfishness is not living as one wishes to live; it is asking others to live as one wishes to live."
—Ruth Rendell

What We Think
Shura's Voice

In terms of mother/daughter relationships this is a tragedy of epic proportion. To some, it may seem almost unbelievable. Yet, like so many human tales, this one is very real.

The socio-historical climate of the time had a profound influence on this relationship. It is the backdrop for this tale and must be understood for the full impact of this story to be experienced.

The drama began in the fifties, a decade which, in the United States, was one of the "worst of times." Some years after World War II a madness seized the country. In a political backlash following World War II, although not immediately after, a Congressional Committee was formed, under the leadership of Senator McCarthy. It was titled the House Un-American Committee, and its mission was to examine the "loyalties" of selected American individuals and groups operating in this country. The committee had developed a list of people and organizations suspected of being "un—American." Various witnesses were called and interrogated concerning their membership, their activities, and their "loyalty" to America.

These were not questions in a passive, information-gathering poll. If the witness replied willingly about his or her activities, ideas or membership, he or she would be found "guilty" of "conspiracy against the government." Nor was this the end of it. If a person "confessed" (shades of other prosecutorial events in history), he or she was then pressured to provide the committee with names of fellow-members. Refusal to name names brought the same charge and punishment.

If the person being interrogated replied in the negative, the committee was prone to call other witnesses to testify otherwise and the person would be cited for perjury. Furthermore, a person reported as having been seen in the company of someone regarded as "un-American" was interrogated in the same way. Again, refusal to comply with the pressure to cooperate usually resulted in some sort of punishment.

The Committee was not passive. Government agents were sent throughout the land to investigate people who had been reported as un-American. It was a time of witch hunting not unlike the days of Salem in the eighteenth century. It was to describe this period that the playwright Arthur Miller wrote "The Crucible," drawing the parallel between those times and these.

Refusing to be intimated, many Americans resisted this wave of political tyranny even when resistance resulted in extreme personal sacrifice. Some, like the "Hollywood Ten" were imprisoned, blacklisted from their fields of work, and unable to get other work. Well-known or not, many citizens were jailed or lost their jobs; their careers ruined. Some, like Charlie Chaplin, who had been a long-time resident but not a citizen of the US, were forced to leave the country. Other people, less famous, were deported. Families were broken up. Some people committed suicide. This attack on the first amendment of the Constitution, which guarantees the freedom of thought and speech, put everyone in jeopardy. The entire basis of the democracy had come under fire.

This was the socio-political climate in which Rebecca and Betty both made their drastic decisions. Rebecca had lived through persecution in Old Russia under Czarist rule and had come to this country seeking freedom of thought as well as opportunity. She had also lived through a similar period in this country after World War I. At that time, the infamous Alien and Sedition laws had been used as a similar backlash to the aftermath of World War I. Then, too, people were jailed, fined, deported for being disloyal. At that time there had been organized opposition to the war itself. Any criticism of government action was deemed seditious and punished.

And so Rebecca had made her decision not to yield to this kind of pressure. This was her way, she felt, of defending the true spirit of

American democracy, for which she had left home and country in her youth.

Betty, too, had a point of view that stemmed from this climate of intimidation. Her husband's government job might be in jeopardy if his wife's family were called to testify. Betty and he were just starting their life together. Her husband's promising career was just beginning. Jobs were very, very hard to find. The slightest accusation against her husband might jeopardize all their plans. Perhaps her husband gave her an ultimatum: them or me. Perhaps she herself gave that ultimatum to her mother. Betty could not, would not risk her marriage and their future.

This dilemma faced many families. People made their own decisions about how to cope. When relationships were disrupted, there was sometimes a family underground through which they could keep in touch. Failing that, there was usually the expectation that when this persecution would end, normal relationships would be resumed. This did occur in many cases.

Why didn't it happen this way for Betty and Rebecca? Did each one feel that the other did not respect her point of view? Did either of them feel that the other did not love enough? Did this rift become permanent because it had seemed like a test of their love? We cannot really know. Nor do we dare to judge.

In a world of fear and terror, when "The world is too much with us, late and soon," as the poet wrote, by what criteria can we judge the behavior of others?

What Do You Think?

Is there a climate of acceptance of ideological differences in your mother/daughter relationship? Does a greater climate consume the relationship? How do you cope?

Letter from Amelia

Dear Jen,

I want to tell you about how Mom and I have come to terms with our differences. As you know, I often felt that Mom did not approve of me and was not kind to me when I was growing up. She would become angry and harsh no matter how I tried to please her.

I'm sure you remember that I left home at age eighteen, immediately after high school graduation. I couldn't get far enough away from her. Mom's disapproval followed me like a shadow. Everything I did seemed to boil down to me trying to prove to myself that I was competent. All my later education, jobs, and training were about justice and fairness to people who were misunderstood and disadvantaged.

Now, at age fifty, it seems to me that as I grew and matured, so too has my mom. I now have a law degree and work as a successful lawyer in the Southwestern United States. Now Mom is proud of me. We seem to have worked out our differences. She is not so critical of me anymore. Maybe we both found middle ground.

I still can't live near her but, from a distance, it truly seems that absence and maturity have made my heart, and hers, grow fonder.

Talk to you soon,

Love,
Amelia

"I've learned that one can never go back...that we should not ever try to go back...that the essence of life is to go forward. Life really is a one way street."
—*Agatha Christie*

What We Think

Jennifer's Voice

Amelia and I have been very close friends since high school. She's grown up a lot, from a very rebellious teenager to a mature, responsible, loving woman who wants to make the world a better place. Amelia had to move away from her mom to find herself before she could come close to her mom at all. I watched her, with empathy, as she used the distance and time apart from her mother as a way of healing her pain. She needed to find a way to make some sense of the hurt.

For Amelia, the world needs to be just and fair. Therefore, her distance served the purpose of acquiring a bird's eye view and a wider-angle lens through which to view the world, as well as herself and her mom. She was able to disengage from her personal hurt and pain and was able to see her mother simply as a woman struggling with her own past. Having reached this level of understanding of her mother, Amelia is more at peace with herself and her life, as well as with her relationship with her mom.

What Do You Think?

Is there a "middle ground" in your relationship? Do you have to search for it or is it self-evident? If you must search, what obstacles might you find in your effort to identify it?

Scenarios of Divorce:
Another Kind of Distance

Jennifer: In divorce, the person who leaves the house leaves not only the spouse, but also the entire family.

Shura: Even when the divorce is relatively amicable between the parents, there are serious repercussions for the children.

Jennifer: No matter how mature the children may be, they see the parents as role models, as their security and their support system. Divorce rocks that boat.

Shura: It takes a great deal of sensitivity on the part of each parent to reach out and maintain a loving relationship with the adult child.

Jennifer: Through such sensitivity, the distance between mother and daughter, as well as father and daughter, can be bypassed.

Shura: Family members must avoid the desire to place blame.

Jennifer: They also should refrain from trying to analyze causes or rehash history looking for reasons. It is difficult enough to handle the present without going into the past. That is just water under the bridge.

Shura: Everyone must make a real effort to reestablish some kind of balance with each member of the family.

"Being divorced is like being hit by a Mack truck. If you live through it, you should start looking very carefully to the right and to the left."
—Jean Kerr

Scenario 1

Twenty-four-year-old Erica, newly graduated from college, was distraught. Her father, Jack, had just announced to her mother, Rachel, that after twenty-eight years of marriage he was leaving her. Erica was confused about her father's announcement. She had always felt that her parents had been loving and supportive, both to each other and to her. She had seen them as a team, planning their lives and living them together.

When they finally did divorce, she became very worried about her own future. She had planned to become a teacher, but became very insecure about her abilities and unsure of her plans. She began to think that perhaps she wasn't good enough to teach.

Despite all her mother's pleas and efforts, she took a job as a clerk in a pharmacy and told her mother she was through trying to make any of her dreams come true. As her unhappiness persisted, Rachel convinced her to go for counseling, which she did. With help, Erica is slowly beginning to feel better about herself. She realizes that her father's actions were not caused by any inadequacies in her. She now understands that she can make plans for her own life and is willing to work at carrying them through.

What We Think

No matter how old or mature a child is, or seems to be, parental divorce has a powerful effect on her, as on all family members. Had Erica's parents discussed with her, either separately or together, their reasons for divorce, she might not have viewed their divorce as a reflection of her inadequacies. The more mature child may or may not ultimately bounce back more quickly, but still needs to be considered in the process.

Scenario 2

When Rachel and Phil married, they lived with Rachel's mother, Leah. In due time they had a daughter, Susan. When the child was four years old, Rachel decided to divorce Phil. He retained custody of their child. The three adults agreed that, despite their feelings, it was important for them all to act in Susan's best interest. Grandma Leah remained living with Phil, and Rachel had daily visitation rights.

Phil remarried two years later. His new wife had accepted the situation and developed a loving relationship with the little girl. She and Rachel were also friendly, so that Susan grew in an accepting adult world.

Grandma Leah realized that her place would no longer be in Phil's home with his new wife. She had to find a way to earn her living. In her late fifties, she opened a small knitting shop.

Rachel had vowed privately that neither her mother nor her daughter were to suffer because she had disrupted their home. For the rest of her life, she visited her mother daily and helped her with the business in every way.

Susan grew in this milieu of respect, support, caring and responsibility. When Leah grew older and more dependent, Rachel and her daughter nurtured and cared for her to the last day of her life.

What We Think

Both parents had recognized that their divorce would affect the development of their young child. All the adults recognized their responsibility to provide a healthy environment for her. To that end, they put aside many differences and cooperated in important ways. Their philosophy and behavior gave their daughter a positive direction for her life.

Scenario 3

Estelle divorced her husband when their only daughter, Carol, was not yet in her teens. It was an angry separation, and Estelle took Carol out of the country. They lived in Brazil, and Carol hated every minute of it. She never saw her father and lost contact with him. Her mother enjoyed life in Brazil and paid minimal attention to her daughter's emotional needs.

As soon as Carol turned eighteen, she left her mother in anger, married and returned to the United States. Theirs continued to be an uneasy relationship, barely maintained over the distance. After some years abroad, Estelle returned to this country, penniless and in poor health. Although she visited her daughter and they maintained contact, their relationship remained extremely limited. Carol felt no responsibility toward her mother. Estelle had to look elsewhere for emotional support in these, her older and difficult years.

What We Think

Neither parent understood Carol's developmental needs or the long-term effects of their behavior on her. In her adult life, she remained distant from both parents. They also remained separated from her as well as from each other. The mother/daughter relationship had lost momentum during the bitter years following the divorce. There seems to have been little or no opportunities for its maturation. This is a story of a family that fell apart, splintered by divorce.

Scenario 4

Elaine's husband died when their two daughters were quite young. She raised them herself and enjoyed their youthful years as well as their successful marriages. In her late fifties, she married for a second time, despite her daughter's misgivings about her choice of spouse. After a few years, this second marriage did not work out. Elaine and her second husband divorced. It was not an easy time for Elaine or her daughters as everyone was regretful. Thanks to her lifelong relationship with her daughters, she regained her balance and resumed a fruitful life of satisfying interests and friendships.

What We Think

Elaine's positive lifelong relationships with her daughters became very important in her later years. She had built a strong foundation for her relationship with her daughters and maintained it through their maturing years. Had her support network not been so firmly and lovingly in place, her aging years might have been bitter and lonely.

What Do You Think?

Divorce occurs under many diverse circumstances and touches the lives of many more people than the two who are separating. Have you been affected by a divorce separation? In what way? How did you handle your feelings?

Define Your Distance

In this exercise, identify the nature of your distance, if any, from your mother/daughter. How did the distance develop? How often do you communicate? What is the mutual understanding about how you maintain the connection? How does the distance keep you separate/ apart? What are the obstacles that keep you apart? What keeps you together? Is there a middle ground? What is it?

Directions: Fill in the columns about what works for you and/or what doesn't. If there is a middle ground indicate it.

WHAT WORKS	WHAT DOESN'T WORK
Ex: Judy used all technologies to keep connected	*Ex:Far away and can't visit often*

269

<u>WHAT WORKS</u>	<u>WHAT DOESN'T WORK</u>
<u>Unconditional Love &</u> <u>Mutual Understanding</u>	<u>Limited Opportunity To</u> <u>Express</u> <u>Range Of Feelings</u>
Ex:Celina and Efraina *believe they will and can* *always be there for each* *other*	*Ex: In " Far " mother is* *alone and separated at this* *time in her life*
<u>Telephone-direct</u> <u>conversation Photos and</u> <u>Videos extend to the other</u> <u>generations and illustrate</u> <u>live experiences Instant</u> <u>gratification</u>	<u>Distance makes everything</u> <u>emotionally one-</u> <u>dimensional, cold.</u> <u>Conversation at distance</u> <u>may lead to</u> <u>misinterpretation and</u> <u>misunderstanding</u>
Ex:Judy and mother used *these to retain connection* *and keep it updated*	*Ex: in "Far" mother* *doesn't want to be a burden*

WHAT WORKS	WHAT DOESN'T WORK
<u>Correspondence</u> <u>Opportunity to retain</u> <u>connection</u> <u>Time to screen ideas and</u> <u>feelings</u>	<u>Time consuming and not</u> <u>spontaneous</u> <u>Give-and-take is limited</u>
Ex: Amelia's Letter: " I still can't live near her, but from a distance it truly seems absence has made both our heartsgrow fonder."	*Ex: in "far" daughters says "Now I'm trying to forgive her and perhaps myself. I'm not sure I know how."*
<u>Basic Family Values</u> <u>Implicit Understanding</u>	<u>Limited Opportunity to</u> <u>Deal With Different</u> <u>Viewpoints</u>
Ex: Bernice &Marian living far apart sharing ideological connections.	*Ex: in "Far" mother says "It isn't easy to communicate at a distance."*

Exercise: Family Sculpture

In this exercise, you diagram the members of your family. Place them according to the distance or proximity as they relate to each other. Distance might be emotional, willingness to and behaving toward fulfilling your various expectations, your communication needs, emotional needs, intimacy needs.

Explanation: Arrow indicates positive connection (both ways in this example). Mother, sister, and I are close. We communicate easily and do things together and for each other. I was the center of the family group. Dad was alienated from us. All communication with dad, to and from, was through Mom.

Now, try your hand at sculpting your family.

Musings
Jennifer's Voice

Distance defines itself in so many ways
Spatial...emotional...ideological
Change and separation offer pain
What to keep? What to maintain?
So many barriers to overcome...Some don't even try
Some create a peace within...Others cry

Shura's Voice

"DISTANCE: *separation in time...spatial remoteness...personal and especially emotional separation...aesthetic distance...difference...disparity.*"
"DISTANT: *far-off...separated in a relationship other than spatial...reserved or aloof in personal relationships.*"

These ideas, excerpted from Webster's Ninth Collegiate Dictionary, are relevant to our thoughts about the mother/daughter relationships. So many ways to be distant, so many ways to overcome distance! As an aging mother, I feel the distance of time as I observe the lives and behaviors of my grown children and their children. Despite the innumerable changes in the outer world, I see, also, the continuity of their emotions in relationships as they grow and mature.

My own grandmother never saw the conquest of space. Their grandmother has seen it and its impact on the entire world. My grandchildren have mastered all sorts of electronic devices that still baffle their grandmother...me! Yet across such man-made barriers are the human universals, and we are somehow able to understand each

273

other, accept each other, even exchange ideas, cope with our differences and support each other despite these changes.

Yes, time creates a distance between generations. It behooves the older person to reach across the barrier with understanding, not with judgment. It is for the older mother to realize that her daughters and granddaughters have yet to experience the currents of maturity. The older woman has learned something between the ages of fifty and eighty. Therefore, it is for her to recognize this and allow the younger ones to cope with the powers of life that assail them and to grow and develop within the context of their time.

This, we older women have already done to the best of our abilities. We are still meeting the challenges of our generation within this altered world. We, too, hope for understanding without judgment from our daughters. This undeniable, pervasive bond between us is a flexible one. It is subject to much interference from the external world and its fluctuating circumstances.

And so, we must nurture this, the primary bond between us, with consistent understanding and unconditional love.

Guideposts for Thought

1.   There are many kinds of distance: geographic, emotional, ideological, legal, etc.

2.   Distance may be viewed as an obstacle to relationship. It can become the reason for limiting or terminating a relationship or it may be seen as a challenge for creative problem solving.

3.   When there is distance, you take yourself wherever you go. You take along a lifetime of baggage, e.g., your background and experiences, value system, coping ways, emotional responses. You also take your hopes, your strengths and limitations, your own expertise.

4.   Distance offers the opportunity to select those elements of the relationship you would like to maintain and those you would like to change.

5.   Each change of situations is accompanied by a range of emotions. It is important to be aware of these and how they affect you.

6.   Distance offers the opportunity to review your communication style as well as the role and relationship patterns in your family.

7.   Boundaries are always important and necessary in proximity or at a distance. In either case, clear boundaries strengthen relationships.

8.   It is always possible to maintain a relationship, regardless of changes in distance, time or space, when the participants are willing or desirous to maintain it.

9.   It is the responsibility of the older person to be patient with the maturation process of the younger one.

10.   Some distance is acceptable, e.g., generational separation, maturation during developmental stages of growth.

Chapter Five
Tendering Nourishment: Care Giving

How do the mothers and daughters weave their tenderness and nourishment through the intricate challenges and demands of their changing lives?

Tender Nourishment,
What Does this Mean?

TENDER: *"Considerate, solicitous, delicate, fond, loving: also, to offer, to present for acceptance"*
NOURISH: *"To nurture, to rear, to promote the growth of, to support"*
—Webster's Ninth New Collegiate Dictionary

The words "tender" and "nourishment" have implications on two levels: there is nourishment of the body and nourishment of the soul. Here the tendering connotes the solicitous offering of nurturing care. Synonyms for "tender" include also "soft, flexible, loving, and compassionate." When people care about each other, the relationship calls upon one's sense of responsibility. This sense of responsibility is established early in a person's life, and we all experience it just a bit differently.

In a perfect world, the baby cries, the parent tends to the baby's need, and as the baby grows, to the child's needs. The child learns, "When I need something, I will be heard and tended." That child grows to be an adult expecting needs to be heard and attended. That child also develops a sense of responsibility for hearing and tending to the needs of others in a caring relationship.

That's in the perfect world. In this less-than-perfect world, there are many bumps and potholes that lie along the path of life. Communication that doesn't work, interpersonal behaviors that don't work, misunderstandings, bad advice, outdated family traditions, depression, anxiety, selfishness, greed, and substance abuse are examples of the barriers that may interfere with the healthy course of a person's growth.

Again, in a perfect world the changing needs of family members are anticipated, as it is clear that everyone is growing and changing. These anticipations prescribe the roles of parents and children, husbands and wives, fathers, mothers, sons and daughters. Yet again, the bumps and potholes of the real world affect these expectations and the opportunities for fulfillment.

A range of diverse circumstances arises to challenge the creative ways in which the family copes. Some are functional; some are not. How do the actors in these dramas play out their roles?

"What do we live for, if it is not to make life less difficult for each other?"
—George Eliot

Unconditional Love
Jennifer's Voice

The color of health is the color of the heart
Pregnant with unconditional love
Fertile soil creating beauty...bearing beauty
Whose fruits sow seeds that blow in the wind
Scattered...dispersed...creating...
Mother Nature's healthy wind blows fertile beauty

What does it mean to feel unconditional love? Does it mean that no matter how I behave, you will love me? Does it mean that no matter how you behave I will love you?

Well—yes. Unconditional love is loving with no conditions attached. It is knowing that the bond is so strong that nothing can sever it.

There are shades of love. Unconditional love is not felt for every person whom we love. For example, I love my child. I also love a friend. If that friend is cruel to me, or betrays me, I may sever the relationship. If my child is cruel to me, or even betrays me, under no conditions would I sever the relationship. However, should the relationship be severed beyond my control, my love will still persist. My expressions of love may take different shapes or forms. My behavior will also be different as the outward relationship changes.

Unconditional love does not mean unconditional acceptance. The loving person may not necessarily accept or agree with everything that the beloved person says, thinks, or does.

There is room in this loving relationship for a whole range of ideological differences, of diverse behavior and emotions. But the presence of such differences does not suggest rejection of the person, the relationship, or the diminution of the love bond. Unconditional love does create and maintain the possibility of lasting, important, positive relationships despite the differences.

However, the powerful impact of that love remains…the bond remains…painful as it may have become under some circumstances.

The nature of such love affects other facets of a relationship, especially the powerful mother/daughter bond. For example, some people live out the concept that there is a price tag for love. Such conditional love as, "I will love you and you take care of my needs," teaches us to mistrust. Experiencing cruelty from someone who, we believe, loves us creates a sense of doubt about others and ourselves.

Feeling the bond of unconditional love creates a sense of safety and good feelings about ourselves and nourishes our ability to trust.

"Nobody has ever measured, not even poets, how much the heart can hold."
—Zelda Fitgerald

Keep My Heart Open to Change

Jennifer's Voice

When I'm scared and unsure
As life unhinges my door
I keep my heart open
As the new and obscure
Are fearfully met
Eyes tearful, cheeks wet
Heart in a knot
I reach deep within
Lest love be forgot

Caring thoughts that I share
Sometimes lead me nowhere
But heart open to self erases despair

Allowing pain to prevail
And the sadness I feel
Will pass like the wind
With the sun at its heel

And I dance in my heart
Knowing now how to start
Staying true to myself
Keeping heart open wide
Freely awaiting
Hope and Peace are allied

JENNIFER ROSVALLY AND SHURA SAUL

Finding my way each day to next day
From doubt to assurance I range
New paths to explore, life begins to mean more
As I keep my heart open to change

How I Learned I Was a Care Giver

Shura's Story

My mother aged as she had lived, gracefully. So gently did she move into older adulthood that I hardly noticed.

When her husband, to whom she'd been married for sixty years, retired at the age of 83, Mom's life changed as well. A brilliant, compulsive, and creative worker, he mourned the loss of this central role of work in his life. His strict daily routine changed, and so did hers.

The changes in her activities of daily living were almost imperceptible. Food shopping was first. Ever since I'd become a mother and housewife, as well as worker, Mom and I had gone food shopping together. When my children were little, we took them along. Many were the times that we were our own small parade—Mom and I, my three little ones, and our dog! After the children were grown, I'd drive Mom to the supermarket and each of us would shop our respective food lists. Then I'd drive her home, help her up with the bundles, and then leave her to get home myself.

Now, however, I found myself walking up and down the aisles with her, helping her make her selections, find and reach the things she needed, then drive her home. I'd help her up to her apartment with the bundles (after frantically searching for a parking space). Al, her husband, would greet us at the door and together they would put things away.

Many times I'd take them both shopping. There were certain shops that Mom preferred for her meats, vegetables etc. I'd drop them both at the shop, and then seek a parking space that was sometimes blocks away. Leaving the car, I'd rush back to the shopping area to help them both. Then I'd leave them standing in the doorway of the shop while I went back for the car.

Some of those episodes were memorable, anxiety provoking, and laughable! A few times I'd return to the shop only to find them gone! Once, they wandered around the corner looking in the windows of other stores. Once they decided to walk into other stores. Each time I had no idea where they might be, and I ran up and down the block, running into stores, looking for two small white-haired people easily lost in the busy crowds. Of course, I always found them, arm in arm, smiling and chatting happily—totally unaware of the panic I had been experiencing during those ten or fifteen minutes of my frantic search!

Sometimes, I would drive round and round to find a certain store that one of them wanted to shop in, but weren't exactly sure of the location. Or Al would want to buy a certain item, and we'd drive back and forth looking for the store that would carry that specific item. To say the very least, patience, humor, and love were important ingredients in those adventures.

Then there came the change in food preparation and nourishment. For years I had stopped by after work to see Mom before going home. Often, Al would already be home from work, and since my own husband worked every evening, I might join them for a light, evening meal. I began to notice that the food being taken out of the freezer was slightly freezer burned. I realized that Mom wasn't doing much cooking, and was "saving" food (often forgotten in the freezer for too long a time) for another meal. Since I myself had a rather hectic schedule that limited my own cooking, I began to take them out for dinner a few times a week. Other nights I'd stop by with cooked goodies. My daughter, who worked in a nearby hospital, began to come in during her lunch hour and bring some nutritious food. Between the two of us we kept the nourishment going.

Of course Mom's capacity for housework became greatly diminished. The first things to go were the plants. In those days I was an indoor plant gardener; It was my pleasure to bring Mom some of my beautiful plant babies. We placed them in her sunniest windows, and she enjoyed watering and tending them. Then, one day she asked me to take them home.

"I just can't take care of them anymore," she said regretfully "I hate to watch them drooping until you get here to water them." Sadly, I carried them home.

That was the beginning. Housecleaning came next. Mom's apartment had always been neat and clean. It was uncluttered, almost stark in its tidiness. I soon became aware of the fine coat of dust on windowsills, wooden furniture, etc. As I was a full-time worker myself, with considerable household responsibilities, I could hardly do her house cleaning. So I approached her, timidly suggesting that we get her some household help.

Her reply was unequivocal. "No. I've always done my own housework," she said.

"Mom," I begged, "Just a few hours a week. Just the heavy stuff. I know this lovely person, Mrs. Duffy, who would be willing to come one morning a week."

After weeks of begging and cajoling, my mother said, grudgingly, "Let her come this Saturday morning and talk to us. Then we'll see."

Well, Mrs. Duffy came. It turned out that the three of them hit it off nicely and they arranged for her to come one morning a week for a few hours. This lasted for a few months.

But when Mrs. Duffy announced that she had to return to Ireland to care for her own old mother, Mom and Al refused to consider another house worker. And they never did.

Laundry chores came next. I began to realize that Mom was wearing the same dress day in and day out—and Al's shirts looked pretty frowsy as well. It turned out that neither of them was going down to the laundry room in the basement of their apartment house. Laundry was piling up in the hamper. Bed linens were not being changed. The only thing I could do was scoop up the laundry, take it home and add it to my considerable mountain of clothing, and bring it back! We began, together, to put the fresh, clean linen on the beds.

Paying bills was another major change. Mom had always paid her few utility bills in person, in cash. That had been her way. Now this became impossible. So, I took them both to the bank, opened a bank account for them and showed Mom how to pay by check. Believe it or not, she had never written a check. Now, in her eighties, she learned to keep the checkbook balanced and pay the bills. Bright and quick, she learned this. Being unsure of herself, she asked me to help, which I did consistently every month.

A final routine that became increasingly important in those years were her visits to the doctor. Mom had always taken care of herself and her husband. Now, however, she needed reminders and help with transportation. So, all doctor visits were scheduled so that I could take her. Al always went along. These visits became outings—with lunch out and an occasional shopping chore folded in. I was fortunate in that I could adjust my work schedule accordingly.

These routines were useful for several years. Ultimately, as we ourselves grew older, my husband and I had to make a major change! We moved permanently from the Bronx to our summer house (now winterized) in Westchester. At this point in our saga, my husband had undergone serious surgery and had been sent home in quite a fragile state, to recuperate. Simultaneously, a long awaited remodeling of my kitchen was in effect. The carpenter and plumber were working in the house. The refrigerator had been moved temporarily, blocking the entrance to our guest room. I had my hands full!

The phone rang. Al's voice was on the other end. "You've got to come and take us right away. We can't stay here another day."

"Al," I wailed, "You must wait until tomorrow. I've got to get the refrigerator moved so that you can get into your room."

"Okay," he said. "What time tomorrow will you be here?"

Of course I picked them up; bag and baggage the next morning— and they moved in to live with us for the next few years, after which later developments required further solutions.

During this entire time, I never thought of myself as a care giver. I was simply helping my mother, as she had helped me all my life!

Some years later, I went to a workshop led by two researchers who had done some studies in care giving. They distributed a checklist for the participants to fill in. All the above items were listed—and, when I had filled it out, I discovered that all these years, I had qualified for the title of care giver!

"After the verb 'to love,' 'to help' is the most beautiful verb in the world."
—Bertha Von Suttner

It was just continuity for
you to go on giving to
your mother as she had
always given to you.

The needs of everyday
life were suddenly
transformed into care giving
without my even noticing!

Are You a Care Giver ?

In each category signify whether you do this with or for the person being helped.

Task	Daily	Weekly	Bi-Monthly	Monthly	Sometimes	Never
Shopping: Food Clothing Other						
Meal Prep.						
Feeding						
Personal Grooming: Dressing Bathing Other						
Finances: Banking Purchases Bills Other						
Mail: Writing Reading						
Household Responsibilities: Cleaning Laundry Supplies Other						
Health Care: Doctors Visits Pharmacy Medications: Set-up Administration						

Task	Daily	Weekly	Bi-Monthly	Monthly	Sometimes	Never
Transportation						
Culture & Rec. In house: reading aloud TV, radio, computer, other Out of house: Visiting Walks/drives Other						

At what point do you consider that you are a care giver?

Becoming a Care Giver

Jennifer's Story

I never actually became a care giver. I was born a care giver. My family role was one that encouraged this predisposition. I think it's in my nature to give care and be caring.

I was the child who, in kindergarten, played with the one retarded boy in my class. No one instructed me to. I just knew the other kids wouldn't play with him. They were afraid of how he looked and acted and I wasn't.

So, now when my mom, who has taken good care of me all my life, needs me in new and different ways due to her changing health issues, of course I will set aside as much as possible to give care to her. This needed change has required some new skills in some internal exercises.

For example, sometimes, I find myself getting very annoyed at her because my mother over extends herself by trying not to ask for help when help is needed. I tell her I can't trust her judgment, and I wish she could just sit back into the need and let me do it, for example, bending down or lifting laundry. Other times, I forget that those things I've come to expect from her all her life as an independent, skilled, and competent woman may now be unreasonable for me to expect, for example, digging into the back of the refrigerator to find food may be too taxing for her.

The most difficult part for me is adjusting to her changes, sometimes even recognizing them. I can't read her mind and she doesn't like to ask for help.

In fact, when she does ask for help, it may suggest that the immediate situation is desperate.

Much of the burden falls upon me to make the judgment call. I don't like that, and we've talked about it, but Mom doesn't want to impose and feels she is imposing even in the times when I don't feel it's imposing.

What Do You Think?

In our diverse roles throughout life, we find ourselves both giving and accepting help and care. Most of us are in both positions at one time or another. Which are you in now? Both? For whom are you a care giver? Who gives you care? Are you getting the care you need ? How do you experience these positions?

My tendency had been to
give you what you would
need. I had to learn to ask
before giving and trust that
you would be honest with me.

It didn't seem like a
choice for you.
It was just natural
for you to give
to me as you
gave to everyone.

"You can give without loving, but you cannot love without giving."
—Amy Carmichael

Accepting Change, Accepting Help
Shura's Voice

I've been a care giver all my adult life. Daughter, granddaughter, wife, mother, friend, the tides of a woman's life lie on the ocean of caring, giving and doing. This outlook was pervasive even in my careers as worker. I chose early childhood education, social work and gerontology. In all my endeavors, I put my knowledge, skills and special abilities into service to the others in my world.

I loved and reveled in all the roles. I allowed others to lean on me and learn to do better. I strengthened my own muscles of self-help and self care. I was always aware of the love and support of a network of friends and family. Mine was a personal commune, a circle of reciprocal give and take.

As I grew older I grappled with the inevitable and unrelenting changes imposed on my body and my energies. I began to learn that my reach exceeded my grasp. I found it necessary to reconstruct my life and yet find ways to feel fulfilled.

Aging is a new phase of life requiring specific changes. I had to change the balance of my daily plans and activities…the very structure of my life.

There are some things I have to do differently such as altered eating and sleeping patterns.

There are some things I have to do more of: more staying at home and less going to other places, more thinking and less doing.

There are some things I have to do less of: less work and more rest, less traveling or driving alone, more riding along with others, less helping others and more accepting help from others.

Especially, too, I must be mindful of my daughter's concerns and the fact that she takes full responsibility for helping me in areas and at times when her help is needed. For me this is quite a switch from clearing my time to help others.

These changes require awareness, practice, yielding some control, and finally…graceful acceptance.

I think that last is most difficult of all.

You had to learn to accept
help because you were the
giver of help throughout all
of your life. That was a
hard thing to do.

I had to learn about the
changes that the aging
process was imposing on me.

"Old age is no place for sissies."
—*Bette Davis*

Gracious Acceptance
Shura's Voice

I was taught from childhood
That "gracious giving's" something good
And so I always did believe
"'Tis better to give than to receive."

Now after years of busy living
Nurturing and gracious giving
Taking is the skill to learn
And I'm told it's what I've earned.

Gracious acceptance, my new art
Hard on habit, heavy on heart
Power once that I could wield
Now in aging I must yield
So much that once I had controlled
As I grow older...older...old.

Care Giving: A Lifetime Commitment

When a child is born, the parent is born simultaneously. The family is created. Parents and baby are involved in new currents of being. A new and different life stream requires new roles, new tasks, new responsibilities related to the entrance of the new person.

If there has already been a family and another child or other children, the family group experiences a process of re-creation and re-configuration. The currents of life flow more broadly. The life stream becomes more inclusive. Everyone moves over and changes a bit. In a healthy family situation, all the members develop a rhythm of co-existence.

All members of the family group require nurturing and care giving. Mothers and fathers care for their children. Partners care for each other. Children learn to care about their parents and about each other. As everyone grows and matures, needs change. The nature of care varies with the needs and circumstances of each individual. There are normal and expected developmental changes which affect everyone. These are anticipated in the growth and flow of family living.

Sometimes, however, a member of the family requires more than the usual or expected quality or quantity of nurturing and care. Because family bonds are so important in the development of each family member, such exceptional needs of one family member will affect everyone else.

"It is only in the giving of ourselves to others that we truly live."
—*Ethel Percy Andrus*

Sally's Story

As Sally tells her story, we see how the needs of one child have affected the lives of all members of the family, and we see, especially the role of the mother as she performs a lifelong balancing act to insure the welfare of everyone. She writes:

My first-born daughter, Laura was a healthy, happy baby. My husband, Harry and I enjoyed her early years and we looked forward to a second child. But Harry was sent overseas during WW II and so we had to wait. My second daughter, Faye was born about a year after he returned.

It was a difficult delivery. I had lost a great deal of blood. My mother took care of Laura and the baby until I became well enough to handle both girls.

I thought that Faye was a happy child, but she was over-active and would never rest easy in my arms or on my lap. She was bubbly—but had difficulty speaking. We learned later, she had hearing in only one ear.

Whereas Laura had been an excellent little student at grammar school, Faye had difficulty learning. From the beginning she became very good at fooling her teachers into thinking she knew her work. For example, she came back from kindergarten one day with the complete alphabet written on her paper.

I said, "Oh! You have learned the alphabet."

She said "No, but I didn't want the teacher to know that I didn't know it, so I copied it from my neighbor!"

During her years in elementary school, I visited the teachers often to discuss her uneven learning patterns and behaviors. Finally, I spoke to her 8th grade math teacher who suggested psychological help. Harry preferred consulting a psychiatrist and we were referred to Dr. B. (Although initially Harry had said he would cooperate, actually his input was very minimal. I have paid, from my own account, for Faye's psychiatric help from that day to this, and made most of the decisions about her care.)

Dr. B gave me one wonderful piece of advice. When I told him the child wouldn't sit calmly in my arms or on my lap, he said, "Tell her you know she's unhappy but that you love her." I did that over and over and these words did calm her down. Now, an adult, she remembers them and the hugs that went with them.

Faye was not a pretty child. She had a prominent nose, crooked teeth and a receding chin. From day one everything about her had to be corrected or improved and, as a result, she had a very low self-image. I started her early on teeth straightening. That took years as the work was interrupted by her admission to college. We had found a small college that accepted her. She did fairly well, but she was not happy there. She quit after the first two years and returned home. We located an excellent orthodontist who did straighten her teeth. At this time, also, Harry found a job for her at our Community General Hospital. Faye was twenty years old.

Faye also wanted contact lenses. The ophthalmologist recognized her many problems and referred her to a psychiatrist, Dr. F. Faye was interested and I agreed. I realized that this was her decision and not another thing being foisted upon her. Dr. F. remained her doctor and helper for years afterward.

Meanwhile, Laura was growing up, leading her own life. She graduated from college, enjoyed a professional career, and was married. Whenever I needed help with Faye, Laurie was always there for us. Meanwhile, my husband's health was deteriorating. He had to retire and needed my help in adjusting to the reorganization of his own life. We moved to a new community. (Until he died, we wintered in Florida to keep him out of the cold weather.)

When we moved, Faye did not move with us. I rented a studio apartment for her and taught her to do her own banking. I furnished her new apartment and stocked it with food and other necessities. Whenever I was away, my good friend, Sylvia, remained available for any emergencies that might arise.

At about this time, when Faye's cousins of her age married, Faye felt she must marry. She had met a young man at a Jerry Lewis telethon at which she had volunteered. They became engaged, and Faye began making all the wedding arrangements by herself. Because both my husband and her fiancé said the marriage would "cure" her completely, Faye stopped seeing the doctor. I was completely outvoted.

A few weeks before the wedding, Faye realized that her fiancé would not be able to manage their finances nor be able to take care of her. Her fiancé telephoned me saying that Faye was acting queerly. I called Dr. F. and he told me to bring her to the hospital immediately. A psychiatric social worker interviewed us. Faye's fiancé readily admitted that he was marrying her for money. Faye was hospitalized for 4-5 months. She was very depressed even after her discharge. She resumed treatment with Dr. F.

After this, Faye's greatest fear was that she might end up being a bag lady. She had three or four breakdowns in the next ten-year period. Each time after her depression, she would pull herself together and get a job. She always worked until her next breakdown. Ultimately, Dr. F. diagnosed her as bi-polar and prescribed lithium.

Through all Faye's ups and downs my friend, Sylvia, her surrogate mother, and Laura remained friendly and supportive. Faye also had other friends. Becky was one who Faye had met at the temple where they both volunteered to help the seniors with Bingo. One night, Becky invited Faye to dinner along with her own nephew, Phil, who was somewhat disabled. Before he arrived, Becky warned Faye saying, "He doesn't walk so good or talk so good." Faye said she didn't care about that.

That evening, after dinner, Faye called me saying, "I don't know what Becky was talking about. He doesn't walk so bad or talk so bad!"

It wasn't long before they became engaged. Phil was selling his house, and they planned for Faye to move in with him in his new apartment. If things worked out, they would get married in the spring.

(By now they had both matured. Faye was 36; Phil was 44. To me they both seemed about 21!)

While Faye was in the process of moving in, Phil's sister came to visit. Faye had a breakdown right in front of her. Phil called me and I came immediately. We had to hospitalize Faye again. Phil never flinched. He went to all family conferences. While Faye was in the hospital, I helped complete her move to their new apartment. When she was discharged, she went directly there. She now knew that she could always depend on him and he knew he could depend on her. So they were married. Faye has not had a breakdown since.

Phil seemed to have a sixth sense as to when Faye might be "going down." He also knew exactly how to cope. They planned to move to Florida when Phil retired. Until then, they lived with hand-me-downs on an extremely limited income for several years. Faye worked, and they put the maximum amount of money toward his retirement. They managed nicely.

Faye went back to college and earned her degree in Geriatrics and Family Health at Empire State College. She continued to work full time until her last year at school.

When Phil retired they moved to a one-story townhouse close to my home in Florida. Faye works as the activity director at an assisted living facility. She loves her work and the residents love her. Phil is president of their condominium. They have friends, a social life and are truly happy.

Laurie and her beautiful family live in a nearby state. I had always told her that she would have to be responsible for Faye when I can no longer shoulder that burden. She did accept that responsibility. It has been a lifetime of care, but my two daughters are now settled and married. They are both a comfort and a blessing to me.

In the human species,
women tend to be
the care givers—
the nest makers.
It is intuitive for
most women to
care for their children.

You're not finished
being a mother,
just because your
child is an adult.

"No life is so hard that you can't make it easier by the way you take it."
—Ellen Glasgow

A Tale of Dilemma

Sylvia describes a lifelong situation requiring attention to one daughter's special needs and recognizes the extra burdens that were placed upon her and her other daughter. However, she does not suggest emotional trauma or scars, but rather an understanding cooperation among the women of the family. They seem to have fulfilled the requirements of their roles towards each other as well as to their husbands and other family members.

On the other hand, in our next story, Kathy expresses a deep conflict within herself arising from a very similar family situation. Because she always helped her mother with the care of her sister, she became torn between their needs for her help and her own need for a full life. Hers is a tale of dilemma.

Kathy's Story

Kathy is a forty-five year-old woman who lives with her seventy-nine-year-old mother and her forty-year-old disabled sister. Her sister, Liz, was born with a birth defect and brain damage leaving her unable to manage any affairs in her life and completely dependent, even in activities of daily living.

The father of the family died when the girls were very young. Mother and Kathy had vowed, together, to remain faithful to Liz and to care for her at home. Kathy had a good teaching job and was satisfied with her career, but not with her life. She never married and has had only a few superficial encounters with men. She never yearned for a child, but dreamed of a home of her own. In deep conflict about claiming her own life, Kathy needed to sort through her own life priorities.

Soon after her eightieth birthday, Kathy's mom suddenly developed health issues of her own. Even though she had been an independent woman devoted to caring for her daughter, she became needy for some care herself. Household chores and activities of daily living became more difficult for her. Consequently, the ongoing attention to Liz's needs complicated the family picture.

Ominously, the writing was on the wall for Kathy. This was now her dilemma. She felt her obligation to continue as care giver to both her mother and her sister. These had been the priorities in her life until now. On the other hand, how could she ever develop a sense of herself…an identity consistent with her own maturity? Many women attain and discover new depths to their lives when they reach their forties. How was Kathy to achieve this?

This story remains incomplete. Kathy is her own personal ethical dilemma, conflicted by her integrity and family values versus her dreams and hopes for her own life. She is challenged to find ways to rearrange her priorities to accommodate everyone's changing needs, including her own.

"Never grow a wishbone, daughter, where your backbone ought to be."
—Christine Paddleford

Gertrude and Vivian

Gertrude's story is a third and very touching example of a mother's lifelong devotion to a daughter with special needs.

Gertrude's only daughter Vivian was retarded from birth. Gertrude's husband died shortly after the child was born. A single parent, Gertrude went to work and cared for her daughter for the rest of her life. As Vivian grew older, she developed other physical difficulties, and was wheelchair bound from the age of forty.

In her older years, Gertrude struggled with several chronically debilitating conditions including congestive heart failure, emphysema and osteoarthritis. Finally, at age eighty-eight, she suffered a stroke and was hospitalized for a long time. During this time, Gertrude paid for a nurse's aide to stay with and care for Vivian. After the stroke, Gertrude remained wheelchair bound. With mother and daughter both in wheelchairs, it became impossible for them to be cared for at home.

Gertrude, who had never permitted a permanent separation between herself and her daughter, now realized the demands of a new and difficult challenge. She had always faced the realities of her life with courage, and now she had to cope with the reality of her own mortality.

She applied for admission to a nursing home in her community, stipulating that she be admitted with her daughter and that they be housed together in the same room. Compassionately, the nursing home complied with her request. Gertrude and Vivian were helped to adjust to their new living situation.

Special attention was given to Vivian's adaptation to the new living arrangement. She needed to learn to accept help from the staff rather than from her mother. With Gertrude's help Vivian made the transition and found her place in the life of the facility.

Less than a year later, Gertrude died. She seemed to have waited for her daughter's acceptance of life in the nursing home and died peacefully in her sleep. The staff helped Vivian to mourn appropriately for the loss of her mother. Gertrude had been successful in her life's endeavor!

The daughter's special
needs complicated the
mother's aging process.

This is yet another example
of a mother not being
finished with taking
care of her child,
even when the
child has grown up.

What Do You Think?

What do you think about these longtime care-giving commitments: about Kathy's personal dilemma, about Sally's family situation, and about Gertrude's control of her life and death? Do you have any personal dilemmas regarding care giving? Do you have a conflict of integrity and priorities of family values?

Family and Friends as Community...
as Support Group

Consider a circle of friends and relatives, people in whom we confide, count on, and need emotionally and physically. This circle is a person's closest community. Some of these people may live geographically nearby, some may live far away. The expectation is that this "family" will respond appropriately to our needs as we reach out to them. They will expect the same of us. We are there for each other at the drop of a hat. There's a rhythm and synchronicity to our behavior. We don't expect perfection from each other, but we do relate through a mutual understanding of each other's needs and within the context of unconditional love.

Members of this circle participate in an ongoing dance of interaction whose patterns and rhythms are dictated by the ever-changing music of their lives. As needs arise, the patterns and configurations are altered to fulfill them. When there is a crisis, the "family" responds. appropriately. Life patterns, living arrangements, constraints and deployment of energies, time, and money often require alterations. Humor, flexibility, and a willingness to give and take become foremost in everyone's thoughts and actions. Some changes may be long term; others may be temporary. The situation itself controls the appropriateness and balance of action.

When such a circle exists, coping and resolving the crisis elicit the highest form of courage and caring in all concerned. The underlying pervasiveness of unconditional love is at a high point in the life of this circle. Some of these ideas are illustrated in the interview with Nancy, an eighty-seven-year-old mother and grandmother and her daughter Sophia.

We Live Together, Yet We Don't

In this interview, Nancy and Sophia, mother and daughter, describe their living arrangement and how they have developed their mature relationship within the context of their needs.

What is the nature of your relationship?

Sophia: I'm the daughter. (Laughs)
Nancy: We live together yet we don't. I live downstairs. I have my own kitchen and door to close. We're individual and yet we live together. We've been together 6 years.

How did that living arrangement come about?

Sophia: After dad died, I was divorced and a single parent living in the city. Mom was in Queens. My daughter started school. It was expensive sending her to private school in the city. I wanted my daughter to have family around her. My sister and cousin moved to the same town in Long Island. I thought we should all live in the same town. The homes were expensive. I thought emotionally, financially and for my daughter's well being it would be wise to pool our resources. It is important for us to have our own kitchen.

So you have a family support group that came together as needed?

Sophia: Yes.
Nancy: We were concerned about my granddaughter.

Sophia: I get up and go to work. We couldn't live here singly, but I'm comfortable knowing that my daughter is well taken care of and I work to get enough money for us to live. But, I want to talk about the other reason we're out here, my brother-in-law (second marriage for my sister). My sister has a son the same age as my daughter. They are like siblings. My brother-in-law was supportive of the family being together. He helped us find this house. It's very emotional for me. We're all here together and we are going to stay here.

So, the care giving goes all around?

Sophia: When my brother-in-law took ill, we helped my sister and their son. They both spend a lot of time with Grandma. They have Grandma, cousins, aunt and uncle.

How do you feel, Nancy, as the Grandmother to this family?

Nancy: Up to this point, I was involved in activities and volunteering in my community. But a grandmother involved everyday is different than a visit. As a visit, it's playtime. Everyday living, it's less affectionate.

Sophia: It's more of her providing a sense of security. Mom was a school volunteer, so she became involved in this community, the children's school lunch program and other community organizations.

So, this arrangement allows you to maintain your own lifestyle and duties?

Nancy: My lifestyle has changed. I like it like this. It's comfortable. If I didn't have this responsibility, I'd be involved in the Senior Center. That's kind of boring. I'm lucky.

You created your own luck.

Nancy: It's interesting you said that. When we decided to do this, you'd be surprised how many people told me not to and were negative about it. Now, my negative friends are in situations that are not as comfortable for them as mine is for me. Now these same people are saying what a smart thing I did.

How do you handle conflicts between you?

Sophia: We stay open. We always sit down and talk about the conflicts. We are able to express our feelings about everything. We are on the same wave length. I think this has all been good for Mom. Social and family responsibilities keep our moms alive.

Nancy: I remember not to shoot my mouth off. I think about how I feel and what I want to say and come up with how to speak about it.

Sophia: Women get older and it's important they don't end up alone in a nursing home. I hope your book helps people.

Nancy: There's sometimes no reason not to go to a nursing home. I think, I don't know if I want to stay home and be taken care of by aides if I needed it. It would make me uncomfortable. I'd probably prefer to be in a place where others are like me and can't take care of themselves and have to depend on someone. I'd find it uncomfortable to depend on a family member. My parents lived to be in their nineties. My father wanted to go to a nursing home. My mother thought it was unthinkable. I'm more like my father.

There's a hope that someday we can create homelike situations and not have nursing homes as dumping grounds for the community. Nursing homes don't have to be like that. We have to change social attitudes and the way we shape opportunities for older people.

Sophia: I guess Mom and I are creating personally what needs to happen culturally.

You're doing it with your eyes open and understanding the barriers and booby traps. Now let's talk a bit about caring for each other.

Sophia: My mother does so much for me. She'll make me dinner while I'll make dinner for my daughter. She does errands for me, so I can be home with my daughter when I'm home. We do laundry together. It's easier for two people to do it. Mom shops for me, accepts packages for me. I have a "wife."

Yet, you're able to maintain privacy?

Sophia: I do things for her. She had a broken pipe in the bathroom. She moved upstairs to me. I took care of the arrangements to fix the pipe as best as I could. When she has trouble with her car or the house, we use each other's strengths. We own the house together. Both our names are on the deed.

When it comes to decision making about the granddaughter, who makes them?

Nancy: My daughter does all the disciplining and upbringing.

Sophia: I tell Mom how to carry out certain things. Sometimes it's too hard for her and I let it go and take care of it when I can.

Nancy: I do what my daughter asks. I may disagree about her upbringing. I don't say anything. Mostly, she's doing well on her own.

Sophia: When my daughter was younger, she would have tantrums. Mom would call me or have my daughter call me at work. I would intervene as much as I could. My mother raised me and she is my role model, so I raise my daughter with the same values. It's fairly smooth.

Nancy: Sophia's more like me than my other daughter. That's why we can get along.

You sound very flexible in managing the curves that life throws your way.

Sophia: We have a strong sense of family values. Even when we disagree, we still know we are connected, and it can never be severed.

Nancy: The bottom line is, "we value family."

And you seem to have a deep sense of respect for each other that works for you!

Nancy: My older daughter had a son who died at age 15. When he was young, I asked him what love was. He'd say, "You have to respect someone."

Sophia: My father always used the word "respect."

Nancy: You live the word and everyone seems to know what it means.

What We Think

This is a story in which the members of the family treat their family as a small community. They relocated to be close to one another and for the cousins to grow up as friends. They pooled their resources to help each other on a daily basis as well as in times of need. They also found ways to maintain appropriate boundaries of privacy and pursuit of individual interests.

This is not a large family. Similar arrangements may be found in many other family groups, especially in large, extended families.

What Do You Think?

Are similar arrangements found within your family? If not, does this plan appeal to you, or do you prefer a different arrangement for yourself? Do you know why?

Finding a Balance
Patty's Story

Whereas Nancy and Sophia created a living arrangement with consideration for the needs of other family members as well as their own, Patty describes how she balanced her needs with those of her mother.

Patty was 37 years old when she left New Zealand to come to New York. She was seeking adventure. Having never married, she felt she should fulfill her life's dream to go very far from home and explore new worlds.

She found a loving, compatible family to live with. They helped her obtain a green card, and she became a nanny for their children. She worked in the United States for eight years until she was well into her 40s. Having no siblings, she had left her mother and father back in New Zealand to care for each other. As they enjoyed their own satisfying life together, they managed well with this arrangement. Patty would speak with them weekly and was able, occasionally, to go back home to visit when finances permitted.

Six years into her stay in the states, her dad died suddenly. Patty was very sad and returned to her mom immediately. She realized that her mother would now be alone and recognized her responsibility to help her through this hard time. Patty reevaluated her priorities and kept her heart open to change. She left her interesting and fulfilling life in the United States to find a new way with her mother. They mourned their loss together.

However, in due time, she found that her mom was able to reestablish some balance in her own life. Patty returned to the United

States to pick up where she had left off. Maintaining her close touch with her mom across the distance, she became increasingly aware of her mother's changing needs as she aged.

After a while, Patty became very torn at not being with Mom, who was now in her mid seventies. She found it difficult to be apart from her and ultimately decided it was more important to her to care for her mom.

Again, she aborted her own adventure altogether, and she left the states. She returned to New Zealand and began a new adventure, caring for her aging mom. Her own needs had changed and in accord with her sense of responsibility, her heart guided her to change the course of her life.

Currently, Patty, now in her late forties, has developed a new work career in New Zealand, that combines satisfaction for herself and the opportunity to care for her aging mother.

She created an acceptable
balance in meeting her own
needs while caring for her mother.

This mature daughter
accepted her filial responsibilities.

*"Never regret. If it's good, it's wonderful. If it's bad, it's experi-
ence."*
—Victoria Holt

What We Think

Patty made her life work for herself because, at each point of change, she accepted the challenge to determine what was right for her to do and what she was capable of doing. Because she was able to fulfill her desire to pursue her own interests, she was then able, also, to find fulfillment in doing what she knew she had to do.

This is balance and balance is satisfying. When a person can follow her dream, as long as it is realistically possible, she is then able to make changes required of her when they become necessary. Coming to terms with the demands of life is a form of balance. Such balance enables one to continue to feel fulfilled.

Patty met the challenges that presented the need to change directions in her life.

Her sense of values and filial responsibility enabled her to find new ways of fulfillment.

What Do You Think?

It is a "given" that nothing in life is "always or never." With this understanding, have you been able to find balance in your life? In what ways? Was it/is it a struggle? If you have achieved a measure of balance, do you feel satisfied? If not, what can you do toward achieving a better balance and greater degree of satisfaction?

Exercise: How Flexible Are You?

In the following scenarios, write about the changes you would make in becoming a care giver. What would you do? What changes would you have to make in your life? What are your alternatives and options?

Scenario#1: Your mother lives in Florida, You live in New York. Your mother is diagnosed with emphysema and needs medical attention. She also needs help in activities of daily living.

Scenario #2: Your mother/daughter has suddenly become disabled or chronically ill.

Scenario #3: Both your elderly parents have become chronically ill and weak and unable to function independently. They live near you.

Scenario #4: A sibling living with your mother/daughter becomes chronically ill and unable to function independently.

Scenario #5: Your mother becomes seriously ill. You are advised she requires nursing attention 24 hours a day, 7days a week. Nursing home placement is suggested.

Scenario #6: Your mother lives in an assisted living facility, and you see that she needs an increased amount of nursing assistance.

Even My Dreams Shift
Jennifer's Story

The altered needs of one family member requires a change in the balance of the entire family

Ironically, as Mom and I began to write this chapter on tendering nourishment, Mom developed some health problems. She felt tired all the time and her normally high energy level waned. This was startling enough for her to consult her physician. After due tests and examinations, it was clear that she would require medical treatment. With this uncertainty of her future health, Mom went forward with the prescribed regimen. As in all treatment, one can never foretell the unique response of the individual.

Responding to this development of Mom's needs became a new adventure for us all. As in any adventure, we couldn't know what lay ahead, nor could we know what obstacles might pop up. The only thing we really knew was that we loved each other and we were all willing to pull together. As for the obstacles, we would persevere and overcome what we could, and find ways to accept what we couldn't control. We were in this together, and no one person's needs would be ignored.

Our family redesigned its arrangements of daily activities to accommodate to the new needs of one of its members. Although our plan required all sorts of significant and sometimes difficult rearrangements, it was fulfilled smoothly and we made it work. No one expressed distress or complaints. We all kept our hearts open to the sentiment of the words, "new, different, rearrange, change, and unknown." There was no panic, no sense of emergency. The pervasive attitude was one of matter-of-fact acceptance of the need for the various changes.

Somehow, through our mutual strength, we learned to cover for each other. Sometimes the needs of one family member would be observed by everyone else. Other times it might have to be the needs of another one of us. We were all willing to be flexible and available to each other, both physically and emotionally. My teenage daughters and son grew and matured in their understanding. Through this experience, we have found ourselves becoming stronger warriors in the struggles of life.

Actually, during this time, my whole family has become a group of "tender nourishers" for each other.

"There are two ways of meeting difficulties. You alter the difficulties or you alter yourself to meet them."
—Phyllis Bottome

What We Think
Jennifer's Voice

So, what does a person have to give up to become a caretaker? What does a person have to give up to maintain the life of a caretaker?

Giving can be very natural and at the same time draining. For me, giving is a way of life. I give to many people all day long. I give to my kids, my husband, my mother, my home, my friends, my clients. People are always saying to me, "I don't know how you do it and stay sane."

I think for me the key to sanity lies in a "cocktail mix" of many ingredients. They include the following:

First: I know my boundaries. They are so clear that I'm able to be fluid about them, and yet I never take onto myself what belongs to someone else. This skill has matured through the years. I needed to learn about myself and what I need, who I am, how I tick. The more clearly I can see myself, the easier it is to see others. Then I can see which issues are mine and which belong to other people.

Second: I feed the tank with gas. Just as a car can't go without gas, I need to fill certain of my needs in order to put my energy out into the world. So, for example, I need to eat certain foods at certain times of the day. I need to exercise and drink a lot of water. I need to sing and listen to music. When these needs are met, I have it in me to put out more for others.

Third: I stay open to change. If something shifts in my life, and I become a caretaker of a family member, I may have to reevaluate myself as a person. What are my priorities? What values do I want to live by? What is my new vision for my life? How can I reconcile these issues with the current family needs? If I am successful at this, I can then feel that I'm not giving up something, but rather changing.

You may ask, "Let's get practical, Jennifer; if you suddenly have to start caring for someone in your life, aren't you giving up your own dream?"

I don't experience it that way. I look at life as a series of dramatic events in constant motion requiring me to stay flexible and willing to shift in sync with them.

Even my dreams shift.

It took tender nourishing
and flexibility for everyone
in the family to adapt.

The new needs of the
older person were met
by changes in the
family as a whole.

*"You don't have to be afraid of change. You don't have to worry
about what's been taken away. Just look to see what's been added."*
—Jackie Greer

What We Think
Shura's Voice

This mother/daughter dyad found new dimensions to their lifelong relationship as they helped each other through a situation requiring medical care and treatment. Jennifer describes how all the members of the family became a circle of support as each one rallied to meet the medical and care needs of grandmother. She notes, also, that this has been a positive growth experience for her teenage children.

What Do You Think?

What are your thoughts about the family as a mutual support system in the tendering of nourishment? Who is in your circle of friends and relative? Have you experienced obstacles and problems in developing such a support network? What were they? How did you cope with them?

Rediscovery and Renewal

A relationship can grow and mature at any age when there is unconditional love. A lifetime of miscommunication can be reversed through a mutual desire to clarify feelings and thoughts.

Interview with Babs and Magdelena

In the following interview, Magdalena, giving care and support to her daughter during cancer treatment, tells how the experience gave her the opportunity to grow and change. At the same time, they rediscovered each other as women and Babs developed a deepened insight and understanding of her mother. Their relationship takes on new dimensions.

Magdalena: For me, the relationship is wonderful. I love her. I care for her. I'd do anything in the world for her. I lost one daughter when she was 2 years old.

Babs: Mom and I have a much better relationship now. We became close because I learned more about you, Mom, as a woman. When Mom and I would drive an hour each way for my cancer treatment and spend at least two to three hours in the hospital twice a week, we had long periods of time together to talk. She'd tell me about herself. Learning about the person, I would get emotional—hearing about her life as a child, young adults, and finally, wife and mother—her joys and hardships. She was emotional too. Mom was organized; head of the household, had to be strong. Mom was more reserved than dad. She was more inward and kept almost everything in.

Did you always feel you had to be responsible, Magdalena?

Magdalena:I had to be perfect. I couldn't reveal my weaknesses.

In the day-to-day, did you, Babs, as daughter, always feel her control of her feelings?

Babs: Oh yes!

Magdalena:Domineering. I wish I could go back, not be so fussy with the house. We should be born old and get younger. I thought I was doing the right thing. I just wanted to help. Maybe it was wrong.

Babs: Mom would get upset. As a child I'd figure I did something wrong. I always tried to be a good girl and do as I was told.

Magdalena:Isn't it sad that I didn't know that?

Babs: We can go forward, knowing what we know now. It's good you're here, so we can go ahead. There was a point, earlier, when I had a problem with my youngest daughter, the baby of four children. She was a free spirit. That was fine with me. She got upset at my mom. Mom offered to talk to Jen about it. Mom was ashamed at the way Jen dressed. She was embarrassed to be seen with her in public, and told her so. She thought Jen was dressing for attention. Jen got angry. She felt badly that her grandmother was embarrassed by her. Jen told me about it. She felt criticized.

Magdalena: I wanted to help her. I realized it wasn't helping her and Babs yelled at me. From that day on, I never got involved.

Babs: I was very upset for my daughter. I accepted her however she dressed. I needed to stand up to my mother to defend my daughter and her feelings. I had never done that before. I went to her house. I couldn't understand why I was so scared, but this was my daughter, and I needed to stick up for her. I got to the door. Mom said, "I know why you are here." I said, "Yes, I'm here because of my daughter." There were loud voices yelling. I don't remember what exactly was said. Then I remember Mom said to me, "You changed." I was going to therapy, learning about myself. Mom said, "You're not my little girl anymore." I was trying to hug her. I said, "You're right, I'm not your little girl anymore. I'm trying to become a woman, but what did not change is that I still love you."

Magdalena: I didn't remember that. I was angry. I didn't seem perfect to my daughter.

When we are angry, we don't see. You never said that to her before. She never said anything like that to you before.

Babs: Mom said that when I left she was still upset. I remember hugging her.

Magdalena: I don't remember that!

Babs: For me, this was the first time I ever defied her. I needed to grow. I needed to find out who I was instead of being what someone else wanted me to be. I was trying to learn to stand up for myself and for the things that were important to me and yet try not to hurt Mom's feelings.

Magdalena: I don't remember how it ended, but it is better now.

It is better, because you are both relating to each other as grown women.

Babs: Mom has since told me about her own life, in depth. Before this, Mom never would reveal anything personal. Now she's an adult relating to me like a girlfriend. It made her more real.

How did it happen that you revealed yourself to her, Magdalena?

Magdalena: Babs asked me and one thing led to another. Her dad always talked about himself. I kept quiet. Her dad was more outgoing.

Babs: Mom would say, "There can't be two of us, outgoing." So Mom held back.

Before this turning point in the relationship, what was the interaction like?

Babs: Mom was always helpful. She was the first one to give and to help out.

How did that make you feel?

Babs: I needed all that, she still does that, but I was still being the young child. I'm 100 % grateful. Looking back, many times I don't know how I could have managed. There was a time when I was separated and Mom and Dad lived next door, and I would date and come home late. Mom said that she was concerned because I'd be out too late and there could be a fire or something could happen to the children. I told her, "I know you don't understand, but this is something I have to do." I felt like I was being watched, critically. A couple of times Mom would be critical of me. One Thanksgiving, while coming into the kitchen she said, "The turkey will be dry."
    Mom wants perfection. I couldn't live up to those perfections. Accept me as I am, with what I do. You don't talk to a friend like that. For me, if I had a friend who didn't make me feel good about myself, I would leave her or him. I took it from Mom. I wouldn't take it from anybody else.

Magdalena:I was hurt and upset when we heard that Babs had cancer.

What obstacles keep you from improving your relationship now?

Magdalena:I don't know.

Babs: I don't know. Expectations from Mom. Pleasing Mom meant things went smoothly.

Magdalena:There was not much interaction in the communication between us.

Babs: There was never any feeling in the talking we did do. There was a habit before bed, a kiss goodnight. If I was upset, they'd say, "Why are you upset? You should be happy!"

Of course, in what each of you describes, there was a difference in perceptions. Mom has a certain way of being and behaving. Everything she does is out of love.

Magdalena:Sometimes, I see now, that hurts the other person.

Babs: The tone in your voice is sometimes critical.

Magdalena:That happens with you too. Tell me next time it happens.

Babs: Sometimes I don't know right away. I need time to absorb it. Mom is quicker.

Magdalena:Not so much anymore. I need to hold back sometimes.

Such changes take time because a person is defended. You don't have the habit of telling each other right away. Needing to be perfect is a burden for both of you.

Magdalena:Don't feel you have to be perfect for me. Everything you do is perfect.

Babs: That's on the surface. We never had arguments. Arguments can be good.

Magdalena:I can't live with arguments.

Babs: It's too bad I never learned to argue or express my feelings. I had no idea of my feelings, let alone expressing them. Now through therapy, I'm in touch with my feelings. Because of my cancer medication, my moods are altered due to the steroids I have to take. I try to remember not to talk too much and to be patient. I'm much more emotional because of my medications. I'm very sensitive.

Magdalena:Me too. I do it at home; I don't express it to you. I cry all alone. I put nice music on, and I go back to my youth, and I cry. Sometimes they are good cries. Makes me feel good. Sometimes I think about sad things, and then I cry and I feel better.

Babs: When my sister died, I was ten years old. I remember the morning I went into the kitchen and my father was crying. I don't remember my mother. Someone said (must have been my mother) that my sister died. I called my girlfriend and cried. So my father was in the kitchen alone crying; my mother was somewhere else alone crying, and we were never together with our sorrow.

Magdalena: I didn't let you go to the funeral. I thought it was best for you. Today, I wish I had let you go. My parents made me kiss my grandmother's corpse in the casket when she died. It was terrible. I didn't want it to be terrible for you.

Babs: Our relationship is much better now.

They outgrew their views
of each other as mother and
the young child and matured
into an adult relationship.

They used the opportunity
of tending to the daughter's
changing needs to learn
to see each other in
a new light as mature women.

"If you've never been hated by your child, you've never been a parent."
—*Bette Davis*

What Do You Think?

Is there some way you would like to turn your relationship around? What would you be required to give up in order to make this change? What do you expect you would gain? What would she gain? What would you like to do? Are you open for this?

When Mother Has Not Been Nurturing

This is a painful subject. It was difficult to interview the women who were willing to share their feelings about these mothers. It was not easy for them to review the distressing events of their past.

A Tale of Two Sisters

Hannah and Maxine are two sisters in their late forties or early fifties. Hannah is the older sister. Both are mothers. Their mother, Florence, is eighty-five years old. Maxine, the younger sister, lives near her. Hannah lives a two-hour drive away. They both spoke to us in matter-of-fact tones as they shared their memories of inadequate parents, narcissism, and cruelty. Although each had somewhat different experiences with their mother, they shared their early suffering. Clearly, they had understood and supported each other throughout their lives, as indeed, they did during this interview.

What is the nature of your relationship?

Hannah: Maxine is the one who has the most hands-on contact.
Maxine: I have a strange relationship with Mom. She's hard to describe. I go by the tone of her voice to know how to respond. She has a certain tone and I know how to respond. I walk on eggshells.
Hannah: She can be prickly at times and lovely at other times.
Maxine: Growing up, I was oblivious to what was going on.
Hannah: Mom called me the practical one. She said my sister was happy-go-lucky. I was moody and sat in corners; didn't want to be bothered.

Maxine: I'm with my mother daily. Sometimes I speak to her several times a day. She has mellowed with age. She had colon cancer. She has tremors.

Hannah: Mom and her sister, our aunt, are alike and they bicker. We hear about it and we get upset for both women.

Maxine: My sister and I experience their bickering in the same way. I didn't speak to Mom for four years because of something that happened. It hurt me and killed me. It involved my father.

Hannah: He made the sacrifices. He took the brunt—babysitting, chores, and cooking.

Maxine: Mom would take a lot out on dad. She was domineering.

Hannah: Her personality—she was dictatorial. If you don't do what she says, there's hell to pay.

Maxine: Mom's mom, our grandmother, had diabetes and was insulin dependent. She lost her toes. She needed care daily. She couldn't care for herself. My parents had to move closer to Grandmother to help. So we moved from Manhattan to the Bronx.

Hannah: Although my aunt lived with my mom, it was my mother who had to be trained to give Grandma the insulin. She took care of her mother. She became distraught at her mother and her mother's siblings, our aunts. She had to get away from the stress of care giving, dealing with our aunts, mothering us, and coping with the stress of dad's health.

After a while, the doctor made my mother go to work. He said either that or he'd put her in a mental institution. I raised hell. I needed my mother and went through terrible times. I didn't know how to handle it. My mother, father, and the doctor sat me down and explained what was going on. I was nine and a half years old. I understood. I had to take care of my sister and suppress my own anger—my personality. I cried for the paternal grandparents I had to leave behind in Manhattan when we moved. My paternal grandmother was wise and kind. She taught me everything. In the Bronx, my mother ran from work to feed her mother every night. Then, Grandma died.

Maxine: My mother shielded me from everything. My sister got the brunt. Even when I got older, they told me nothing. If they didn't want me to know something, they'd speak Yiddish.

Hannah: They couldn't do that to me. My paternal grandmother had taught me Yiddish.

Maxine: We don't tell Mom things today. We discuss them between ourselves.

Hannah: Mom had a habit of trying to turn me against my sister. She'd try to get me to argue. My father taught me to never stay angry with my sister.
So the relationship with dad counterbalanced some of Mom's influence.

Maxine: She would try to convince us that dad wanted things a certain way, but it was she who wanted them that way!

Did you think something was wrong with you?

Hannah: At the time I thought something was wrong with me. You had to be careful how you dressed. If you didn't dress to her liking, she'd make you feel bad. She matches everything all the time. She'd match her clothes, and she'd buy all her shoes and clothes to match.

Hannah: Yes, her taste is the only taste. I was wrong if she didn't like it.

Maxine: My father got pleasure in putting Mom on a pedestal. Mom would make dad feel this small.

Hannah: Dad sacrificed—sometimes went hungry to buy her clothes. In her eyes, if someone at work would borrow money from dad and have to wait until payday to pay him back, she'd yell at him, "You're a fool." He ended up coming to live with me. We were living in the suburbs. Mom threw Dad out, and he had no place to go. He came to me. He went back to her. He died in 1995. Dad would forgive and forget.

Does your mom need any care now?

Maxine: Mom is eighty-five now and very independent. Even if she needed help she wouldn't accept it. She forces herself to do things. She wouldn't want anyone to take care of her physically.

Does she live alone? Who takes care of her house?

Maxine: That's where she needs help. She has someone coming in. I shop for her and cook. She demands it. She lives alone. I'm not allowed to be tired. I have to give up everything. I'm not allowed.

Hannah: My sister is a mother, a widow, and a mother-in-law. She's also studying for her master's degree. She runs errands for our aunt. She's being run ragged by Mother.

Maxine: Mom tells me how great my sister is and how terrible I am. Even though I'm the one, now, who does everything for her. Now, my daughter lives with me. My mother molded my daughter to be just like her. Now my daughter became my mother all over again.

Hannah: I ran away from home three times before I was six years old. I tried to run away in my teen years. I had to get away from the beatings. The last one I got when I was 26 years old. Mom had long, clawed nails and gouged the inside of my mouth. I still have the scars. She had stiletto heels that she used as a weapon. She would kick me with them, throw me down, and kick me in the back. She'd pull off my belt and use the buckle to hurt me. I have physical and mental scars.

Maxine, how is it for you now, taking care of your mother when she is not nice to you?

Maxine: I'm ambivalent, angry…but I don't let her know. This is what I'm supposed to do. This is my personality. People don't understand how I feel. I don't care how much you hurt me. I still have to do what I have to do.

Sounds like you're like your dad.

Hannah: When he died a part of me died.

How do you feel about Mom now? How much do you have to do with her?

Hannah: She never told me she loved me. Or held me or kissed me. Never read to me when I was young. Nothing I ever did was good enough.

Maxine: I don't know what I feel for her. My mother—I don't know if I love her. She never told me she loved me. Thank God, Mom got to be eighty-five. Do I love her? No. I have no reason to. Do I care what happens to her? Yes, she's my mother.

Hannah: I would cry buckets of tears if anything happened to her. Not because I'm sad, but because of what we never had.

There is something. You do care about her despite something you never had from her...your birthright...her love. It seems that both of you went on to live your lives the best you could in spite of her. Mother is a powerful person in a girl's life. You have acknowledged that relationship, despite all the sadness you've described.

What We Think

Hannah and Maxine are war buddies. Their mother was violent, narcissistic, and demanding. A difficult woman to live with, she abused her daughters physically and emotionally. Each sister was treated somewhat differently and each coped differently. Maxine, the younger, learned to adjust to Mom's views through Mom's verbal cues. She protected herself emotionally through becoming adaptable and flexible.

In a sense, Maxine was protected by the presence and assertive behavior of Hannah, her older sister. Hannah, the firstborn, never accepted the fact that her mother would not and could not attend to her healthy needs for a mother's nurturing care. Hannah insisted on expecting that her needs be met. Even as a child, she was open and communicative about it. However, her dad asked her to understand her mother's needs and to sacrifice her own. Hannah tried to repress her needs, but she was never really successful. To this day, she continues to suffer from the emotional scars that her mother inflicted upon her as she was growing up.

Hannah did have a lifeline, her paternal grandmother who is remembered for her wisdom and kind nurturing. Even this was neither perceived nor valued by her parents. They broke her lifeline by moving away. However, Hannah retained the emotional and intellectual memory of this experience and later replaced it in her own adult life.

The sisters stuck together through the difficult years of their maturation. Consistency and continuity have been important for them and they found these in their relationship. It is interesting that Maxine reports that her own daughter picked up the flaming torch of her grandmother—becoming difficult, demanding, and hard to live with.

It was important to these two women to express their memories. In spite of their non-nurturing mother, they have gone on to live fruitful lives. Maxine is responsive to her mother's needs. Hannah, who bore the brunt of earlier problems, is married. After the interview, she told about her loving relationship with her husband, son, and mother-in-law.

The emotional impact of these interviews was experienced by the interviewers as well as the sisters. We were all left with after-thoughts and feelings to sift and sort. We were all drained. To survive and cope with such tormenting experiences, and to find ways to create a fulfilling life, are indeed a form of courage that is rarely noted or acknowledged.

These two sisters really
stuck together to maintain
their strength, sanity and
sisterly relationship.

This mother was inaccessible
to her daughters and distorted
all the family relationships.

What Do You Think?

What feelings were aroused within you as you read the material in this section? What are your thoughts?

Daughter to Mother

Jennifer's Voice

You say you need me now
Perhaps you think it's true
How can you expect my kindness
When hurting me is all you do

You never do acknowledge
The nasty things you say…
I never felt safe, or trusting
You never made me feel that way

I grew in a world of anger
Unpredictability and pain
I felt your rage and jealousy
Disapproval and disdain

Now at eighty-five you need me
To provide for all your care
You say you are my mother
The obligation seems unfair

For you never acted motherly
And you never cared for me
So it's tough to give you comfort
And provide for your safety
Conflicted as I am within
Responsibility is strong
I need to feel I'm doing right
Although you did me wrong

So I'll do what makes me peaceful
Put punishment aside
My integrity determines
That from you, I cannot hide

I can count the number
of times that you've
been to my house.

She's the only mother
I know who wants
to be a burden
on her children.

It's What I Do…It's in My Nature
Interview with Eva

Eva shares memories of her mother who did not nurture her. She, too, as an adult has come to terms with inadequate parenting, and she has made corrections in her own life as a mother and a professional. Although she does not describe the physical cruelty and extremely erratic behavior of Florence, the mother in the preceding story, Eva makes clear the non-supportive behavior of her mother.

Describe the nature of your relationship with your mother?

At the very end, my mother was on medication, antidepressants, and anti-psychotics. For the first time in my entire life, she was available. She was less paranoid and depressed so she could engage in rational conversations. Prior to that, conversations had been limited by her depressed, paranoid thinking.

When the veil caused by these conditions was lifted, she was available on a whole other level. For example: I moved her to New York from Florida so that I could attend to her after my father died. That way, she wouldn't be isolated and I could do what I had to do in my life. She took the antidepressant, anti-anxiety medication just for the last few months of her life. She was already living in New York and in an assisted living facility when she began to take it. The move from Florida had taken place before she started the medication.

After that, she was available for me to talk to her more rationally about her care. Prior to the medication, for example, she saw a pair of her pants in her closet and insisted that someone came in and put them there. She would cut them up. The aide who was with her couldn't stop her, and she wouldn't have clothing. Physically, she couldn't go shopping. If I'd shop to buy her clothes and brought her something, she might not like it. She valued her looks. Having nice clothes mattered to her.

Why wasn't she on medication earlier?

She refused medication all her life and had shame about mental illness. Finally when she depended on me in later years, I told her I couldn't take her behavior. It was only after she had taken an overdose of Xenex in an attempt to commit suicide, while she was at Kittay House, that I was able to get her to the psychiatrist there. I'm not sure how much of it was for my sake and how much it was that she wasn't ready to die and was shaken up by her own suicide attempt. Something shifted and my mother went for help.

My mother was very bright. She had been trained as a pharmacist. It was never her wish, but her father wanted to open a pharmacy and she was obeying him. In the fifties, women were supposed to be housewives. Our relationship for most of my life was geographically distant, she moved away when I was in my late twenties. Most of my adult life, it was on the phone with occasional visits. When she was younger we'd go to Florida to visit and she'd come here to visit. In the later years, we'd only go there.

How was it on the phone?

During her rare, calm moments, I knew she wished me well. She wanted me to be happy, but these moments were infrequent because of her neurosis and delusions.

When I was a child, my mother was completely disinterested in any of my interests. If I tried to talk to her about school, or my friends, or other things in my young life, she would say contemptuously, "I'm not interested in that." Her disinterest continued for most of my life. For example, I brought my Master's thesis for her to read and she didn't read it. When she was older, she became very interested and wanted to know me.

During the Florida/New York years, was there ever anything she needed that you had to take care of?

When she got older, my father got sick and less able. I had to take care of their finances. My father refused to have my mother's name on the bank accounts because she was unreliable, impulsive, and capable of outrageous behavior. She didn't mind; she wanted him to run things. She resisted me getting her name on the account, but my father became blind and she needed to pay aides and such. I had to arrange for physical care. They were lucky though, because they lived in a community where they had access to support.

As your parents' needs unfolded, how was it determined that you would be the one to take care of them?

I think I assumed the responsibility because I was the caretaker child. My sister's role was to be the pretty, irresponsible one and my role was the not-pretty, practical, dependable one. Also, they trusted me and they didn't trust my sister's judgment. When they did their will and healthcare proxy, they made me the healthcare proxy and power of attorney before my sister and didn't tell us. They kept it secret. They were afraid of my sister's anger. They made her the executor. So, while they were alive, they made me in charge, and when they were dead, she could be in charge.

Were you ever in need of anything she could have done for you?

It never would enter my mind to go to her for anything I might need. When I was younger, they helped me financially when I needed it, but once I became an adult, I was on my own.

How about your mother's interest in what goes on in your son's life?

Her narcissism won out. She had a favorite grandchild and a second favorite, my nephew and niece. She would baby-sit overnight for my sister's children, but when my son was born she announced she wasn't going to baby-sit overnight anymore. Once, when I complained to her that she showed no interest, she was surprised. She said that she thought she did show interest. For proof, she showed me that she carried a note around with her that my son once wrote to her. When she was older she would express joy in seeing him and he showed a lot of caring and interest in her.

Another example of her narcissism is that when my father was alive and they were living in Florida, the apartment was hot. My family was visiting and all of us were roasting, but she didn't want the air conditioner on. The way I handled it was to tell her, "You have two choices. We can leave the air conditioner off, and only you will be comfortable while the rest of us are roasting, or we could put the air conditioner on, you can put on a sweater, and we could all be comfortable." She got angry in response, and she said I was starting trouble.

Did you ever consult your mother about decision-making?

I didn't respect her point of view. We never had that kind of relationship. The attention I got from her was based on criticism about my appearance. Looks are what mattered, and I didn't have it. She never offered an opinion about anything else. Only once she gave her opinion about me changing professions. It was unsolicited. Without any curiosity about why I was doing this, she told me I shouldn't change because if I didn't change my profession I would end up with a good pension.

When I was little, I couldn't understand how my mother could be like two different people. She was sometimes the nice mother and sometimes the bad mother. I thought that there was a secret or hidden door in the front closet that the good mother would go into and the bad mother would come out of. I understood very early on that something was wrong with her, not me.

In later years, I would call her on everything. I was not afraid of her controlling withdrawal and anger. That was a change for me from the early years when I tried to avoid upsetting her.

One nice thing was that my mother let me know she liked my personality even though she didn't like the way I looked. The other nice thing was that my mother was capable of getting hysterical with laughter. I enjoyed laughing together with her.

I was going to ask about the dying years.

I have a certain comfort level in dealing with death and dying. I can talk about things and deal with them. I worked in a hospital and I am involved in spiritual things. Both my parents were in a hospice program and I could talk to them about it. They both needed a mother and I became their mother. I didn't have emotional mothering from my mother. I never got to have a mother; I only got to be a mother.

How was it to be mothering your mother when she was dying, considering her lack of mothering to you when she was alive?

It was natural. That's what I do. Whatever my programming is, there wasn't a question. It was my sense of responsibility. It's in my nature, even when it's a loaded issue.

Now here's a piece, towards the end, about singing and dancing. When she was approaching her ninetieth birthday, about five years before she died, at age ninety-five, I was visiting her in Florida. As I dreaded the usual family fights and tensions should the family get together to celebrate her ninetieth, I said to her, "Let's put on a show." She liked the idea.

When her birthday came, we were all at her apartment in Florida and we did perform. My father did a comedy routine. My mother and I sang a duet—"Look for the Silver Lining." When we did a tap dance together (she tapping with her walker) to "I'll Be Down to Get Ya in a Taxi, Honey," my sister wanted to join in. My sister had not wanted to have the show, and she hadn't prepared anything. My mother got annoyed at her and didn't want her to interfere with what we'd rehearsed. It was familiar for my mother not to consider others' feelings, just her own.

My mother didn't have room in her heart to let us relate together; it had to be about her, always in the middle.

She also recited Shakespeare: a rare occasion for her to share her intelligence, rather than her paranoia, depression, and anger.

Now I'll tell you something my mother did do for me before she died, because she was freed by the medication to do so. Somewhere inside herself she wanted me to have a good life and not be deprived. While she was on hospice towards the end of her life, my chorus was invited to sing in a concert in Germany. I wanted to go. She was able to acknowledge that I had been incredibly attentive to her during the last couple of years and she wanted me to go. I alone was taking care of nursing home placement, aides, finances, trips to Florida, selling her house, and arranging her move to New York. I couldn't share these responsibilities with my sister.

My mother said she wanted me to go to Germany. The hospice workers told me that the dying process had begun. I wanted to go with my chorus, but also wanted to be present at her death if possible. I didn't want her to be alone. She knew of my conflict and told me that she wanted me to go on the trip. I told her I would go and I asked her to still be here when I returned. She asked me if I wanted her to promise. I said yes, so she promised.

Then she said, "I promise, but I don't know if I can keep the promise. It's in God's hands, not mine."

I did go to Germany, and she was still there when I returned.

The actual end was sad. Her dying wish was that my sister and I should get along. I told her it's not going to happen. She was very upset. I later thought about it and decided that I wouldn't lie, but would frame the truth in a kinder way. I told her I'd do what I could. She was relieved. She took that to mean I would take some action to make it better. I didn't mean that, but that is how she interpreted what I said.

The day before she died, there was a meeting about her care in the nursing home where she was living. Both my sister and I came there to attend.

My mother was so happy we were all together in the same room at the same time. She asked my sister, "Are you talking to Eva?" My sister, in a hostile tone said, "No." The next day my mother died. The sad part is my sister remembers my mother dying, thinking we will get along. She doesn't remember the nasty, "No." My memory is the look on my mother's face when she said, "No."

Here's the thing; I never told my sister.

What We Think

Even though Eva's mother had not been nurturing through her life, Eva found it possible to accept her mother as the woman that she was. Eva came to terms with the realization that she would never be nurtured and mothered the way she would like to have been. Through this deep level of understanding and acceptance, Eva was able to find ways to build a satisfying relationship with her mother, even though it came later in their lives. Such acceptance on Eva's part evoked a loving response from her mother to the point where she generously released Eva to go on her trip with her choral group.

By offering positive understanding and acceptance to her mother, Eva evoked a positive and accepting response from her mother.

What Do You Think?

Have you been called upon to offer nurturing in spite of the fact that you yourself had not received it? What feelings did this evoke in you?

Exercise Questionnaire

Taking Care of a Mother Who Did Not Nurture You

1. Describe your relationship. Has it always been like this?

2. What, if anything, has occurred to change it?

3. What is there in your relationship that has enabled you to make the changes required by the circumstances?

4. What obstacles exist in your relationship that make it difficult to give to each other?

5. How do you cope with these obstacles?

6. What did you have to give up to make the necessary changes? How do you feel about it?

7. How do you think the person receiving the care feels about it?

8. Looking back at the change process, how do you feel about it now?

9. What ultimately happened that brought circumstances to this point at this time?

Care Giving Is a
Do-Whatever-It-Takes Kind of Job
Interview with Carole

Carole is a fifty-eight-year-old woman who spent seven years of her life caring for her mother during her later years. She talks about the cost-and-gain to her of this commitment.

Tell us what it was like for you to take care of your mother all those years.

It was a continuation of a lifetime of taking care of my mother on an emotional level. When my mother started needing physical care as well, it became my life, especially my emotional life. It was intense. Before the physical care, I could just walk away from her when I needed a breather.

For years it was so intense and all consuming that after my mother died, I went to the doctor about myself. As the nurse was asking me questions about "my condition," I realized that the answers I was giving her were not about myself; I was answering them about my mother. I had spent so many years repeating her medical history to nurses and doctors, and being consumed by her treatment, that I no longer existed other than as her care giver. My needs didn't exist.

Describe what you did to take care of your mother.

From the time I became an adult, my mother and I had lived in separate households. When she became incapacitated and could no longer care for herself, my husband and I moved her in with us and assumed responsibility for all her activities of daily living. Twenty-four hours a day were now devoted to our caring for her needs.

As her physical needs increased, our housing needs changed. She required different kinds of physical arrangements. For example, when she needed a wheelchair, we needed to buy a one level home. We had lived in a 1450 square foot home. We bought a house with two separate levels. There was a room for a housekeeper/attendant to live in and help us with the care. The house was so arranged that my mother could live there like a queen. She moved in.

One day, she received a phone call from a friend who had moved into a retirement home. Her friend advised her to move there instead. So, she announced to us that she was moving out to live in this retirement home. We had just come back from vacation. We had just bought this new home for her to live with us at her request, and now, she suddenly decided that she wanted to leave!

My brother moved her and her things out of our new house and into the retirement home. Soon after she arrived there, we realized that she'd had unrealistic expectations of us. She expected us to spend as much time with her there as we had when she lived with us, but my husband and I had to work. She had no consideration of our needs. And then it turned out that within a few weeks she was miserable. Her friends were not interested in spending time with her. People who lived in rooms adjacent to hers were dying. And soon after she moved in, two people committed suicide by jumping off their balconies. After several months, my mother became really sick and her attempt to live in the retirement home ended. She moved back to our home. She was never direct with us about what she needed or wanted.

Our responsibilities deepened again. At about the same time, my father-in-law became blind and came to live with us. Again, we needed new accommodations to meet their diverse needs. We sold and bought another house. At one point, after sustaining a stroke, my mother slept in our bedroom for six weeks because she could not be left alone, and the new house had not yet been set up appropriately for her needs. Ultimately, we set it up for her comfort. She lived there with us for the next four years until she died.

As her care givers, we were always sensitive to her feelings about having become dependent. After her stroke, my husband and I took her out for dinner to celebrate her leaving the hospital. I bought her a new outfit so she'd feel better about the way she looked. We took her for pizza because after the stroke she couldn't use utensils. She could eat pizza with her hands. My husband and I walked on either side of her so she wouldn't have to use a walker. We wanted her to feel good about herself. We went out of our way to tend to her every physical and emotional need. We anticipated her problems, compensated for them, and forfeited our own needs constantly.

During the time when my mother had the stroke, she became disoriented. The hospital wanted to put her in restraints. They were concerned that she might fall. I told them they could not do that. I moved into that hospital room for three days and nights. When I found that I could not sleep in the chair provided for me because it was bad for my back, I asked my husband to bring some bedding and I slept on the floor of her hospital room.

During those three restless nights, I realized that, when I was only sixteen years old, my mother had left me alone in the hospital and in pain. Now, here I was sleeping on the floor of her hospital room to make sure they didn't tie her up. She never gave that kind of concern and commitment to me!

One night, later on, I told my mother that I was sorry that I was acting like her mother, always telling her what to do. ("Take your medicine, take a shower, put your feet up...") My mother looked at me and said, " I wish you were my mother." When you have a mother who is as vulnerable as a child, you don't have a choice.

What other parts of your life were affected during the time you were caring for your mother?

My life and relationships with friends changed. Certain friends wouldn't come by anymore. We couldn't accept invitations from others. It was difficult for us to get away from home to socialize. My mother really liked having people around. When we'd have friends come over I could never be alone with them, because she wanted their attention and felt insulted if we did not include her. And I felt I'd be denying her the social opportunities she wanted if I didn't include her when our friends visited.

Outside the home, we would take her in the station wagon, and we always had to double-think about what we might need. We went with a wheelchair, walker and commode at all times. We would take her out shopping. Once we took her to a supermarket in her wheelchair. While there, she had a sudden attack of uncontrollable diarrhea. I took her into the bathroom to wash her up. I had to change her clothes. We had no fresh clothing with us that time. Fortunately, my husband was wearing sweats and an extra pair of shorts underneath. So, he took the pants off and gave them to her. Anyone in the supermarket who might have noticed us must have thought he was a masher, constantly going in and out of the women's restroom with plastic bags! We laugh about it now, but it was a critical incident when it happened!

If you needed to, would you do it again the same way?

I'm still the same person I was. Integrity dictates that you behave a certain way. This isn't just "I'm gonna lend a friend some money." Care giving is a do-whatever-it-takes kind of job that requires 24/7 attention. It consumes you and limits you. This is a defined sustained emergency.

Yes, but lots of people handle such emergencies differently, would you do it differently now?

Some people place their mothers in nursing homes. Others leave them at home with 24 hour aides. Much of the time, they end up feeling guilty. Part of the problem is that there is no good, happy outcome for this end-of-life kind of situation.

People are wired differently from one another. I did what I had to do. This is how I am. My mother, herself, wasn't wired that way. Maybe that's why I am. I know how bad it feels to be on the other end, when there is only limited commitment to another's needs. Because I didn't receive the kind of nurturing I needed, I became the nurturer myself. The bottom line is that it is better to maintain your integrity and do what you feel you need to do, even if it's life draining for you. Yes, better to do it that way than not to.

I have no regrets about how I treated my mother. If I would ever feel that I had put limitations on my care giving or had negative feelings about how I cared for her, I could never have gotten over that. For me, this was and would be again, the only way.

What We Think

Carole says she has no regrets about the way she took care of her mother and would do it all again. Even though she gave up a lot of her own time, money, energy, enjoyment of life, bought and sold several homes, and lost some friends, she still feels fulfilled in having behaved the way she did to care for her mother. No matter what anybody thought, she remained true to herself and retained her integrity. She also exhibited great sensitivity towards her mother's needs. She took care of the basic necessities of life and made sure her mother's dignity and sense of self were supported.

What Do You Think?

How are you wired? How far would you, in a similar situation, be willing to go? What compromises would you be able to make? What is not negotiable for you?

No matter what anybody
thought, Carole retained
her integrity.

Despite enormous personal
sacrifices, Carole has no regrets.

We Did the Best We Could

Arlyne's Story

Both Arlyne and her mother wished she could have died at home. They did the best they could.

My mother came to the United States at the age of five. She was the youngest of ten children. Her father had owned a farm in Austria Hungary and her family was well educated both in secular and religious schools. My mother was both educated and proud of her college degree. She spoke English, German, Yiddish, and was intellectually gifted. Classical music and good literature were part of my upbringing. Although my father was not educated in the United States, he was extremely well read, interested in world news, music, and history. He was also extremely handy at fixing things. Before I was born, they lived in a doorman building in the Bronx and my brother had a Jamaican nanny.

The depression changed all that and I was born into a fractious home where money issues played an important role in my parent's disagreements. There were also family issues which divided my parents. My mother's family lived in our apartment house and across the street from us. My father's mother also lived in our apartment building. Family members were always in and out of our apartment. Although the other relatives in our vicinity had no children, it was my parents who took my mother's sickly mother to live with us. She shared a room with my brother and myself. My brother is seven years older than I am and my mother idolized him. He was an obedient child who did whatever she wanted him to do. He was bright and self-absorbed. He experienced me as an intruder and either ignored or rejected me.

The financial and family issues burdened my mother. Since I was a more assertive child, and angry at my mother's rejections, she often vented her anger and unhappiness on me. She could be hysterical, vengeful and uncontrollable. Nevertheless, although our relationship was often difficult, it was always honest.

In my adulthood, when my father became ill with dementia, my mother turned for help to me and to my partner Arthur. She chose us as we lived near by, and she felt that she could trust us to do what she asked. My brother and his family lived far away. My mother had difficulties with my sister-in-law and she felt that my brother could not stand up against his wife's insensitivities.

It was difficult, in terms of the time it took, to take care of my parents. Although we explained very carefully about the expense of the help my father needed at home, my mother did not want him to go into a nursing home as long as there was money to pay for home assistance.

But she didn't know how to deal with the help that she needed in order to keep my father at home. This was her choice, but helping her manage the help, and keeping everybody satisfied, was almost another full time job for us. Since both Arthur and I worked, and I was also going to school, these tasks made it a very busy and time-consuming effort.

At one point, my mother was hit by a car and hospitalized in Brooklyn. She required special nurses and we, who lived in Manhattan, had to travel to the hospital every other night to pay for this care. However, my mother made an amazing recovery. After a number of months, she was back home and in charge.

We pointed out that my father's situation was getting worse, and suggested placing him in a nearby nursing home, but my mother would not consider this idea. By the time it became impossible to keep my father at home without the help of a male aide, the nearby nursing home was out of the question. A cousin was on the board of the Baptist Home and Hospital in Brooklyn which was very far from where my mother lived. The care there was excellent and my mother finally accepted the reality that my father had to be admitted to a nursing home. She traveled by car service to be with him daily and their remaining funds were spent in that way.

During this time, Arthur died of cancer, and my mother and father remained solely in my care. My father died shortly after Arthur's death, and my mother gradually needed more and more help. She was in her late eighties and physically limited by a heart condition. My brother came every few months; he did nothing but visit. With the little monies that had remained for my mother, we managed her care at home. Finally she became eligible for Medicaid and I was able to get round-the-clock care for her. All this I arranged.

During this period, my mother would begin her relationship with the home care aides by enchanting them, but then she would begin to resent the fact that they were doing her job, running her house. Her attitude was psychologically understandable, but she would become nasty and suspicious toward those who were helping her. If I pointed out that they were really quite accommodating, she would become furious, accusing me of preferring them to her.

I knew how difficult it was to get good help and understood her feelings but she would become relentless. Time and again it became necessary to let some of the help go, and request new aides. This was very difficult. As nice as the aides were, she would ultimately become angry with someone for something. When the third regime had to be let go, I threw in the towel and accepted the fact that my mother would have to enter a nursing home. My brother saw this as a positive move. He had little idea of the physical and mental limitations inherent in my mother, nor of her deterioration; nor did he seem to understand how much she wanted to remain at home. She entered a nursing home close to where my brother lived and worked. However, it was about a two-hour trip, or more, for me. I had hoped that, with the help I had arranged for her, my mother would live out her life in her own apartment. Nevertheless, for me it was also a relief from the burden that had been very stressful for many years.

My mother deteriorated further in the nursing home, and when I came I had to feed her. I would take her to the garden in her wheelchair and she would try to converse. She was sometimes very articulate and at other times withdrawn. Ultimately she suffered a stroke.

One day I visited her with my brother and also departed with him. However, as I lived so far away, I felt that this might be the last time I would see her. Even though I had left, I decided to return and to spend some time alone with her. I lay on her bed, holding her. I kept telling her that I loved her. I assured her that if she needed to leave us, we would all be well. I just held her, and stroked her, and after awhile she seemed to be sleeping. Then I left.

She died two days later.

What We Think
Shura's Voice

Arlyne and her mother both hoped to arrange their lives to enable Mom to die at home. The series of events, described by Arlyne, is experienced by many mothers, daughters and families in similar situations. An elder parent dies and the spouse remains alone. The daughter (or another family member) assumes responsibilities to support the continuance of the parent's independent living. Then, a new set of circumstances demands increasing assistance to the old person. The daughter herself has experienced changes in her mid-life that require her to make changes and new adaptations in her life. Nevertheless, she continues to monitor and support her parent's needs. Home help becomes difficult to arrange and sustain. Financial resources become strained. The health of her parent is in steady decline, requiring increasing and intensified care.

Finally, placement in a nursing care facility becomes mandatory and the search begins for an acceptable facility. This becomes an enormous problem. The health care system in the United States is extremely limited in its offering of long term care. Social policy is bureaucratic and not individualized. Medical, financial, and availability considerations are primary in the final decision. There are also time pressures if the old person is in a hospital awaiting discharge. Social, cultural, family and emotional issues are low priorities.

Leaving one's own home to live in a nursing home is a major traumatic change for the old person as well as for her family. The nursing home is a facility where residents must accept an environment and life style quite different from the one to which they've been accustomed. A resident lives with and is cared for by strangers. She must conform to rules and daily routines over which she has little or no control. There is little or no privacy. She has had to yield so many taken-for-granted ways of her life in exchange for the nursing care she needs now.

The facility may be located in a neighborhood distant from her home. Out-of-doors, she may view a world totally different from the one she has always known. Even the most loving daughters and family members may find visiting difficult. These fundamental changes have a powerful emotional and psychological impact upon the old person and her family. The mother/daughter relationship is challenged. Both must understand the changes and respond with patience, courage and love.

Even without an accompanying verbal commentary, Arlyne's emotional struggle is clear. Despite earlier difficulties in the relationship, she was able, because of her unconditional love, to help her mother die. It is remarkable and heroic that she and so many other mothers and daughters live through this experience with grace and love.

What Do You Think?

Have you ever had to cope with the issue of placement in a health care facility? What were our feelings and how did you cope? If you haven't dealt with this concern, how do you think you would feel about it and how might you cope?

In spite of all the problems,
the daughter fulfilled all
responsibilities with her
unconditional love.

This enabled her to release
her mother and
ease the pain of separation by death.

*"A woman's life can really be a succession of lives, each revolving
around some emotionally compelling situation or challenge, and
each marked off by some intense experience."*
—*Wallis Simpson, Duchess of Windsor*

About Grandmothers and Care Giving
Shura's Voice

In my kitchen, there hangs a plaque, given to me by my daughter-in-law. It reads, "Just when a woman thinks her work is done, she becomes a grandmother."

The young women who see this plaque, laugh about it. The mature mothers smile thoughtfully. The grandmothers who come in to my kitchen nod their heads in agreement.

National statistics tell us that millions of children in this country are receiving their primary care from grandmothers. This number does not include grandmothers who "child sit" a few hours after school while their grown daughters are at work. Nor does it include grandparents who visit on weekends to ease the childcare burdens of their daughters and sons. Nor does it include grandmothers who come by when someone is sick and needs a hand; or when there is a new baby and grandma comes to her daughter's house for a while to help with the older children; or when the daughter incurs excessive expenses and grandma offers needed emergency funds.

The statistic refers to those children who receive consistent daily, weekly, monthly and year-round care from grandmothers because their own mothers either work full-time, are chronically or mentally ill, or unable to care for their children because they themselves are on drugs, or living away from home for some other reasons.

These roles of grandmothers cut across ethnic and financial lines. I know grandmothers who are very well off financially who are raising their grandchildren as their own for any one of the above-mentioned reasons. Some daughters of the youthful generation of the sixties became addicted to drugs on well-known and costly college campuses. Some bore children but were unable to care for them. Many of these children are now living with grandmothers who do care.

Such a grandmother is Ava, whose beautiful daughter Sarah, became addicted to drugs and bore a child. Sarah's addiction was so severe that she was unable to care for her baby Helen. Ava, who had been working full time and preparing for her own retirement, assumed complete care of Helen. Sarah was in and out of rehabilitation programs for some twenty years. Sometimes she disappeared altogether and Ava didn't even know where she was. Finally, Sarah was able to resume a life of some normalcy. By this time, the "baby" was in college, thanks to her hard-working grandmother.

Such a grandmother is seventy-five-year-old Clara, whose oldest daughter Jeanette suffers from mental illness. Jeannette's baby, Dorothy, is being raised in Clara's home. Dorothy calls her "Mama," although now, a young teenager, she knows that Jeannette is her birth mother. But Clara, her grandmother, is her mama.

Such a grandmother is seventy-year-old Nora, whose daughter vanished into the streets and returned home briefly with her baby daughter, only to return to street life after leaving baby Tammy with her own mother. Nora, a wizened widow, herself on Medicaid, has been raising the little girl who rarely sees or even knows her birth mother.

Such a grandmother is Sophie, whose daughter Ellie, died shortly after her out-of-wedlock baby was born. Sophie, a woman well into her seventies, has been raising the baby as her own.

These are only a few of the grandmothers who are known to the authors. Ethnically, two of these women are African-American and two are Caucasian. All the grandmothers had been in the work force earlier in their lives. Only one is a professionally trained person. These grandmothers are widows themselves, and have already dealt with the severe loss of their own roles as wives and lovers. Now they are fulfilling the maternal roles that their daughters would have performed, had they not been lost to family life for one reason or another.

These stories can be told and retold with as many variations as there are individuals who have lived through similar circumstances.

"For no actual process happens twice; only we meet the same sort of occasion again."
—Suzanne Langer

Exercise: Guided Imagery

Take three deep breaths. With each inhale feel the oxygen filling your lungs with cleansing, relaxing air. Then hold for one second and exhale. Imagine your exhale is shaking loose and freeing the tension in every part of your body. It starts escaping through your windpipe, into your mouth and out through your lips. Now, allow all the muscles in your body to relax.

Adjust your position so that you are even more comfortable and able to release even more tension.

Now imagine yourself in a shrunken version and you are entering your own body through the skin. Travel into the veins and enter the bloodstream.

Let's take a ride through your bloodstream as you enter your heart. Notice the color, the shape and size of your heart. Take time to enjoy the rhythm of your heart's unique beating. Now, visualize all the love in your heart. What color and shape does that present? What and who does it include?

Consider whether you are willing to shift that love and expand it to include more than its current contents. Are you ready to imagine including strangers in your community? What does that feel like? Is there a physical sensation to this opening? If so, what is it? Notice and observe the nature of the changes in shape and size of your heart.

Now can you expand it even more to include the state in which you live? Again, pay close attention to the sensations and the changes that your heart is experiencing.

Can you open your heart to include your country? And now, when you are ready, the whole planet earth?

Can you even include people who have done you wrong? Keep noticing the nature of all the changes you observe as you do this exercise.

This opening of the heart for all people on the planet is what we refer to as compassion. Can you experience compassion in your heart for all that exists in your view each day?

Musings About Care Giving
Shura's Voice

The universe tends and nourishes itself, as do all living things. Care giving and tender nourishment are dimensions of our humanness.

We care and tend in so many ways; for each other, for plants and pets, for beauty, thoughts, and ideas. We nourish in so many ways; bodies, minds, hearts, souls, friendships, relationships.

The care giving of mothers and daughters must be understood within the context of their lifelong relationships. As human beings are so marvelously diverse, so too are these relationships and their responses to the challenges of their unique lives.

How strong are the bonds of family! How powerful the ties that bind daughters and mothers! How powerful are maternal and filial responsibilities!

Whether the bonds are loving ones or not, whether responsibilities are fulfilled or not, the emotional accompaniments are powerful and undeniable. They persist throughout one's lifetime.

Life is a continuum of changes and changing needs. So too, is care giving a process of changing phases. Whether the care is given to a child or to an elder, we must be mindful that changes and individual development affect and alter both the care giver and the person receiving the care.

Time, ill health, and dependency needs bring stress to both individuals. Sometimes even the most loving relationship is altered by the strain of the ongoing, unrelenting needs demanding attention. Even the kind mother falters. Even the kind daughter tires. The love remains the same but the ability to provide the needed care may wane.

Thanks to our culture of individualism, geographic mobility, and the consequent erosion of the extended family, today's families have a different face from those in earlier times. When an elder needs care, family members are not always available or accessible. Even when they are, they need help and respite at times so as to give good care.

Community resources such as health care agencies, visiting nurses, case managers, individual companions or home health aides are not always enough. Sometimes the elder person's needs require continuous, round-the-clock nursing care. For such needs, the nursing home is usually the only resource.

The family may be in great conflict about the decision to place a loved one in a nursing home. They may feel as if they have failed a responsibility or an expectation. They may be deeply concerned about the nursing home's competence to meet needs. They may worry about how the person feels about being in the nursing home, about a stranger tending to intimate needs. Is he or she being handled with care? Should we be doing more? There are widespread financial, legal and social issues to consider.

The person receiving the care, whether at home, in a facility, or at a distance, copes with an equally difficult set of feelings. Is this what I've become? Why can't I take care of myself? My body is betraying me. Why must I put up with strangers? Why isn't my family more available? I wish I could be in my own home.

Ultimately, everyone wonders, "Why is this happening to me? What have I done to deserve this?"

Whatever the specific circumstances, and whatever the existing relationships, the current dependency needs demand priority attention. The family bond is very strong

Through the many years of working in a nursing home, I have learned about the power of this bond. There are daughters who love their mothers, daughters who do not approve of their mothers, daughters who have never gotten along very well with their mothers, daughters who don't even like their mothers.

There are mothers who nurtured their daughters, mothers who didn't nurture their daughters, mothers who didn't approve of their daughters, mothers who don't get along with their daughters.

382

There are families who have lived for years with anger and disapproval. There are families who have lived their lives with love and caring.

Also, there is a social stereotype that describes uncaring families who dump their older parents and ignore their needs. This point of view stigmatizes families who have no recourse and intensifies feelings of shame and anxiety.

Most important this stereotype interferes with appropriate planning for the person who needs this care, as well as the family.

Whatever the circumstances of family life and relationships, it is amazing to me to realize how so many people are able to cope with grace under so much adversity.

Song About Two Mothers
Duet
Shura's Voice

-1-
Let me tell you about my mother
Who gave me life and love
When I was a little girl
Fed me and clothed me
And put my hair in curls

Taught me and played with me
Scolded in the gentlest words
Tended me so tenderly
Taught me to laugh when Life's
absurd

Showed me beauty in the sunlight
And how to sing a song
By precept and example
She taught me right from wrong

CHORUS

Now she's old and fragile
And needs my tender care
And though I tried—
She did decide
That she'd do better here

So here she is, within this place
To my chagrin, to my disgrace

It was so hard to let her go
I love her so…I love her so
I love her so

-2-
I'll tell about my mother
From whom I never heard
Since my earliest memory
One tender, loving word

Her sharp, sarcastic witticisms
Were clearly cutting criticisms
To make me feel absurd

She taught me wrong from right
To my chagrin, to her delight
I was always wrong and
She was always right

CHORUS

Now she's old and fragile
And needs my tender care
And though I tried—
I did decide
Better if she lived here

So here she is, within this place
To my surprise, to my disgrace

It was so hard to let her go
Though I dislike her so…
I love her too

385

Guideposts for Thought

1.   Care giving, under any circumstances, is a task; whether a loving one or not, it is a difficult task.

2.   When it's difficult, due to the nature of the relationship, one must cope with the emotional and psychological barriers.

3.   The path to overcoming the obstacles involves patience, humor, being flexible and recognizing responsibility.

4.   Change requires awareness, practice, yielding some control, and graceful acceptance.

5.   The powerful impact of the mother/daughter bond, although sometimes painful, is over-riding.

6.   You may be a care giver, or the receiver of care, without realizing it.

7.   Acceptance is the other side of the care giving coin.

8.   Developing and utilizing family supports and community resources are needed for care giving.

9.   One needs to open one's heart to creative problem-solving in care giving.

Chapter Six
Death, Loss, and Bereavement

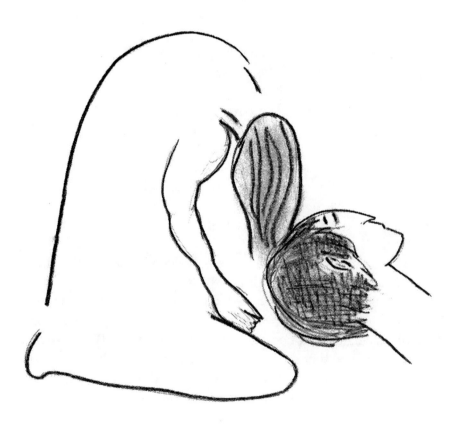

Two Views:

The Fingers of Death
Shura's Voice

Death has long fingers
To bring the Gift of Loss
Whose heavy breath still lingers
Nor does it leave
The while we grieve
The time we mourn
Remaining long beyond the time
When Hope and new life are reborn

Looking Forward After Loss

"It is a cliché, but life is short. One only becomes aware that there
has to be an end sometime, after about the age of fifty.
I try to look upon the time I have left as an opportunity, not a threat.
And a chance to be my own person, rather than the half of a pair.
I am just trying to look upon this time as a new and different period,
with all the happy times and good feelings behind me like a comfort-
able, cozy cushion. That gives me the confidence to go on."
—*Christine McDonald*

Dimensions of Death, Loss, and Bereavement

These inevitable portions of the experience of living affect our lives in many ways.

In this chapter we blend our voices to present the perspectives of mature daughter and older mother. Some are remarkably the same; some are different, reflecting the unique view of each as seen through the lens of her different point of development.

We focus on four elements: change, facets of loss, the redistribution of balance, and considerations of death and our own mortality.

About Change

We agree that change is the only constant in existence. We also agree that every power, circumstance and situation in existence retains the intent to maintain itself. Therefore, change, implying elements of the unknown, is a threat to the status quo. Being on the threshold of the unknown is a source of anxiety. Change can be positive or negative. It may trigger fear even when it is awaited with positive anticipation

A Daughter Writes

I perceive anxiety in my body. My chest tightens and I get the sensation of excited energy vibrating through my arms and torso. Worried thoughts with negative predictions flood my mind. These sensations suck me in and prevail over my common sense. My behavior becomes an ongoing attempt to soothe the discomfort that pervades my being.

Sometimes I cope by becoming aware and allowing the experience. I pay attention to the vibrations of energy and examine them in great detail. Then, and only then, does the anxiety begin to dissolve and there is some relief in anticipating the change. The journey becomes acceptable and now I experience the freedom of my adulthood.

A Mother Writes

The anticipation of change triggers these major questions: Will I have the strength to sustain it? What adaptations will be required of me? What must I give up to manage the new and unknown circumstances? Who else will be affected? Will anyone I love be hurt? How can I protect them? What can I do to help? I am willing to make changes but am I able to conform to their demands? Am I required to change plans and ideas? Do I still have the power, the intelligence, the versatility to meet the challenge? I call upon all the wisdom of my years to help me work through all that now lies before me.

Facets of Loss

We consider several losses as we proceed through the journey of life.

Loss of Mother

Every daughter has or has had a mother. We agree that love her or not, enjoy her or not, nurtured by her or not, the bond is powerful and undeniable. When she dies, we respond emotionally. Sometimes our business with her has remained unfinished. We must come to terms with that. Sometimes we feel we have done our best in the years of our relationship and feel fulfilled even as we mourn her loss.

Eruption of Repressed Emotions

When a parent dies, the entire family reacts in profoundly different ways. It is as if the very foundation of a house has been unearthed. The reactions of the family members will vary in expressions of a wide range of emotions. All the unresolved, unexpressed historical issues rise to the surface and are acted out in variations of unexpected behaviors.

For example, repressed sibling rivalry may erupt into heated arguments and even into legal actions between or among each other. Old anger and hurt surface fiercely. These may focus on the money, property or other assets left by the parent. So much of the emotional response to this loss is colored by ancient history, yet the family members are generally not aware of this. It is helpful to become aware of these feelings and the depths to which they extend. All feelings, no matter how manifested, are normal and part of the response to the severe loss. It becomes important not to devalue oneself or others. This is a time for compassion and respect.

Feelings of Abandonment

Loss of mother, father or someone almost as close, may be accompanied by feelings of abandonment. It may feel as if this important person has left us here on earth, stuck with the drama of loss. It is helpful to become aware of such feelings and to realize that it was not, most probably, the intent of that person to die and leave us behind. To restore some sense of balance, we must review the legacy this person has bequeathed; tangible or not, useful or not, acceptable or not. To understand again what this person has meant to us in our lives, becomes a kind of healing. It helps to relieve some of the weight of the loss itself.

As we revisit the lost relationship, we also begin to reevaluate the gift of life that remains ahead for us. We may be able to close the gap that the person has left, and reconstruct what lies ahead.

This is not an easy task. It may take time, patience and effort to achieve.

Loss of Peers

We have no control over our friends dying. These downhills of life are among its many sharp turns. This loss is one of the most difficult of human experiences.

A Daughter Writes

I have experienced several sudden deaths of people under the age of fifty-five. My first response was shock and disbelief. *How could this be?* I thought. People of my age are not supposed to die! A friend died of colon cancer. After the shock, I began to consider what led to the demise of this intelligent, middle-aged man. He had been a physician. He'd had symptoms for some time. He should have known, should have caught it. He didn't have to die! Such a loss as this one, and others, led me to a deeper appreciation of all that I do have in my life. I have a safe home, health and sustenance, a loving family, good friends, and work that I enjoy. How lucky am I? Yet the drama of life continues to roller coaster with sharp unexpected turns. Death becomes part of life's equation. I begin to realize that although I am healthy now, I must take care of my body more carefully. I don't like this process of losing my friends.

A Mother Writes

My sense of loss is painful as I reflect on the dwindling of my peer group and the ways in which I have lost some friends. My dearest friend of long standing died after a long illness at home. Her husband who had cared for her died soon after. This has happened to three more couples with whom my husband and I had spent many happy times. Another friend and neighbor of many years now lives in a nursing home in a faraway state. A girlhood chum lives quite far away as well. As we are both drivers, we had always managed to meet half-way. Now we are both unable to drive the distance and remain telephone friends. The roll call of personal losses continues to include many others. My world becomes smaller each time. Every friend is remembered. The passing of each leaves a gaping space. It remains as I continue my own journey to its destination. This experience is an inevitable part of growing old.

Closure
Concluding Dialogue

Shura: Closure is about being able to go forward in your life after you have experienced a severe loss.

Jennifer: It is a process during which we attempt to put to rest some of the feelings of the loss.

Shura: In no way does it suggest that the sense of loss can be eradicated, or that you can forget the loss of a person important to you. When the loss is important, it can never be eradicated. The person who has been lost is never forgotten!

Jennifer: However, in time, the emotional severity of the loss may assume a different location on the person's emotional map.

Shura: In time, the impact of the loss is not always in the forefront of your consciousness.

Jennifer: Closure involves acceptance—acceptance of the loss—of the change—of the pain—of whatever has developed during the mourning of the loss.

Shura: You can achieve some measure of closure when you have evaluated the essence of the relationship and its meaning in your life. Then you can begin to live with that meaning after experiencing the loss.

Grief

Jennifer's Voice

The dark days of grief
Come upon me
Like a storm at sea
Tossing my ship about the relentless waves
They haunt me, the motion of time
Rocking me—shaking me—no rest
The dark days of grief
Stab me in the gut—the center of my being
Seeking blood
I can only surrender
As the pain overcomes my soul

The dark days of grief
Move into my home
Shadowing the windows with sadness
I can't see out
I stay within
I'm lost to the darkness
An unwanted guest refusing to leave
The dark days of grief
To whom I must surrender
And spend those days of grief in darkness
Until it decides…ENOUGH

Exercises Regarding Change

1. Twiddle your thumbs:

Fold your hands together, fingers intertwined. In this position, roll your thumbs around each other. Keep doing this for twenty seconds. Now Stop!

Holding your hands in the same position, roll your thumbs around the other way for twenty seconds.

How quickly were you able to make the change? What thought process enabled you to do this?

2. Arms Akimbo:

Fold your arms akimbo; that is, cross your arms over your chest, right hand to left shoulder and left hand to right shoulder. Now slide each hand down from the shoulder to grasp the other arm, and tuck one hand under the opposite armpit.

Settle into the position comfortably. Which arm is folded over the other? Is your right arm over the left arm or vice versa? Where are your fingers? What are they touching? How are you holding your shoulders at this point? How comfortable are you? Hold this position for a moment or two.

NOW: Maintaining this position of akimbo, change the position of your arms. If the right arm was folded over the left arm, now fold the left arm over the right arm or vice versa. How does it feel now? Does it feel different? What change(s) are you experiencing? How easy was that to do? Are you more or less comfortable? Is it the same level of comfort as before the change? What thought process did you have to go through to make this change?

What thoughts about change are suggested by these exercises?

Remembering Mothers

As the mature daughters remembered the loss of their mothers, they also began to recall many aspects of their relationships that have remained important to them. Both Jennifer and Shura, as well as the speakers themselves, found each session fraught with emotion and learning.

Reminiscing in this way brought forth new perspectives which were helpful.

For Mama
Shura's Voice

You understand, Mama
Not for me your grave
And headstone
The desire to lie there
Was yours

That is not you
Encased in pine
Beneath the gleaming granite
Beneath the earth
The grass, the ivy

You are not there
Where people place a stone
And shed a tear

No—it is here
In the blinding radiance
Of our heart-memory
Mamatchka

Your every word of wisdom
Your kindness unforgotten
As your love's flame
Is remembered

Every living moment
In the pulsing heart throb
Of our daily lives
Here you do remain
Mamatchka

Finding Peace
Interview with Amy

Amy and her mother engaged in a lifelong process to achieve a friendly, loving relationship

What was the relationship with your mom like?

I don't want to sell her short. It was rocky when I was younger. I was headstrong and independent. In my later years, Mom was like a foundation for me. Everything I published, my writing, and lots of my artwork, was at her house. After she died, I went through some of the things in her house. She had saved all of my work and appreciated it.

In my mom's house, I also found letters that I wrote to my Grandma. That's a significant part of my history. My mother was always there to "qvell" about me and encourage me. She was proud of me. I don't have children of my own but there was someone for me who thought I was special and not ordinary. When others in the world might have treated me poorly, I knew my mother would offer me kindness and wisdom.

My mom was outspoken and an activist. I always admired that. My mom liked that I was outspoken and that I stand up for what I believe in. Even now, I'm 50 years old, but I still need that kind of unconditional support. I don't have children but I had Mom. My Dad went to G-d at fifty-three years of age, after having been exposed to asbestos and radiation in the Navy.

You don't have children, and now that your mother is dead, you are not a child. How do you feel about that?

I feel disconnected. I'm searching for ideas. I'm lonely for my mother. I would talk to her and hear her loving voice say, "Hi, sweetie."

Look, it wasn't always wonderful, but the love went very deep. As an adult, I know that my rocky history with Mom was motivated by her unfulfilled dreams and her fears. She once told me, "If I had my life to live over again, it would be yours." What bigger compliment could she give me?

My mom has been a lifeline for me. I have sisters, but they don't fill the same need. Although Bonnie and I are very close and dear to one another, my mother became my best friend in later years. Even though she had been cruel to me when I was young, she apologized. I accepted her apology and from that we developed a relationship based on love, truth, and acceptance. When I disagreed with Mom, we would air it out, not sweep it under the rug. She confided in me; I listened. I enjoyed my mother's values about giving. I was proud of her with all her imperfections. She was a good human being; she valued friendship and worked hard.

How did it come to be that you cared for your mom while she was dying?

I had to come to care for her. My mother gave me life and now it was a question of her life. I slept beside her on the floor at her home. I kept watching to see that she was breathing. One of my sisters was difficult, distant, and harsh—like an adversary during that period. My other sister and I grew closer together and joined forces for strength. Bonnie's husband wanted more of her presence during that time. He was not entirely supportive of her involvement with our mom and me. But in spite of that, we climbed an emotional mountain together. It was unquestionable. Because I was staying with Mom from out of town, I was physically with her. I felt that I should be there and be her advocate. What was more important? Where else could I be? How could I have been doing anything else?

How did you reconcile your feelings with the historically bad treatment from your mom?

My mom gave me life. She also abused me and I was afraid of her at times. She used to tell me that she had eyes in the back of her head and knew everything I did. She told me that she was a witch and that scared the crap out of me! As a child, I learned to run away from her. That actually was a good thing because it gave her time to cool down. I learned that giving her the time to cool down was the best thing I could do.

What made your relationship work in your later years?

Airing the old issues and working it through, not being afraid to confront her about her hurtful behavior, forgiving past hurts. We shared a reciprocal, respectful and honest dialogue.

Mom owned up to her part in it all. We were both willing to start building trust based on the new information we had about each other.

There was honesty; connecting with the unconditional love, seeing each other for who we are. Mom allowed me to see the little girl in her. We each appreciated the good-and-well meaning in the other. We got past our own obstacles. We were both very vulnerable!

Do you have any regrets?

I wish I could have advocated for her medical treatment at an earlier point. I wish I were closer to her physically in the later years. I considered going to Florida to be with Mom but my partner didn't want us to. I earned my Ph.D. in December; Mom got sick in January and died.

I also regret that when she was dying and I did go home for a few days to take care of matters, I found that they had taken her out of ICU. I wouldn't have allowed them to do that had I been there. That made for more conflict with one of my sisters who is a doctor and completely defended the medical institution's decisions. I was living my own life and was far away.

During the short time she was ill, were you conflicted about being away?

The doctors said she was fine, even though she had shortness of breath. Mom used to walk for miles, but the shortness of breath was hindering this activity. The doctors did not take care of Mom. They did not effectively diagnose her medical problem. It hurts so much because I believe with quality medical care Mom would be alive today.

When I was with her, I told her I loved her a lot. When I did come home to stay with her, sometimes I'd drive her crazy and then I knew she was better and it was time to go. Now, I appreciate her. I know that I admired her and she knew it too. It's painful to be without her. I'm trying to make the most of my life.

Your relationship with your mom was an amazing learning experience for you. We learn from experience and adversity, don't we?

Yes!

"When you can't remember why you're hurt, that's when you're healed."
—Jane Fonda

What We Think

Jennifer's Voice

For Amy, connections with her mom and grandmother were her continuity. Amy had chosen not to get married and not to have children. At this point in her life, she is feeling disconnected from family. Her feelings of disconnectedness are intensified by the loss of her mother who had been her lifeline to a sense of family.

Amy overcame a very stormy relationship with her mom. Ultimately, she came to appreciate her as a woman with her own issues and struggles. Through this process, she learned tremendous lessons in how to make a difficult relationship work. Amy is going on with her life, making the most of what she does have. She still feels her loss and bereavement by her mother's absence from the planet, but she learns from her adversity and continues to strive to make herself a purposeful and whole individual.

What Do You Think?

Are you challenged by a stormy relationship? Do you understand the challenge? What is your reaction to it? Are you coming to terms with it? If so, how?

Ambivalence and Regret
Interview with Corinna

Corinna describes her conflicted feelings for a mother whom she truly loved How did these conflicts come about ?

What can you say about your relationship with your mother?

It was stuck at a certain time when I moved to break away from family. She was always there to help, but when she started getting sick, I felt guilty being away. There was always a sense that there wasn't much time left. She'd want me to come see her and it was difficult for me to establish other relationships, do other things. I felt like I had to wait to see what happens. It made me feel selfish.

My aunt validated my feelings, confirming to me that my mother needed her family. She had grown up with a rough family. All my mother wanted in her life was a family of her own. My brother died young at age 19. Then her needs became more intense. She was overprotective of me. She understood it was her hang-ups, but still I was overprotected. My father was a lovely man, but Mom did not know how to stick up for herself. She got stronger as she aged. I love that my mother never stopped working on herself. I told her I appreciated that in her and thanked her because it helped me to not accept certain things. You can't give to someone and expect a certain behavior in return. When you give, you must just give it away. Otherwise it's too much pressure. I loved my parents so much, but after my brother died, I felt like my family wasn't my family anymore.

When your mom got sick who took care of her?

My father. At the very end, I was there. In the process, I was trying to avoid. I was afraid of getting too close. I was fearful I would get close and she would die and I'd be abandoned. It was hard for me to be there for her. I felt guilty, but I also felt that if I were there, I'd be locked into being there and I'd be unable to go anywhere else.

I feel sad about my relationship with my mother. I could and should have been more generous. I really wasn't there for her the way a person who cares for another person should be. I was afraid, and I'm not sure why. On her death bed, in one of my last conversations with my mom, she told me, "I don't know what is going to become of you." Then she saw me dealing with the hospital staff and told me to come close to her. I put my head by her head and she said, "You'll be okay."

When it comes to my mother, there is a blind spot. I don't remember things when I think about her. I feel I was a disappointment to my mother. I didn't live my life happily. I didn't like the life I was living. I don't like my day-to-day life now. My mother didn't want me to become a baker. She felt it was not a socially conscious thing to do and she worried about my aging. She thought I would get tired and ultimately not be able to bake. I realize now she just wanted me to be happy. I think as I get older and mature, I realize my parents were just people with their own problems doing the best they could. This insight makes it all easier for me.

What do you miss most about your mother?

Sitting in the kitchen and talking. Cooking together. We related through projects.

"Perhaps now and then a castaway on a lonely desert dreads the thought of being rescued."
—Sarah Orne Jewett

What We Think

Jennifer's Voice

Corinna lost a dream of a cohesive, happy family when her brother died young. Mother became over-overprotective. Corinna felt that her expectations were unreasonably high.

Corinna is in a lot of conflict. When a person must deal with ambivalence, guilt and conflict, it is very difficult for her to be at peace about anything. Corinna describes the loss of her mother and father as being laced with love, sadness and regret. She discusses having a blind spot about her mother. She felt she let her mother down, not living up to her expectations. Her guilt and avoidance about her mother have left her with unfinished business about their relationship. Her mother died leaving her with no closure. This is a difficult feeling that may haunt a person throughout her life.

In the end, Corinna was able to mature to an understanding that her mother was just a person with her own conflicts and problems. She understood the ways in which she was different from her mother and even understood what she needed.

Perhaps Corinna was equally disappointed in her mother for not having been able to give her what she needed. Yet, she was able to appreciate what Mom could give her and could help her make the most of her life.

When we lose our dreams, do we move on to new dreams, or do we settle for what we have and focus on struggling with the loss?

What We Think
Shura's Voice

The loss of a child is one of the most intense, tragic losses a mother may be called upon to endure. Corinna's mother lost her son at the height of his youth, just as he was entering young adulthood. Devastated, mother wants to protect her other children from a similar fate. She is deeply invested in seeing her daughter enjoy her youth and achieve the full flower of adulthood.

This story illustrates some of the possible effects on the entire family when death interrupts the expectations of normal living. Each family member responds with intense feelings that need exploration and understanding. Mother, father, brothers, and sisters need support and assistance when they must cope with such a terrible happening.

In a loving family the feeling of parental love and caring, such as Corinna describes, is very important. The family's love does bind its members closer and offers much help and needed support.

Sometimes, however, they do not or cannot help each other appropriately and their feelings are left to fester over time. Each person is left to live life as best he or she can. Mother's anxiety and depression interferes with her ability to help and guide her daughter as she might have done, as her daughter wished. Coupled with Corinna's own sense of loss, the problem is exacerbated for mother and daughter.

Love is important. Love helps. But sometimes, as in such situations, love alone may not be enough to give the help that is needed.

What Do You Think?

Do you experience ambivalent feelings? What losses have left you with unresolved conflicts? Do you feel you have achieved closure?

To Her Dying Day
Interview with Elizabeth

Elizabeth continues to seek her mother's approval even after her mother's death.

What was the nature of your relationship?

I am conflicted. The relationship is a mixed bag. I knew my mother loved me and was generally proud of me, but I also often felt controlled by her. When I made a decision she didn't approve of, she usually pushed me until I changed my choice to what she wanted it to be.

Didn't you ever rebel? Not even when you were a teenager?

I was never really a hell raiser or really rebellious. When I did rebel, I just kept it to myself. I was looking to avoid conflict. As a result, we appeared to be close on the surface, but were never really close. There were times when my mom got very upset because she wanted to talk about what was going on in my life, but I kept her at a distance. We both missed out on the relationship we both wished we could have had.

How did you feel inside?

I was probably angry, but I didn't feel bad. Like most teenagers, I thought, "My mother doesn't know anything, and I'm gonna do what I want to do." I'm still rebelling. I never grew out of that. With Mom, I was always trying to have it both ways, making an effort to have her approval while wishing I could say to her, "This is how I feel, but thank you for your opinion." Then I could have moved on knowing I was being true to myself. I'd like to be mature enough to say this even now in situations with other people. It is still a struggle.

What were your conflicts when her dying process began?

Huge. I knew she was dying. We never worked through these issues together and I never became mature enough to take a stand and feel like an adult next to her. I needed to make peace with that. I need to make peace with the fact that she is now gone and I never will have that respectful, mutual, mature relationship with my mother that I really wanted.

When I was caring for her, I didn't realize what I now know. It wasn't that she was trying to control me. It was just that she did not want to relinquish control over her own life. She was conflicted about being dependent and needing to rely on others who might not do things the way she wanted them done. I think she was torn between being thankful for my efforts and not wanting to be a burden.

I was keenly aware while she was dying that she had given me so much and now I wanted to give back to her, to somehow complete the incomplete. To make up for lost time. That was my agenda.

It's painful for me now to realize that I didn't understand her needs. There was so much misunderstanding and so much we couldn't say to one another.

We fell into old patterns. For example, I made her meals, and she always worried that I was going to put too much oil into the food. So when she'd hear something that I was cooking, begin to sizzle, she would get upset, worried that the oil would make her nauseous. She didn't understand that the sizzle was me browning meat. I didn't understand that the kitchen odors would permeate into her bedroom. She was uncomfortable and never explained that to me. I never understood. It was like that when she was well and continued while she was dying. This was continuity for her. She knew that change was coming and she was holding on.

Tell us about her dying process.

She was diagnosed with lung cancer in July and she died in November. My sister-in-law, my brothers and I were taking care of her in the hospital in Florida. She was very weak and sick. But we couldn't remain in Florida, what with our kids going back to school and the adults working. She had improved a bit, and was strong enough to come to my house in New York and we cared for her here. She loved Florida and she was uncomfortable and cold here. She never liked depending on others.

I wonder if the decision for her to come to New York was for her or for us. I'm not sure it was the better place for her to be. The question was, "Is it better for her to be cared for by paid professionals in Florida and be comfortable, or to be with her family?"

When we brought her here we still had hopes for treatment. She had been getting radiation and it gave her some relief. Although it made her feel sick, she bounced back and recovered for a while. This gave us all a false sense of hope.

She started chemotherapy treatments in Sloan Kettering and she was weak and in pain again. She wanted it to be over quickly. In her Florida home, she had a book that gave instructions on committing suicide and now she regretted that she hadn't brought it with her to New York.

I saw each day I had with her as a gift to be savored. But she wanted to be dead and not have to go through the dying process. I don't blame her for wanting it to be over.

The cancer was inoperable and advanced. She had spent her whole life with a cough, so when she began to "cancer-cough" no one looked into it. Now I go into my shower in my cold, chilly New York home and I think about how uncomfortable she had to have been in this shower. My regret is that we didn't work on the relationship while she was alive and well. I carry around the memories of caring for a sick lady who was uncomfortable.

Being with her own people was worth something. I'm sure her not telling you is consistent with her not approving, not giving you that. She was herself until the last minute. You wanted it to be different.

So I walk around with this feeling. At what point would it have been possible to try and work this out? I never could have confronted her to work it out. It was only possible for me to let go of it and mature and move on. I still can do that, but haven't yet.

That is how you stay connected to her.

My house was full of stuff my father brought from Florida. I feel a need to go through it all.

It's the first bond in your life. The bond never breaks, even if you say, "The hell with you." There's so much power in the bond. Your task now is to come to terms with yourself. Your mom was a tough lady who was in touch mostly with herself, knew what she wanted, and let people know.

I feel like my life controls me and I don't control anything. I don't make an effort to control anything except maybe my own kids. The difference between my controlling them and Mom controlling me is that fifteen minutes later, I realize how I behaved and I tell them I'm sorry. I tell them I made a mistake and shouldn't have behaved that way.

You learned to give in to Mom, not try to speak up or take control. Was there anything else you learned from her point of view? Anything that she had that she funneled to you through the "control?"

I learned a lot from my mom, some of it good, some of it less so. I learned that family is more important than anything. I also learned to be judgmental and to try to control by being passive-aggressive, even though I know that's not good. I don't want to be that way.

How about unconditional love?

Yes, I know. I learned never to give up on the people I love. Even though my mom may not have approved, I knew she loved me and was proud of me. I also knew if I needed anything, my mother would be there in a minute. She'd be hugging, kissing, helping, giving money, doing whatever she could. There was unconditional love. I just didn't always recognize it as unconditional. If I had been honest and confronted our differences, she might have accepted them. She even admitted to me that there were things I was doing in my life and in raising my children that she wished she had done. That was gratifying to hear. Now, I still have my father.

What role did he play in all this and may still be playing?

It was very hard for him. He didn't know how to help when Mom was sick. It was just very hard for him to see her suffer. He really loved her. He supported my mother.

He supported me in the same ways that she did. Sometimes, I think he is disappointed in me, but I think our relationship could benefit from the same honesty and maturity that would have helped in my relationship with my mother.

It's rough to grow old and lose your partner.

I regret that there are not more happy memories. There is a lot of ambivalence in my memories. When I look at myself in the mirror, I see my mother. My hair is gray, her hair was gray. It's getting straighter as I age, more like hers. I look at my gray, less-curly hair, and I think of Mom.

What We Think
Jennifer's voice

Elizabeth speaks of being disappointed with herself at not having worked through her relationship with her mother while she was alive. Yes, this is a very difficult position to be in. Elizabeth's maturing process has a life of it's own and one cannot do what one cannot do until one is ready. Elizabeth has to live with that. As a teenager, one needs to separate and find who she is as an individual. Elizabeth's separation process slowed down because she felt conflicted. She was a good daughter, but to be a good daughter to her mother, she felt that she had to compromise her own integrity. She felt that she was required to behave in ways that were not true to herself. Until she could let go of the need to be the "good daughter" in her mother's eyes, and just be okay as herself, she could not be free to move on toward her own development as a woman. When the time came for Elizabeth to help her mother die, she was called upon to take the role of caretaker. At the same time, Mom was struggling with her own ability to be open to the changes she needed to face about herself.

Elizabeth's regret that she had not worked on the relationship while Mom was alive and well is sad for her. She feels that all she can do now is mature and let go of those feelings so that she can move on. However, one can't just "let go" of strong feelings. One must accept the feelings that rise, all of the feelings. After all, we can't control feelings. They just happen. They are just passing storm fronts.

In spite of all this, Elizabeth says she knows her mom loved her. Elizabeth's attempts to grow up and move on, to make peace with her relationship with her mother, were all stunted due to her mom's rigidity about keeping the status quo. When faced with the dilemma of being true to oneself versus being true to an old family pattern, it is important to stay true to oneself as much as possible.

What Do You Think?

What memories does this story evoke in you? Do you have any regrets about your relationship? Can you come to terms with them?

Sometimes a child seeks her
mother's approval continually
no matter how old she is.

And pays a price in
her own maturity.

Too Little and Too Late

Kathryn's Story

Her mother's harsh criticism left permanent damage to Kathryn's self-esteem

"You'd be so pretty if you'd do something with that stringy hair."

"You'd have such a nice figure if we could get that butt down to size."

"Push your glasses up. Pull your shirt down. Sit up straight, don't mumble, look at me when I'm talking to you!"

My mother, Joann, had been a lovely, coltish girl with a sweet nature, a quick wit, and clouds of admirers. I, Kathryn, had always been too shapely, too smart, too shy, too different. Joann, had also been molested, abandoned, and the other half of a hopeless marriage designed to get her out of her torture. Out of the frying pan.

As a girl, I felt I could do nothing to please Joann. Nothing I did was quite right, quite perfect, quite impeccable. In short, never good enough. I was good. She acknowledged that by telling me how proud I made her and what a joy I was, but somehow her actions invalidated her words. She'd pluck at my clothes, smooth at my hair and cluck when she saw my outfits. A look of disgust came over her face when I'd bend over revealing my size and shape.

"You're not really going to wear that. It's just covered in lint!"

I adored her. For as long as I can recall, we were joined at the hip. We'd shop together, go to movies together, and go to lunch together—be girls together. She had never had a chance to be a girl, so I was her last hope. As a consequence, she took a piece of my girlhood from me. I spent my life trying to please her. I wanted to be good enough. I

419

wanted to make her proud of me. I wanted to take that pain of her childhood and spread it over with all the excellence I could muster in order that she not hurt, if even for just a while.

Our mother/daughter relationship was frighteningly convoluted. It was difficult to tell who had which role most of the time. I grew up being the mother more often than not. Always the different one and the outcast, I knew that I could fix myself if I could fix my mother, just as she knew that her own repair lay in me. We loved each other, hated each other, and needed each other desperately. I grew up neurotic and a compulsive over-eater. I swallowed the pain and put a nice weight on top of it to hold it down. She became more and more ill with diseases like asthma. The metal band around her chest was the cage of her soul that kept her always gasping for air and life. All we both really wanted were acceptance and forgiveness.

Last summer she looked into my eyes, seeming to see the real me for the first time in 40 years. "You know, you are the best person I have ever known. You are simply a good person right through to your heart."

That was all it took. The stringy hair became lustrous and glossy, the figure was womanly rather than grotesque, and all the lint was decoration not schmutz. My eccentricities became charming and fascinating for the first time rather than weird and strange. All the criticisms and put downs and all the inadequacy fell off like rain.

Six weeks later, the band constricted, her breathing gave up the struggle, and her soul finally left that tortured cage. I adore her even more, and will never be quite complete.

"When she stopped conforming to the conventional picture of femininity she finally began to enjoy being a woman."
—*Betty Friedan*

What We Think

Jennifer's voice

Spending your life trying to please the mother who sees you as an extension of herself and doesn't like herself to begin with, is a very unfulfilling, frustrating, and fruitless experience. It's common for women who are tough on themselves and have their own unresolved issues to be tough on their daughters.

It is impossible for a daughter to compensate emotionally for her mother's unresolved issues. The trauma with which Joann grew up was translated into perfectionism and self-hatred. Apparently, she never worked through these early hurts and became a tormented woman who, as Kathryn describes her, felt her suffering through her body's inability to breathe sufficiently and her emotional incompleteness.

I'm sure Joann did not plan or even want to create an unhappy, critical life for her daughter. No mother intends this. If such a mother raises a child and then turns to this child to be mother to her, to complete her, to nurture her, then that child suffers too. In the end, Kathryn did get to hear the words from her mother, words she had longed for, words of acceptance and love.

Yet, Kathryn realizes that this does not complete her. She has no true closure with her relationship with her mother. Kathryn describes herself as having been cheated of her own childhood, as she lived her life designed around her mother's needs. Where was there room for Kathryn's needs? Kathryn's story is a very common story.

What Do You Think?

Have you experienced anything like this? What needs were you trying to meet in your relationship? What happened to your needs?

Even though she thought she
had a breakthrough she
felt incomplete.

The damage to her from her
mother's criticism was
permanently imprinted
on her sense of self.

Bonnie's Dream

Bonnie sent this e-mail a year after her mother's death.

My mother passed away January 24, 2003, as you know. Her loss has left a huge hole in my life. I keep feeling such disbelief that she is no longer here with us and I find it amazing that one as bright, lively, and intelligent as my mother could be gone. So I keep wondering where she is, how it could possibly be that she in not here with us—it's astounding to me.

A few weeks ago, I had a dream about her. I was driving through a small town and looking for a parking space. One came along and I happily pulled in, front grill to the curb so that I was directly facing the sidewalk and had a good look at the passersby. Suddenly, my mother was walking along the street looking really beautiful, wearing a turquoise dress with a white print, so flattering to her and she had a big smile on her face. I leaped out of my car and called out to her. "Mom, Mom, wait for me!" I quickly caught up with her and I could feel the thrill of seeing someone whom I miss terribly. She didn't seem to be as surprised as I was. It was almost as if she just saw me yesterday.

I asked her the question that'd been on my mind since she'd been gone. "Mom, what have you been doing? Where have you been?" I practically cried at her.

She looked at me and said, very matter-of-factly, "What do you mean? I've been here. I'm always here with you."

That dream gave me a level of comfort that I hadn't felt since she was gone. I knew it was true because from time to time I do smell her perfume just waft by me at the oddest times in the oddest places. Thanks for letting me share this with you.

Bonnie

What We Think

Jennifer's voice

Dreams are wonderful windows to the unconscious mind. Like imagination, which daytime dreams are, nighttime dreams can be a source of torture or comfort. We can't completely know and don't control what is in the unconscious mind, but through our dreams and by watching our behavior, we can have clues as to some of what goes on in there.

In this case, Bonnie's unconscious mind offers her comfort through nighttime images about her mother, reminding her that she is always there for her, even when she thinks she isn't.

Dream Exercise

Observe some of your dreams and log them below. If you have trouble remembering, let it go. Develop a curiosity about what is in your unconscious mind. Ask yourself questions about behaviors you observe in yourself. Keep a log of these things. If you are really stuck, sit down with your journal and write several pages of stream of consciousness and see what comes out. Even if you think you have nothing to say your unconscious mind could surprise you.

"It's the most unhappy people who most fear change."
—Mignon McLaughlin

What Do You Think?

Your questions…your log…your stream of consciousness.

Pamela's Dream

Pamela describes her peaceful recollections of her mother who died two years ago.

My mother and I had, in large part, a very painful relationship. I was often madder at her, more than I was at my father, who beat me physically. When I was fifteen, I said to my mother, after a very nasty argument, "You don't like me." She replied, "You're right; I don't like you, but I do love you." Despite a continuous sense of not being liked by her, I was there in a minute when she needed me. These days, when Mom visits me in my mind, it's the best of all there was. She's only laughing, telling me the problems are not hers anymore. And I feel peace.

I had a dream. There was a fire in our house and I ran in to carry my mother out. Dad ran in to go after his books. As long as my mother was alive, I permitted myself to put away my rage at my family so we could gather and be together. As the daughter of a feminine-conscious woman, even when I was a child, if I was angry with my mother, I came to her defense and took care of her in spite of my anger.

I always understood my mother as a woman. As an adult, and for many years until my brothers were able, somewhat, to take over, I knew that there was no one else to intervene or care for her when she felt victimized by my father's rages and anger.

"We must be the change we wish to see."
—Mahatma Gandhi

What We Think

Jennifer's Voice

Isn't it interesting how Pamela's relationship with Mom can be stormy all her life, but when Mom needs her she is right there. Her sense of responsibility to Mom surpassed everything else, even her anger.

Isn't it interesting that Pamela can miss Mom after her death less than her family does because she enjoys wonderful visions of Mom's visits where Mom is laughing?

Isn't it interesting that Pamela and her mom could be at battle during their lifetime together, yet Pamela can feel so much at peace with her mom's death?

She feels such peace because the turmoil of battle is now calm. The visions of Mom are now in her control.

Pamela can enjoy Mom in the manner that is available to her, through her imagination. She can retain all the wonderful memories, imagined or not, while excluding the things she doesn't care to remember. Our imagination is a wonderful human attribute. It can be a source of torture or comfort

Isn't it interesting how Pamela chooses it for comfort?

.

What We Think

Shura's Voice

Family relationships are a complicated mixture of many emotions. Love and anger may vie with each other, especially in the consciousness of the young child. These emotions are experienced throughout one's lifetime, in whatever ways we may find for ourselves. As we mature, we begin to examine this mixture and identify the emotions we want to maintain and those we prefer to minimize.

Pamela describes the mother/daughter bond she has always felt. Her dream describes its power as being very important against the backdrop of a male presence, which seems to have valued the intellectual over the love elements of his relationships.

In her journey through life, Pamela seems to have found a way to cope with the turbulence she describes, and to achieve some level of peace that she was seeking. It would appear that, although she describes her relationship with her mother as "extremely difficult," their bond was strong, important and somehow helpful to her in her own search for meaning.

What Do You Think?

What thoughts or memories does your imagination offer for torture or comfort? Do you try to control these thoughts?

She always understood
her mother as a woman.

No matter how angry
she was at her mother,
she always came to her defense.

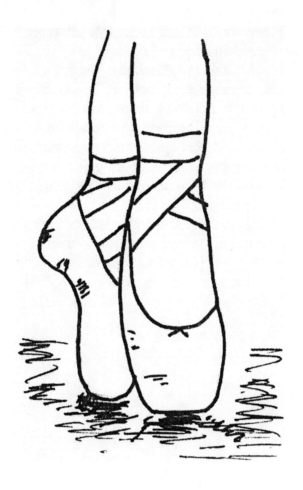

The Redistribution of Balance

We have discussed the importance of staying open to change. Change is inevitable. Death and the losses that accompany death are among the most glaring, inevitable changes everyone must face. Each time a change occurs, a loss occurs, and an opening for a new opportunity occurs. As the old saying goes, "When God closes a door, he opens a window."

When the loss is the death of a significant loved one like mother or daughter, life becomes empty. My heart fills with grief. I have lost the ability to be in her presence and to receive whatever I always had received from the person who has left me.

For some people, the wound of loss never heals. For some, the depth of the connection can never be reproduced. This change is painful and difficult, laced with suffering. At some point in this process some level of acceptance develops, allowing the person to move on. We find something to fill the void. Perhaps, when we are ready, we take stock in the substance of our lives, and we develop a new appreciation for it. Our focus shifts and we realign our relationships to ourselves and to our existing circle of family and friends.

This does not suggest that we no longer feel the impact of the loss or no longer miss the person we have lost. It just means that we are guided toward an emotional equilibrium or balance in relation to the new world around us—the world without that person. This allows us to move forward.

What Do You Think?

Have you seen this happen in families? Has this happened in your family? Has it affected any of your relationships? In what ways?

Diagram of Loss and Balance

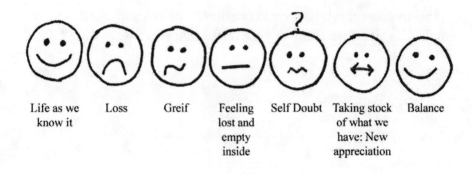

| Life as we know it | Loss | Greif | Feeling lost and empty inside | Self Doubt | Taking stock of what we have: New appreciation | Balance |

Exercise

Draw your own diagram of loss and balance illustrating your own experience.

When Husband and Father Died
Jennifer's Story

When dad died suddenly in his mid-seventies, we were left completely unprepared. Deep, painful grief fell upon all of us.

I was not prepared for the emptiness of that experience. I, the mother of three young children, felt that my own childhood was over. I was scared and did not know how to integrate the loss of my dad into my everyday life. I searched for some meaning in this terrible loss.

Mom, also in her seventies, had been his best friend since age twelve. Now she was left alone to rattle around in their big house. She was in her own pain. She was not at all prepared for the long journey of widowhood that lay ahead. Although she and I had always had a loving relationship, I felt a desire to be even closer to her. My desire to ease the pain for both of us motivated me to devise creative ways for spending more time with her, to shift my energy and focus onto what I could retain in my life, rather than on what I had lost.

My days as a working mother were already filled with a myriad of duties in addition to my full time job. Now, I built in time for lunching with Mom so that she wouldn't be eating alone, and so that she would eat properly. I also began to accompany her on medical appointments when necessary.

We began to blend our mutual interests in poetry, music, visual arts, group work and psychotherapy. Our time together became satisfying to both of us. We attended conferences together and offered conjoint workshops on these subjects. A fascinating new relationship developed. We became partners in creative endeavor. Ultimately we published a book of our poetry and created a dramatic production, which involved my entire family.

When Mom's blood pressure acted up, my twelve-year-old daughter, Danielle, was so worried that she insisted that Grandma not sleep alone. Since our homes were a stone's throw from each other, Dani decided to sleep in Mom's house. Quietly and firmly she moved into her grandmother's house. Now our lives became entwined on a new level. Our ability to share and care for each other has continued to enrich my life and my mother's, as well as to enhance the experiences of my entire family.

Shura's Story

When my lifetime friend and husband of over fifty years died suddenly, I wondered how I could survive. I felt I didn't even want to.

My survival, I feel, derived from my responsibility to my family and the love I received from them all: two sons, one daughter, their respective spouses, and eight grandchildren. They made me understand, from the beginning, that I could not subject them to further loss. I could not ignore their loving overtures toward me and their efforts to convince me that, somehow, I would find ways in which my life could continue.

They all lived quite nearby. My daughter's children, young as they were, could as always, come walking up the hill anytime. In the beginning, my daughter and son-in-law saw to it that I would never enter an empty house alone. My daughter made certain that I would skip no meals. My granddaughter moved in to live with me. A new and profound relationship developed between us.

To this day, they include me in all their family activities. We shop together for meals, for gifts, for whatever the children might need. We share the problems of daily living. We plan together for family holidays and celebrations.

Also, we have become colleagues as well as friends and family. We work together on projects of mutual interest, like co-authoring this book.

Yet, it is also important to note that we respect each other's needs for privacy and peer relationships. We are careful not to intrude on these.

We encourage each other's independent interests at the same time that we share their pleasures.

We have established a graceful balance. I am fortunate and grateful.

A Bonus of Time
Alicia's Story

Alicia assumed responsibility toward her mother after her father died. This act culminated in a special gift to both of them.

I was always close to my father. My two brothers were closer with my mother. I always thought that my mother favored her sons, and that my father favored me. Before my father died, my mother had been suffering from congestive heart failure and he'd been taking care of her. The night he died, she was taken to the hospital in severe cardiac failure.

It seems, however, that the daughter becomes the care giver. It isn't that the sons don't care. They just don't seem to know what to do. After my father died and mother was alone, my younger brother tried to live with my mother, but the plan didn't last for more than a week or two. I found myself going, every weekend, to Pennsylvania where my mother lived. Finally, my mother needed a great deal of care and couldn't be left alone. I was frantic.

My fiancé, Michael, said, "Bring her up here to New York. We'll take care of her." I brought her home with me. Mother was grieving the death of her husband and leaving her home. She knew that things would never be the same for either of us. I knew it too.

She was in and out of attacks of congestive heart failure. Her physician in New York performed an angiogram, and told me that he really couldn't do anything to improve her health. I took her home, sick in my own heart, to think we couldn't do anything to help my mother. The very next day, the doctor telephoned me to say that he had located a cardiologist/surgeon in Valhalla Medical Center who was willing to operate. When we consulted with him, he described the particular procedure he was suggesting. It was an eight-hour operation and the risk was very high. There was a ninety percent chance that she might die during the surgery.

My mother wanted to discuss it further. The doctor sent me out of the room saying, "You are a daughter. I want to speak only to your mother, very directly."

I left the room, quite frightened. When I was recalled, my mother turned to me and said, "Well, I'm going to have the surgery. If I do this, I may live. I may also die during the surgery. But if I don't have the surgery, I'll probably die soon anyway."

My mother didn't die during the surgery. After being discharged from the hospital, she came to my house for several months of recovery. That's when she and I began to have a closer relationship. I remember taking her home from the hospital. It was in October and the leaves were changing color.

She looked out the window and said, "I never thought I'd ever see another fall."

I said, "I'm glad you did." And that was the beginning of our new relationship.

She told me how before her surgery she'd been afraid to be alone. I had known this. Now, she told me, she was glad to be alive. I sensed in her a new feeling of independence and freedom. I was so proud of her. She had survived.

I remember one important incident. Prior to surgery, I had taken her shopping in the mall. She wasn't able to walk much, and so I put her in a wheelchair. Now, after the surgery, we went back to the mall. I wanted to get the wheelchair for her. She said, "Oh, no, I don't need the wheelchair. I'm walking!" There was a big sale of bright tee-shirts. She bought one of every color and said, "I'm going to wear them all!" She really wanted to live. She had come through her illness and very serious surgery. She could have died many times, but she survived.

When she was well enough, she moved back to her home town in Pennsylvania and entered a senior residence. She loved living there. She resumed a wonderful relationship with her sister. They would go out together. She could come and go as she pleased. It was wonderful for me to visit her in her own small apartment. We'd send out for dinner. We'd watch TV together. We became closer and closer.

One day she went to see her physician in Pennsylvania. She told me he looked at her and said, "My goodness, I never thought you would survive!"

She told him, "I would not have made it through if my daughter had not intervened, brought me to New York, to Valhalla, and back to her home for recovery."

It was the best two years and seven months for her and for me. In those last years she enjoyed a happy quality of life and we both enjoyed our wonderful relationship with each other.

"We must remember that one determined person can make a significant difference, and that a small group of determined people can change the course of history."
—Sonia Jackson

What We Think

Shura's Voice

There is amazing strength and resiliency within human beings. When we have allowed ourselves to mourn and grieve, when there is support in our world, we can return, renewed, to live without the person we lost.

In Alicia's story, the entire family was, as are all families, lost and bewildered when their vital, active father died. Alicia tells us that hers was a profound and powerful relationship with her father. She suggests that her relationship with her mother was something less than that. Having lost her dad, Alicia is aware of her mother's grief and bereavement as well as her own.

The mother/daughter bond takes on a new dimension as Alicia finds herself in a new care giving and supportive role towards her mother. This creates a new sense of balance between them and within the family unit as a whole. Establishing this different and healthy equilibrium enriched the lives of both women.

What Do You Think?

Have you ever bargained for more time with a dying loved one? With whom did you think you were bargaining?

What We Think

Jennifer's Voice

As a daughter myself, I find it striking that Alicia was lucky to receive a bonus of an extra two and a half years with her mother who had almost died several times. Alicia's intervention in caring for her mom earned her this time and gave her the opportunity to enjoy it. In telling her story, Alicia reveals her keen awareness of how special it was to have this opportunity. Just think about it! If you could, wouldn't you bargain for more time with a loved one who is dying, be it a week, a month, a year?

The bonus time together
was the best two years and
seven months for both of them.

She accepted responsibility
and extended her mother's life.

Loss of Self
Shua's Voice

We lose ourselves in many ways...in joy, in sorrow, in love, in anger, in thought, in wonderment. Sometimes we say it aloud. "I've lost my way...my looks...my temper..." Sometimes we think it. "What day is this...what am I supposed to be doing?" Sometimes we feel it and don't quite understand it!

This happens to everyone at one time or another. When things or people around us change, we may become bewildered and lost. In times of illness, loss, or death, the feeling of losing oneself can become very powerful and threatening.

When the mature mother ages, she changes and must find her altered self and make her way through new, untrodden paths in her life.

The mature daughter also faces changes with which she must cope. She also becomes aware of the changes facing her aging mother, to whom she has been bonded through life.

Both women are challenged to deepen their understanding of themselves, of each other and of their lifelong relationship.

From time to time, each may feel lost in the process. Each needs to find herself in order to go on.

Caged Bird

Jennifer's Voice

Caged birds can't fly
Only dreams of sun on wings
Hopes of clouds and sky
Cages are pitiful things
Caged birds can't fly

Sad times, clipped wings
No hope
Only dreams for you
This bird won't even sing

I've got a blind spot
I wanta hitchhike to the sky
I wanta spread my wings
My expectations are so high

I've got a blind spot
But not so blind I can't see
I've got clipped wings
I've been holding on so long
The music of my spirit
Sings sweet a sadlike song

Lost dreams of flight
There's no more flight for me
I guess I'm here
I'm just down here
Only wishing I was free

Who I Am

Dorothy's Story

We just completed two performances of a play reading of *Coming to Life*. The audiences were fellow residents, friends and relatives.

We now call ourselves, "The Williams Players" and hope to be ongoing. I generally received high praise for my role. The role was Louise, a complaining, old biddy—complaining about her daughter, fellow residents, and even the price of organically grown bananas. Another character in the play says to me, "Face it, Louise. You're damaged goods. You're a cranky old biddy with a crooked old body and a personality that scrapes off wallpaper!"

I tried to feel the role. I told myself, "At least I am not that character in real life, but I can pretend." I acknowledge that I can barely get around physically without experiencing shortness of breadth. True.

One psychiatrist recently told me that my life-long will and intellect no longer serve me. So who am I? What can I rely on at this stage? There's still enough gray matter but I often find myself apologizing with the apt phrase, "My brain is leaking." In the play Louise, wants respect. So do I—in real life. And I'm not getting it as often as I'd like.

Between my being hard-of-hearing and my diminished attention span and short-term memory, I'm often uninteresting and useless to the community, to my family as well as to myself. Dwelling on past accomplishments is not helpful. By finding things to commit to (like these recent months devoted to play reading ensemble), I can still make a difference. I embrace being committed and accountable here, to this over-70s "Womenshare" support group: to Nina, Anne, Helga, Jane, Joy and Gro.

I don't like the fact that when I read the paper or magazine or even a few pages of a good book, I tend to fall asleep. Daily dinner table exchanges are usually superficial and boring. I'm no good at small talk. We can always rely on "Anyone but Bush" slogans or what the doctor said. That's the extent of it. Visits with members of my family are pleasant enough. They are marked on my calendar and fleeting.

The egghead in me constantly searches for substantive friendships and substantive activity. I have yet to accept my limitations—for example, no more attending protest marches at a time when the need to cry out is greater than ever! I'm conscious of my mortality and seek to make the most of whatever time is left for me. Yesterday, I applied for tutoring the kids at PS 75 across the street. Oh, to be useful again!

"What you have become is the price you paid to get what you used to want."
—Mignon McLauglin

What We Think

Shura's Voice

Dorothy is grappling with many major changes that accompany the aging process. She identifies the losses as she is experiencing them. She also realizes that some of the losses are creating a major impact on her persona, her self-image, her very self.

Being hard-of-hearing creates a distance between yourself and others. Communication becomes more precarious. One is not always certain one has heard correctly. The uncertainty creates a hesitation that was not experienced before the physical problem developed. The easy give-and-take of conversation, so taken for granted in earlier times, now becomes precious.

Listening is sometimes so difficult that the person opts out of ordinary conversations. It gets too hard to follow. It is tiring. Fatigue accompanies some other physical changes, such as the altered functioning of some vital organs, especially the heart and lungs. Dorothy says she tends to fall asleep when she is reading. It has become difficult to concentrate. Also, her body needs more rest and takes it whenever possible without her permission!

Dorothy worries about being useful. Yes, we older women, who have been so active and useful on so many levels when we were younger, worry about that a great deal. I believe we must give a great deal of thought to what we mean by "being useful."

What did it mean when we were workers, wives, mothers, and active in our various communities? What does it mean now?

What We Think

Jennifer's Voice

Shouldn't we consider who we are on a continuum, as a series of reincarnations within one lifetime? We then can consider, "That's me in my twenties. I was a 'comment...comment...comment...memory.'" Then we can think, "That's me in my thirties. I was a 'comment...comment...comment...memory,'" and so on. Snapshots of who we were develop into photos of who we are now and then morph into who we become later on.

We become a mixed stew of experience that culminates over time. Considering ourselves useless because we aren't as productive in the same ways as we have been at one time is only one way of looking at the past and using it to evaluate the present.

Many circumstances of living have made us change. We need to consider all the circumstances, including the current conditions, when evaluating who we are in any given time.

It is not helpful to criticize or judge ourselves. It is useful to observe ourselves without judgment and make the most of what we can see, in whatever ways we can. At the same time, we may appreciate the range of human emotions that surface through the changes.

What Do You Think?

On the continuum of role changes throughout life, who are you now? What does "being useful" mean to you?

Exercise: Who Am I?

Think about the various incarnations in your life. Draw a series of pictures of who you have been in the past and who you are now. Then, fantasize about who you expect to be in the future.

Identity

Shura's Voice

And who am I now…now I am old?
I've been so many different people in my time

Daughter, mother, friend, sweetheart, lover, mate
And now, happily, grandmother
Worker, helper, comrade, teacher, mentor, learner, leader
Writer, poet, pioneer, thinker of thoughts,
Teller of tales, dreamer of dreams

Each role unique, diverse in depth
In layers of emotion
In diamond-dipped dimension
Exciting, challenging
My life a whirl of work
Relationships, ideas

Living is change…inventing…creating
Nor have I feared or faltered
In search of self…integrity
Now, I tire easily…Mind and body out of synchrony
One lightening…one languishing
What of self is lost ?What, like my name, remains?

And to learn…the new is difficult to do
I sift and sort through memory
I turn and toss in vanity

Magnetic threads thrust to the past
To reinforce integrity whilst I reinvent myself
Reshaping my identity
To find what has become of me

Who am I now…now old?

Depression, Confusion, and Dementia in Mid-Life and Old Age

Some Extreme Ways in Which We May Lose Ourselves.

Depression in Mid-Life
Jennifer's Voice

During mid life, many women find themselves experiencing loss in unfamiliar ways. There are developmental and situational explanations.

First of all, the hormones that have been driving us for forty-some years are shifting drastically. They cause physical as well as emotional changes. The menstrual cycle begins to shift. Sometimes a period is skipped entirely. In the past year, I myself have experienced this. The first time this happened, I refused to believe that I wasn't pregnant. I took two pregnancy tests and still didn't believe or trust them. I finally went to my gynecologist's office and insisted on a blood test. Only when I was told it was negative, then and only then did I believe that my time of change had arrived.

These physical changes may be coupled with such situational changes as the grown children leaving the nest. Of course, we recognize this as the empty-nest syndrome. This normal event is also coupled with a range of parental feelings. The mother may feel abandoned, rejected, and no longer needed. She may become depressed.

Yet, this is a normal stage for the growing child. Separation from the parent is a developmental task for the adolescent child. Some parents may find it so difficult to bear, that they may want to move geographically close to wherever the child is going for example, to college or to work. However, the parent is called upon to allow the separation, for it is timely, appropriate and the way that the grown child begins to learn and practice what has been taught.

This stage can be unusually depressing for some women who may be reliving their own early separation, which may have been painful for them. Other changes in her life may also cause a woman to become depressed. She may be concerned about her changing appearance, or the need to find new roles and activities, or perhaps to resume a career or to change one. These are not simple adaptations to make; a person may feel lost and depressed while negotiating these changes.

Confusion about oneself and feelings of being lost often accompany this disturbing process and the depression that has set in.

Depression in the Later Years
Shura's Voice

There are similar drastic changes in the life of the older woman. Her physical appearance is changing, as is her physical stamina. She finds herself slowing down, able to do things at a different rate of speed. Aging brings with it some physiological changes which develop at various times during the years. There are also changes in her social life.

Some of these may be positive, some difficult. However, they all require adaptive skills. She may become a grandmother. Certainly this is a positive, new role. But it is a complex one, requiring her to learn how to relate to the new baby's mother—her own daughter or daughter-in-law. Retirement, her own or her spouse's, brings with it a host of changes in the organization of life and life activities.

Whether in mid-life or in the later years, change requires understanding, negotiating, adapting, and accepting. The emotional work that must be done may be accompanied by feelings of loss and sadness, depression and uncertainty, and even confusion.

These are times and circumstances that call for support from those around the person who is living through the process. Sometimes, professional help may be needed. There is no shame in accepting help from any source that is available. Like any other development in life, as these changes are mastered, the feelings will also be mastered.

Normally, the pain of loss softens, the depression is eased, the confusion clears, the person goes on with her life, and begins to achieve and enjoy the new stage into which these changes have thrust her.

Depression
Shura's Voice

I've been down where hell fires burn
While anger ripped my heart
Believed I never would return
From this passion torn apart

Stifling sobs and sobbing breath
Desperately demanding death
Tears of fear engulfing
Shroud me, sinking in the sea
The waves rise high, the tide pulls back
I lose the sky, the water's black
The breakers break, the wild waves churn
My body aches, my body burns
I'm pulled and pushed, waves wind me round
Limp I lie and spiral down
Certain that I drown—am drowned

Wondering now that I am dead
Why these dreams wind through my head?
Whence this light within my eyes?
What power levitates my rise?
Beyond the breakers now I float
The sea is calm, the sky is blue
Life propels me once again
And I find that I've come through

I've been down there and writhed with pain
And learned it will be so again
Yet know I now for I've grown wise
I'll fall again and agonize
But I have learned
Once more I'll rise!

About Dementia
Shura's Voice

DEMENTIA: *"Condition of deteriorated mentality."*
—Webster, Ninth New Collegiate Dictionary

This condition may affect a person of any age. When it does, it changes that person's communication and his/her relationship to self and others.

The demented person suffers several losses. The first of these is a loss of self. Such a loss is threatening and destructive to the personality. Also, the person feels that the world around her is altered and that she herself is lost within it. It begins to seem chaotic and mystifying. She can no longer find or create any sense of order in this different world. The person responds to this threat in varied ways. She may become withdrawn, repressed, fearful, anxious, angry, abusive.

A second major loss is the inability to recognize and express one's feelings. This is often coupled with inappropriate language and/or altered behavior. The changes in the person are puzzling and unacceptable to those around her.

When dementia strikes the older mother, her daughter, like everyone else in the family, is deeply affected. Not only has the person lost herself. Her daughter feels that she has lost her mother.

Just as the expressions of dementia differ, so do the responses of others. It takes time for a daughter to recognize and accept these changes in her mother. It takes a great deal of effort for the mature daughter to find her way through her mother's confusion, disorientation and altered behavior. It is even more difficult to find ways to negotiate the mysterious maze of barriers that have developed between them.

It is important to remember that, although the capacity for intellectual thought and expression is lost, the emotional dimensions of the person are not lost. The demented person experiences a vast diversity of feelings that, for the most part, she cannot express appropriately. Somewhere inside of this "stranger," there is still the mother who has been there from the very beginning of her daughter's life.

Some daughters withdraw. Some seek help from others. Some may begin to learn the new patterns of mother's behavior and to find ways to circumvent the barriers.

It is a troubling, baffling, frustrating, difficult, distressing time for both.

It's the non-stricken
person who becomes
confused about this!

Yes, people tend to forget
that even though thoughts
may be confused, the stricken
person still has emotions.

Dementia—My Grandmother

Jennifer's Story

My grandmother slipped slowly into a dementia over a long period of time. I don't even remember how long or when I began to notice it. I believe I experienced a degree of denial about it. It was painful to watch, like watching time disintegrate your favorite painting—fading of the colors, flaking of the edges until the painting is hardly recognizable.

My grandmother had been like a second mother to me. I loved her dearly. When she was in the nursing home, the fading seemed to worsen. I would visit her weekly. At some point she began to address me by a different name. This, too, was painful. My defensive response was to pull away emotionally. Ultimately, she began to call me by her niece's name, consistently. I looked into her eyes and the grandmother I had known was gone. She thought I was her niece.

I told my mother, "She doesn't know me anymore."

My mother replied in a kind, sympathetic voice, "She knows you are someone she loves. She knows you are her people."

That didn't really seem like enough to me. I had built such a strong, close love with my grandmother since childhood and, now, thirty-eight years later she didn't know me!

On the day that my parents told me my grandmother was dying and that I should go to her to say goodbye, I rallied. I just stepped out of the hurt. It was as if I had taken off the "hurt dress" and put on a new dress. I went to see her. She was sitting in a room with many other old people. Some were in wheelchairs; some were talking aloud to themselves or to imaginary others. The room smelled musty, like old furniture that had not been cleaned in years.

I sat down beside my grandmother. I looked into her eyes. They seemed sad, but not vacant or distant. I proceeded to tell her how grateful I was to her—that I felt that she was the best grandmother anyone could ever have had. I thanked her for her kindness and patience through the years. She had been looking down as I spoke. I touched her hand and she looked up into my eyes. For the first time in years, I knew that she knew who I was.

Her eyes had determined clarity in that moment. Then she smiled softly and whispered, "Thank you." That was all she said. I kissed her and left. I knew that would be the last time I saw her. I felt sad but complete. I knew now that my grandmother knew I was there for her, as she had been for me all those years. I had an opportunity to honor her for her contribution to the person I had become.

I feel so bad. She doesn't
know who I am. She calls
me by someone else's name.

She knows you love her.
She knows she belongs with you.

What We Think

Shura: It is certainly very hard to see anyone we love struggle with dementia. You feel you have lost that person.

Jennifer: As demonstrated with my grandmother, I was always surprised and distressed that she didn't know me. I wanted to avoid this new person in her body. I wanted my grandmother back.

Shura: Still, when you spoke to her as herself, with the love in your voice, your grandmother responded to you in her own old voice, as you would have liked.

Jennifer: It sounds as if you are saying that love and kindness are anchors in the confusion.

Shura: Actually these are anchors common to all human beings. They bring out the humanness of the demented person, as they do in anyone else.

What Do You Think?

Have you experienced dementia in anyone close to you? How did you deal with it?

Loneliness and Loss

Shura's Voice

What time is it?
What day?
What season of the year?
I am the child seeking mother
Or no—
I was the mother
Now the child is gone.
Where are they all
With whom, for whom I live
Or lived?
For whom I cared and care?
Who cares for me?

An alien face appears,
Strange hands place food upon my dish
And somehow minister to my needs
Til early evening ends
As shades
Linger into long and lonely night
The day, and alien face, both fade.

My mirror mocks my frightened face
Panicked eyes in empty space
Seeking them, the active ones
Who filled my life—each day.

And who am I, and where,
What time, what year is this
Anyway?

Doctor: Your daughter tells me that sometimes when she speaks to you, you seem confused?

Old woman: Doctor, whenever my daughter speaks to me, I'm always confused!

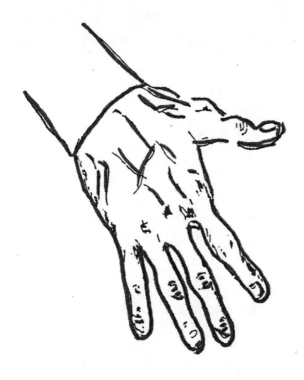

When a Stranger's Help Is Needed

Sometimes, during the dark days of loss, death and bereavement, the emotional burden combined with the concrete tasks conspire to make it too much to bear.

All kinds of help may be needed at these times. It may seem that there are never enough people in the family to share the burden.

Yet, for some who have cared for each other through many critical times, the idea of yielding the care of a loved one to a stranger becomes monumental and threatening.

Who can care for my loved one better than I? And if it is too much and too hard for me, how can anyone else perform the needed tasks?

Bereavement, the acceptance of loss after death, can be a bewildering, challenging, fearful time. How to cope with the terrible loss, whether it is sudden or expected, becomes a challenge for those who must.

The pain of the challenge intensifies the pain of the loss itself. Yet, the survivors find ways to continue with their lives. Some accept help. Some do not.

Help and intervention can be forthcoming in many ways and on many levels. It is not an easy task to help a person at this time.

Helping hands and helping hearts must be sensitive and understanding.

Support must be patient and compassionate.

Monitoring Mother's Care
Letter from Celina

Hi, Shura and Jennifer,

Thank you so much for understanding that I could not bring myself to write about my mom's experience in a Florida nursing home for a short-term rehabilitation stay. She had a total knee replacement and as you know I totally fell apart. The thought of seeing my mother so completely dependent, and the responsibility for making sure that she obtained the best in terms of rehabilitation (as I am her health care agent), was overwhelming for us both!

As you know, I pulled Mom out of the facility after two days. This was an impulsive, emotion-filled decision that could have resulted in an unsafe discharge plan. However, I just could not understand the lack of compassion in the nursing care at this facility. My poor mother was simply appalled at the lack of care, not just for herself but also for the other residents who were there.

I was quite amazed at myself. I am a Licensed Clinical Social Worker with many years of experience in dealing with these situations. Yet, at this point, I was helpless! My best friend, Shelli, flew in from New Jersey to help me create a safe discharge plan for Mom. We worked together and we were able to get Mom home. We arranged for a visiting nurse to monitor

Mom's health. Most importantly, we obtained in-home physical therapy services. Mom has progressed tremendously since then. We all feel that if possible, it is important to try to obtain care at home. It is quite preferable to being in an unfamiliar environment. Mom was absolutely fine, four months after surgery. Now, she is looking forward to flying into New York to see her grandson Alex graduate from college.

I guess I did write about this bittersweet topic after all!

Celina

What We Think

Shura's Voice

Celina describes the emotional impact of seeing her mother in pain and receiving what she considers inadequate care and treatment. She is surprised that she, herself, a seasoned professional, has become so emotional that she cannot plan adequately for helping her mother. She is fortunate that she has a friend who can help her.

It is not unusual or surprising that, despite all training and experience, a person feels helpless in the face of a loved one's needs. Leaving the care of a loved one in the hands of strangers can be extremely threatening. One's own behavior is affected by one's emotional response to this experience.

When we feel that we can develop better planning and treatment for our loved one, it becomes frustrating to deal with the bureaucracy, rules and regulations of the nursing home or hospital. The helping professionals may become threatened by the family criticism and may not communicate compassionately with the distraught family member. The family member, in her emotional state, may not express herself tactfully or show any understanding toward the professional care giver.

This is a situation of tension and emotion. It is important, here, for the health care professional and the agency itself, to realize that they are helping the family as well as the patient. They are called upon to extend their professional skills to both appropriately.

What Do You Think?

At times, emotions make it difficult for all of us to make decisions. We may need help during those times. To whom do you turn for help? How do you feel about asking for such help?

How Nanny Came to Live in a Nursing Home
Jennifer's Story

I called my grandmother Nanny. We were always close. I visited her several times a week whenever my schedule allowed. Nanny loved to cook for me and her cooking always had a special texture and flavor. I like to think of this as Nannyflavor. It was wonderful. As Nanny got to be in her 90s, we all noticed that she began to become more and more forgetful and unable to cook for us. She'd forget to cook for herself. She started blacking out because she'd forget to eat.

We realized she needed a new level of care. My mother and father invited her to live in their big home in upstate New York. She did come to live there for a while, three years actually. The experience was very disorienting to Nanny. She was very distressed by her relocation and the feeling of dependency that she connected to the reality that she was not living in her own home. She would walk around the house at night searching for my grandfather who died several years earlier. My mother tended to her lovingly.

Nanny would become very annoyed at herself and at my mother for this arrangement for her care. They had a talk about it. Nanny was feeling very threatened by the idea of living in my parents' home. She herself said, very definitely, that she would prefer to move to a nursing home. She felt she could maintain her independence there.

My mother felt sad and rejected by this plan. Still, Nanny was clear and definite about the way she wanted to plan for her future aging period. She saw the nursing home as a place where she could control her destiny. She felt she could find peers to relate to there and not be limited to the house unless one of us took her somewhere. This had made her feel confined and dependent.

I found this point of view interesting. Most grandparents of my peers were expressing the opposite sentiment. They wanted to be surrounded by family and loved ones. They wanted to die at home. Nanny clearly wanted to call her own shots and not be conflicted by anyone else's agenda. So my parents honored her wishes. They arranged for Nanny to move into a nursing home of her choice. She thrived there for three years until she died.

"Continuity gives us roots; change gives us branches, letting us stretch and grow and reach new heights."
—Pauline R.Kezer

What We Think

Shura's Voice

This was one of the most difficult and painful acts of my entire life. I felt that I had somehow failed as a loving daughter. Even though my head told me that this was clearly my mother's choice, my heart would not allow me to feel differently. Here I was, a seasoned professional, having helped others through this critical situation. Yet, I myself was beyond help or reassurance. I did have mild discussions with my mother about this, but they were not very satisfactory. Albeit gently and lovingly, as she was always gentle and loving, she reiterated her desire to control her own life.

I had to content myself with frequent and pleasant visits, and the constant reassurance that she was receiving the care and treatment we both wanted for her. We spent many hours reviewing her life experiences and thoughts. I took copious notes and have since shared them with my own children.

My mother was her own woman to the very end. That thought does comfort me.

What Do You Think?

Have you been in the position of yielding care of your mother/
daughter to another? How did you feel? Can you ever imagine facing
this problem yourself?

I know, Mom, you felt really
sad when Nanny decided to
go to live in the nursing home.

I do understand that my
mother was her own
woman to the very end.

Honoring Grandma's Advanced Directive
Notes from Granddaughter Celina

My grandmother, Julia Perez was in a nursing home for approximately 16 years, as she suffered from Parkinson's disease and a life-altering stroke. My mother, Efraina, had the most difficult time making the decision to place Grandma in a nursing home. Mom had to accept, quickly, the reality that her mom was totally dependent on others for day-to-day living. I was quite instrumental in helping my mother make this decision about her mother. Since I myself was a young social worker at the nursing home, I assured Mom that I would do the best that I could in caring for Grandma.

My grandmother was able to sign a Health Care Proxy as she said to us, "Do not hook me up to machines, and I do not want to be fed by a tube." Both my mother and I were Grandma's health care agents. We knew that, one day, we would have to honor Grandma's wishes. Parkinson's is an insidious disease.

Ultimately, Grandma was transferred to a nursing home in Long Island, where Mom lived. Mom wanted to be closer to her mother. My mother said that visiting Grandma in the nursing home was the equivalent of going to church on a regular basis. I would visit my grandmother almost every weekend in Long Island and at the same time, give my mom support.

The time arrived to operationalize Grandma's advance directive. (Tears come to me as I write about this.) Grandma had a difficult time swallowing even pureed food because her swallowing reflexes were frozen by the Parkinson's disease. She just could not swallow her food. Clearly, it was utterly painful for her as she tried to swallow even ice cream, her favorite! We reminded the nurses and the doctor that

Grandma had given specific instructions in her health care proxy regarding artificial nutrition. Despite their hesitation, they adhered to her wishes as it had become necessary for Mom and me to take a very firm, insistent position!

Grandma has other children. My mom was her youngest. Mom and I had to educate her son and oldest daughter about her advance directives because they did not have a clue about Grandma's wishes. In fact I told Grandma's children, "If you visited Grandma regularly you would know exactly what she wants and does not want."

Mom and I were at Grandma's side upon her death. It was so very sad to watch her die as per her own wishes. It was the hardest job ever to act as her health care agent. However we knew what we had to do. My mother, the daughter of Julia Perez, my grandmother, is my hero because as painful as this was for Mom, she was able to honor her mother's wishes.

At Grandma's funeral, there were many family members who kept asking my mother and me, "Why did you let Julia die?" My mom and I just looked at each other silently because we knew the real reason. We were the only people closest to Grandma who listened to her wishes. Mom and I knew that we were about the only people who were able to fulfill Grandma's wishes. We did not care what the rest of the world thought.

"You must do the thing you think you cannot do."
—Eleanor Roosevelt

Cousins and nephews
criticized the decisions
of Celina and her mother.

Despite the pressure
they honored
Grandma's directives.

What We Think
Jennifer's Voice

It is a very honorable, but difficult, matter to be in the painful and responsible position as health care proxy for an elder. By naming the proxy, the elder has expressed an implicit and explicit faith in her/his judgment and ethics. The expectation implicit in this responsibility is that the proxy will honor the wishes of the patient.

You love that person and selfishly don't want to let her go. At the same time, you must honor her clear wishes about her care, treatment and ultimate death. The person desires a minimum of suffering in these processes. The most loving thing you can do for anyone is to help a loved one in his/her dying process.

Both Celina and Efraina loved Julia and courageously honored her wishes. Sometimes, family members who have not been involved in the ongoing process of the patient's care, her illness and her dying don't always understand the process. The health care proxy may be placed, by them, in the position of being blamed or scapegoated. Often these are the members of the family who haven't been as emotionally involved with the patient.

It is important to listen to these family members, to sympathize with them and also to educate them. This can be difficult to do and sometimes not even possible. Sometimes anger takes over and can't be overcome.

What Do You Think?

Have you been in the same position? What did you do? What would you do, if you were?

About Doulas

The word "doula" comes from the Greek, meaning "slave."

Death and loss are profound human experiences during which people need help of many kinds. The dying process evokes many poignant emotions including fear, loneliness and isolation. People help each other through such times. Person-to-person support is important in softening the trauma of dying for the dying person and in easing the pain of loss for the dying person's dear and near ones.

The need for such mutual aid has long been recognized in most cultures. The ancient Hebrew word for funeral, "levaya," means "to accompany." In the twentieth century the hospice program, developed by Emily Saunders, recognizes a trained volunteer as well as that of a spiritual advisor as important members of the death and dying team.

A doula is a volunteer who is trained to help people in transition through such major life passages as birth and death. Some doulas help new mothers through labor of birth and also to adjust after the baby is born.

Similarly, a doula may assist during the process of death and dying, and afterwards to the experience of loss. A doula may visit a dying person and talk about whatever he or she may wish to discuss, her interests, or how she lived her life. Such a visitor helps the dying person to continue to experience the life process until it is no longer possible. The doula can help the person feel less isolated, less alone, less frightened at the prospect of dying. She can help the person evaluate the life that has been lived, and reiterate its meaning. This keeps alive one's personal dignity as a human being.

The doula can also help the family and significant others during this process and also, afterwards. As a silent witness she can encourage them to express their thoughts. She will listen to their various expressions of sadness, grief, and validate their feelings. She can soften the pain of the loss. She can help defuse the feelings of anger and frustration that often accompany the loss. She can help the family restore some balance in their relationships.

In these troubling times, such a person can be a great comfort as well.

"Life begets life. Energy creates energy. It is by spending oneself that one becomes rich."
—*Sara Bernhardt*

My Experience with a Doula

Shura's Story

My husband died in my arms, suddenly, when we were on vacation in Canada. It was dusk. We'd been sitting in front of our cabin with our daughter, her husband and our grandchildren, watching fireworks and quietly enjoying the evening. My husband had been rather tired all day, but he was in good spirits. He suddenly felt a twitch in his chest. I put my arms around him and within the next three or four minutes, he had collapsed completely. We called the ambulance from a nearby hospital, but decided not to wait. As he was carried into the car, my son-in-law continued to administer artificial respiration the entire way. Nevertheless, my husband was dead on arrival at the hospital. My son-in-law left me there and went back to the cabin to inform my daughter, and to return for me later.

Meanwhile, I was received by a very gentle French-Canadian physician who performed the post mortem examination. After answering all his questions, I sat alone in the deserted corridor of the hospital admission wing. It was almost midnight. I was stunned and numb, not thinking, not weeping, almost not alive myself.

A woman, probably in her late forties, came and sat beside me. The physician had summoned her from home to come at this late hour and sit with me. She was soft and calm as she told me she would remain with me as long as I needed her to be there. She listened as I told her what had happened. She comforted me with her very presence and her calm acceptance of the trauma I was experiencing. She asked no intrusive questions. She just allowed me to express my feelings or to be silent—both of which I was doing intermittently.

After a while, I was able to ask her who she was and why she had come at midnight to sit with me, a total stranger. She told me that this was her work—to help others in the time of death and loss. She never used the word, "doula," and presented herself only as a helping person.

I told her that she had indeed been helpful to me during a very distressful hour. She had made it possible for me to endure that first hour. I thanked her for her kindness. When my son-in-law returned, she left me with him.

I never knew her name. I never saw her again. I have never forgotten her.

Eva Tells About Her Mother's Doula

My mother had a doula with her while she was dying. She was a friendly visitor who would talk to my mother about art and music. My mother values literature and music. She enjoyed talking with the doula about these interests. My mother felt that uneducated people were beneath her, so she would not engage in meaningful conversations with the aides who assisted her, but she did appreciate having this doula with whom to talk.

"Service is what life is all about."
—*Marian Wright Edelman*

Facing Mortality

At some point in the maturation process, each of us learns that all living things must die. This knowledge achieves new and more profound dimensions as all growing personalities develop. A young child may lose a cherished pet and mourn the loss. Later on, the impact of death becomes increasingly meaningful as we experience the death of an older relative, perhaps a sick friend, or people in the news.

Coming face to face with the death of people who are important to us is a difficult challenge. Facing our own mortality is the ultimate challenge for each of us.

How each person copes with death in her individual and unique way is often not easy to discern. But somehow, the challenge is met and we find ourselves saying farewell to significant people in our lives. Here we offer some vignettes and stories of the ways in which some women coped with their own mortality, their own death, the ultimate loss of self.

Three Determined Women
Their Stories

Pearl, Josie and Margaret were close friends with Jennifer and Shura for many years. Here are the stories of how they choreographed their own mortality.

About Pearl

Pearl was a strong, bright woman in her seventies. Artistic, creative, and talented, she had spent her adult life teaching sewing to blind people. A mother of two daughters and grandmother of four, she had always been active. She was also very caring. Among other jobs she had worked with residents in a nursing home. She was always willing to extend a helping hand to a friend in need, always graciously and with matter-of-fact humor.

Pearl had strong views on many subjects and expressed them openly, definitely, firmly and often even defiantly. She was never afraid of telling others what she thought and coping with whatever consequences might ensue. She had been a heavy smoker in her young days, but had not smoked for some twenty years. However, after her seventy-fifth birthday and her annual physical check-up, her physician advised her that she had developed lung cancer. It was incurable and inoperable.

After seeking another opinion and doing some research on her own, Pearl decided against the recommended invasive treatments of radiation and chemotherapy.

She said, "Wherever I go, whomever I consult, I'm told to 'fight the cancer.' Well I'm not going to." Instead, she developed a health routine of her own. She exercised daily. She ate selected foods in measured amounts. She visited with her children, grandchildren, and beloved

494

friends. In short, Pearl continued to live life her way and cherished every moment until she died.

When her time came, she went to the hospital for three difficult days of care, and died there. Just as she had controlled her ways of living, so she controlled her way of dying.

About Josie

Josie was a college professor, a writer and artist. She had been a life long activist in many social causes. She had been a heavy smoker and never stopped. Because of her cardiac problems, she had to retire from teaching long before she wanted to. Although she had many creative skills, such as painting and sculpting, which would have enriched her retirement years, she declined to practice them again. When she required by-pass surgery, the surgeons refused to operate unless she stopped smoking. She complied before the surgery but, despite all admonitions, she resumed it afterwards. Even during post-surgery rehabilitation, she sneaked cigarettes defiantly.

Some time after treatment, her mobility became very limited. Her husband created the necessary physical adaptations to care for her at home and assumed all duties. Soon, Josie experienced a series of admissions and discharges to and from the hospital. Ultimately, her devoted husband hired a home health aide to assist him. Diabetic and vision-impaired, Josie took to her wheelchair and television set. A lifelong telephone pal, she stopped calling her friends, although she was happy when an old friend or two visited.

Her husband had promised her that he would never move her to a nursing home. One day, she was admitted to the hospital in great pain and in a coma. Her husband, son, daughter and a lifelong friend were with her all day and evening. When everyone else had been told to leave, the compassionate nurses arranged for her husband to remain. Josie expired during the night.

Although no one in her world had approved of her defiant smoking, and her unwillingness to adapt to the demands of her deteriorating physical condition, Josie had it her way!

About Margaret

Margaret was an attractive, vibrant, well-dressed, well-groomed woman in her early seventies. Her first husband had died of cancer when they were both very young. Left with two young sons, she went back to work to make a new life for them and for herself. She developed a new career in which she was quite successful and much admired.

Sometime later when the boys were grown and on their own, still youthful and attractive, she remarried. Although her second marriage lacked the romance of her first, she maintained an acceptable life style. She and her husband moved to another state and built a new home for themselves. Although living at some distance from friends and family, she continued her relationships with them all.

At one point, she began to develop some physical problems requiring medical attention. Even at a distance, her friends and family began to realize that she was suffering from some ailment. Communicating by telephone, they urged her to consult physicians and to follow doctors' orders.

She assured everyone that she was doing just that. When they inquired about certain physical examinations that she seemed to require, she assured them she was attending to all needs. She reported all the positive and negative test results to anyone who was interested. Everyone thought that she was doing the right thing.

No one realized that she had not been telling her friends the truth. No one realized that, on her own, she had decided that she was suffering from the same type of cancer from which her first husband had died. No one realized that she had rejected the medical care that could have alleviated the totally different diagnosis of the doctors. No one understood how deeply she feared losing her health, her beauty, her vibrant aliveness. No one understood that she preferred and had chosen death.

"I have not ceased being fearful, but I have ceased to let fear control me."
—Erica Jong

What We Think

Jennifer: These women achieved control of the uncontrollable to the extent that it was possible.

Shura: It is a given that we all die. But these women chose the ways that they would live until they died.

Jennifer: It's facing the fact that you are mortal and letting go of the fear that this knowledge creates.

Shura: Each of these women identified her priorities and then lived their last days, weeks or months accordingly.

What Do You Think?

How do you feel about your own mortality? In what ways do you express these emotions? Do you think about this for yourself…for someone close to you?

Young Woman: Oh, Mrs. Fisher, you shouldn't be smoking. It's very
             bad for you!
Mrs. Fisher: So, darling, I'll die young

How My Mother Rose Died
Shura's Story

Mama had been living in the nursing home for some time. She had been relatively content with her care, and had never complained to me or to anyone else about anything or anyone. I worked close by and saw her daily. At each visit, she greeted us with smiles and left us with hugs and kisses.

One day when I was visiting, I asked, as always, "How are you today, Mom?"

Instead of her usual pleasant, cheerful reply, she looked at me seriously. With the closest expression to a frown that I had seen on her face in the past three years, she replied, "It's no good here. I have to get out of here."

Alarmed, I asked, "What happened, Mama?"

She replied, in a tone I probably hadn't heard in her voice since I was a child, "Do I have to account to you for everything?"

Meekly, I answered, "No, of course not, Mama."

Our visit continued, pleasant as usual. Mama did not seem abstracted or distressed. Our conversations were always loving and interesting. After the visit, riding home in the car with my husband, I said, "I think my mother is getting ready to leave us. She is preparing to die."

Then, I told him about that brief interchange. He said, "You're right. I think we'd better get everyone in the family to visit this weekend."

By Saturday, Mama was already quite weak and lay quietly in bed during the visits.

She was gently responsive to her visitors but not actively conversant. My husband and I came with our adult children, their spouses, and our grandchildren, her great grandchildren. Our oldest son Mark, however, was working in Boston and was not in town. When

500

I phoned him he told me he would be getting back on Monday and come to see Nanny then.

Everyone was very somber. The little girls, standing at the foot of the bed, were weeping softly. Although noone verbalized the thought, this was clearly a goodbye visit. Everyone kissed Nanny and hugged her. The room was full of our love and Nanny clearly knew it.

When they had all left, I sat with her and said, "Mom, everyone in the family came to see you today, except Mark."

She said, "I know. It was nice to have them here."

I continued. " Mom, you remember Mark, don't you? Your oldest grandchild?"

She said, "Of course I remember Mark."

I continued. "Well, he is still in Boston, but he is coming home on Monday, and he will visit you. Mom, will you wait for him?"

"Of course, I'll wait for him," she said.

And she did. On Monday Mark came, and his whole family came with him. Again there was a soft, quiet visit with Nanny. She was sitting in the wheelchair when Carol, Mark's wife, said, "See, Nanny, we are all here."

Mama looked up at them and said, "Yes. You are all here except me!"

After they left, Mom was helped into bed. She lapsed easily into sleep.

The next day, Tuesday, I came in to see her several times. She was in a coma. The nurses were keeping her comfortable, as only good nurses can do. When it was time for me to leave, I said "Good-bye my sweet mother. I love you." I kissed her and left.

That night, just as we were ready to go to sleep, I told my husband, "I'll just phone the nurse and see how my mother is doing."

I dialed the number and the evening nurse answered. "Oh," she said, "I was just going to phone you. Your mother expired just a few moments ago, and I am about to telephone the doctor! She slipped away very quietly."

And that was how my lovely, sweet, wonderful mother died. She was in her late nineties!

The Flower That Bloomed Too Late

By Gitel Rivkeh Kuselewitz*

Yes
I feel that I've arrived a little late
But now I'm here, I wish to live
And Living means doing
Deriving pleasure from myself
And others from me.
To bloom, perfume, adorn, inspire
Display myself;
Look at me! I am here!
And even a bit "special!"
For being late,
I am, therefore, somewhat unique

So come and gaze upon me
Feast a bit upon the sight of me
My scented fragrance, my perfume,
For my being here will not long endure.

I feel, I know that autumn comes
With gray days and chill winds
And I am weak
My strength at ebb
And I will wilt
Yes, Yes,
Wilt and disappear.

* Translated from the Yiddish by Shua Saul; from *Reflections at Midnight*—*a* bilingual volume of poems written by Gitl Kuselewitz when she was well past her seventieth birthday, published in 1976 by her daughter, Blossom Neuschatz.

When God Sat on Grandma's House
Beatrice's Story

I don't even know how old she was, 87 probably, but what was interesting is how she orchestrated it. She just did it. I have a strained relationship with my mother. A difficult one. My grandmother was dying and I went out to California from New York to see her while she was still coherent. I knew my mother would be there at my grandmother's house, so I planned to stay with my aunt. I knew I would have to see my mother, but at least it would be limited to daytime visits with Grandma.

When I got to my grandmother's house, I was surprised at how excited she was to see me. I hadn't seen her for three and a half years and hadn't spoken with her for about a year of that time. I didn't even know, till I got there, how much it meant to me to see her. I never thought my grandmother understood me. She was a very conservative, religious, born-again Christian woman. It worked for her because it was genuine and had helped her through hard times. My grandmother had been married to an abusive, alcoholic man who died young. They lived in a barn and picked apples not unlike the characters in *The Grapes of Wrath*. There's always been this kind of wisdom about her. She was a survivor and had done well generally speaking, as did her children.(Except my mother. My mother is critical and you never know, when you see her, if you are going to get the happy person or the discontented one.)

I digress. When I was helping Grandma to lie down to rest in her bedroom, she took my hand and said, "I want you to stay here. You need to be with your mother." I honored her wish. I stayed there with my mother the whole time. Then, my grandmother also, somehow, located my brother, who had been estranged from the family for the past 12 years. My brother also came to my grandmother's house and the three of us, my mother, my brother and I were together for the first time in I-don't-know-how-many years. My brother is six foot three and 250 pounds, and he was sitting on the front lawn with me crying. He looked at me and said, "Could you believe she did this? She did this. I feel like God is sitting on Grandma's roof."

She made it so we were all together. She would sleep and we would be talking, cooking meals, cleaning. She created a sacred space for us. She orchestrated her own send-off in the way she wanted to see it happen. She also had my aunts and uncles (most of them lived near her) in and out of the house. I even got to see cousins I didn't even recognize because it had been so long.

There was a lot of joy and laughter in the house. She would come out of her room and sit in her rocker/recliner and enjoy it, then go back to her bed. She was in a lot of pain and taking a lot of medication. Some days were better than others. We shared old stories and memories. We talked about joyful things. I felt I meant a lot to my grandmother. She would let me help her in the bathroom and to take a shower. She was, ordinarily, a woman with a lot of pride; I knew this opportunity for me to help her was special. My grandmother had been my "saving grace" in my childhood. She was the one who loved me. She taught me to sing, sew, play the piano. I recently rediscovered my sewing skills. I showed my grandmother some of my embroidery work and she shared with me some of her work. I enjoyed remembering that she was the reason I now sew.

It all came together for me in that one week in August. I came home feeling transformed, clean and light. There was something very right about it all. She had given us all this last gift. She also left me her Bible at my request. The one with all the comments and underlining in it. She died in October. My grandmother, although we were very different from each other, impressed me as an amazing woman.

What We Think
Shura's Voice

This grandmother created the departure that she wished for herself. The power of her love and understanding for everyone in her family is very clear in this story. Although separated for years, they came together willingly because of her strength.

There are unspoken messages in actions such as this one. Beatrice was amazed to find that some of her thoughts and ideas had become clarified after her grandmother died. She regained some memories she had forgotten and a renewed understanding of her own maturation. Each person in the family undoubtedly found a different, yet appropriate, message for herself or himself. This is clear in her brother's exclamation.

One of the greatest wishes of people facing their own mortality is to hope that they would not be forgotten. Beatrice's grandmother achieved this wish through her wisdom and power.

What Do You Think?

How do you feel about your own mortality? In what ways would you want to be remembered?

She gave her family this
last gift of getting
them all together.

She wanted to be
remembered after she died.

Guideposts for Thought

1. Change is inevitable. It is a given.
2. Death and loss are equally inevitable.
3. Change is often accompanied by a sense of loss.
4. There are many kinds of loss; death, dreams, unfulfilled desires.
5. Change often creates confusion during which a person may feel a loss of self.
6. During times of change, emotions run wild.
7. Some emotions may surface which had not been recognized before this time.
8. Change and loss create imbalance. A redistribution of balance is necessary to restore a sense of normalcy.
9. A support system is always needed, especially in times of loss.
10. It is important to develop skills of coping with all change, pleasant and unpleasant.
11. It is essential to develop a tool kit of skills for adapting to death and loss.
12. During times of change, it can be fruitful to re-examine the ways in which one has coped, to re-evaluate their effectiveness and to develop new skills of coping and adapting.

Chapter Seven
Roses and Thorns:
What Works and What Doesn't

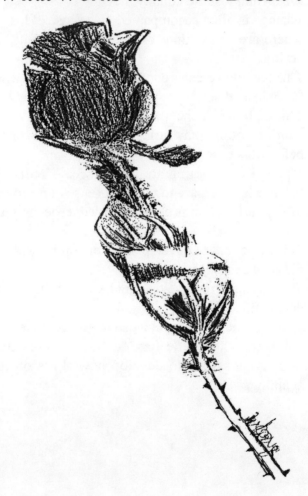

Roses and Thorns: What Makes It Work?

There is a famous poem by the German poet Goethe that tells of a young boy who sees a beautiful rose. He wants to pick it but is cautioned to beware of the thorns. He does not heed the warning and, of course, pricks his finger.

This is a tale of any human relationship: the sources of pain must be heeded if its beauty is to be enjoyed.

What makes a relationship beautiful, or even tenable? What works? What does not work? These questions are not easily or glibly answered. Developing and maintaining the relationship is a lifetime process of understanding oneself and the other person within the context of both their lives.

How do you know when a relationship is "working?" It is working if both parties are satisfied with it. It is working if they have found ways to cope with important differences. Put another way, it is working when they find and develop the commonalities that have the potential of pulling them together. It is working if there is mutual respect—if there is an understanding of one another's needs. It is working when each person realizes and accepts the willingness and desire of the other to be in the relationship. Such acceptance must be reciprocal.

Conversely, how do you know when a relationship is "not working?" It is not working if either party is dissatisfied—if one or both cannot find ways to cope with important differences—if there is no understanding of one another's needs.

The process involves experimentation. There are no recipes for relationships, only ingredients. How much of what ingredient will create the unique mixture required to achieve the desired resultant masterpiece? Ingredients vary, of course. Timing is also important; one must not overcook or undercook. Patience is necessary. It takes a long time to nurture a relationship.

These are generalities that apply to any human relationship. But what are the unique complications for mature daughters and their mothers who are growing old?

So often the daughter still views the mother with the eyes of a child. So often the mature daughter is still the child in the eyes of the mother. What is their history? There has been a lifetime of complex interaction that now requires understanding, insight and new levels of maturity.

Life happens. There are so many changes between childhood and maturity, between maturity and the older years. There is so much to experience, so much process to be processed, so much change to understand.

Sometimes we can hardly tell the roses from the thorns!

Roses and Thorns

Dialogue

Shura: In this chapter we include stories by people who either felt they had made it work or they had tried and couldn't make it work.

Jennifer: What I realized in these interviews is that for a relationship to work, it is necessary for at least one of the two persons involved to want to make it work. That person needs to have the skills or learn the skills to make it work, and then to apply them. The other person needs to be willing to follow along.

Shura: Sometimes, no matter how hard that one person may try, she may not be successful. That can be very painful.

Jennifer: It's a leap of faith. If you want a relationship to succeed, you must be able to accept the other person's limitations as well as your own.

Shura: It is also a matter of expectations. What are you looking for in this relationship? Does the other person have it to give? What is her idea of the relationship? What does she want out of it?

Jennifer: You have to be on the same page for it to work. Both mother and daughter must want the relationship and there must be some agreement about it.

Shura: Sometimes the ideas may be shared implicitly; both mother and daughter working at getting along, each in her own way. However, there are times when someone may need to be explicit about what she is looking for and what her expectations are. Then, a situation may be clarified or resolved.

Jennifer: That could lead to a dialogue between them through which both may feel further gratification.

Shura: If they can develop healthy communications—well, that's one very good way to make it work.

What Makes It Work?

Shura's Voice

One day our neighbor came by to read her story in this manuscript and to check its accuracy. She was surprised to learn how much collaboration there had been between Jennifer and me, and for how long.

"Gosh," she exclaimed, "You must be at each other's throats by this time!"

We were astonished at her comment. In retrospect, after she left, I began to think through the series of experiences that my daughter and I have shared as collaborating professionals.

We had begun by co-leading workshops at a few national conferences. Here, we combined each other's individual expertise to make the workshop unique. Jennifer, the musician, and Shura, the writer, played appropriately different roles in the leadership. Our first joint workshop focused on the creative arts as therapeutic agents. Jennifer sang. I read poetry. As the session progressed, the attendees became active participants. While we talked, they, as a group, created a paper scene of people and buildings. The workshop ended with everyone dancing to the music we had brought. The points were made. The session itself had become a creative arts experience. Our collaborative career had been successfully launched!

Several other, different workshops ensued. Each time, we employed the successful formula of pooling our respective abilities. We were invited to present our poetry as an intergenerational dialogue at a national conference on "Aging and the Arts." This resulted in our co-authored collection of poems entitled *Harmonies* which ultimately blossomed into a multimedia dramatic production including poetry, song, music, dance, and film. *Harmonies* was performed at a number of venues both in the states and abroad, where the entire cast of ten women participated in an Italian-American cultural exchange.

Were we ever "at each other's throats?" I don't think so. Why not? How did we make it work?

I think the first part of the answer derives from our adaptation of the concept of unconditional love. We were each aware, without even verbalizing, that we did not want the project to interfere with our loving relationship. We would keep the boundary of professionalism, in its best sense of teamwork, and maintain it as separate from the other aspects of family life.

Second, we shared a sincere desire to work together toward a successful goal for each project. These two principles were and are the basis of each joint undertaking.

I can identify a few other important ingredients that derive from this foundation. We have a sincere respect for each other's talents and skills. We maintain a positive attitude toward each other's work. We accept each other's suggestions for improvement and changes without feeling diminished. We are not competitive. Rather, we work as a team, in the best sense of the word.

At times there is a difference of viewpoint, even a disagreement. We discuss the issues as rationally as possible aware of the creative process and its attendant emotions, we try not to hurt each other's feelings.

Sometimes, at first, we are not successful. We have developed a way of coping with such situations. We cool it until we can let it go and get past it.

We are also able to separate and go our different ways. These collaborative projects do not consume all our time, thought and efforts. We have separate lives that occupy and fulfill us in other ways. We maintain clear boundaries that we respect and support. We can also laugh about things after they happen.

I think, truly, that our ability to work together, to continue to live together and enjoy each other derives from our mutual love, our healthy relationship and mutual desire to go on with our projects and our plans.

As I describe this process, I realize that so much of it pertains to our mother/daughter relationship as a whole. Our ingredients for a fulfilling relationship include, but are not limited to, basic love, shared values, mutual goals for each other and the family, solid boundaries with respect, appropriate support, and healthy humor. It really works, at least most of the time!

Who asks for, or expects, perfection?

What Makes It Work?

Jennifer's Voice

One day our neighbor came by to read her story in this manuscript and to check its accuracy. In the conversation that followed, she was surprised to learn how much collaboration there had been between Shura and me, and for how long.

"Gosh," she exclaimed, "You must be at each other's throats by this time!"

I realized that her reaction was a reflection of how she thought she might have felt, had it been her mother collaborating with her. Still, it gave me pause to think about why it was not only NOT true, but that this collaboration had actually brought us closer.

Through the two-year process of writing this book, I have gotten to know my mother even more deeply. I have also gotten to know myself more deeply. The collaboration has become a vehicle for learning new dimensions of the relationship. As a child, my mother would correct my writing for school and I thought that I needed that because my writing was not very good. Now, mature, I count on her professional editing skills, which I regard highly.

This collaborative process of writing this book was woven through and around the complications of our lives. For example, one day early on, we were working on titling the chapters. At one point, I had to stop working to take my youngest daughter and her friends to a movie. Mom came with us and we dropped them at the theatre. We ourselves took our notes with us, went to a local diner to work while eating lunch. Then we sat in the car outside the theatre, continuing to work while waiting for the girls. We happened to be struggling with a title for this very last chapter of the book.

A police officer came over to us to see why we were sitting there. He asked if we needed help or were we okay. We told him why we were there and what we were doing. He chatted with us about his own teenage daughter and her current ups and downs. He said, "Sometimes you get the roses and sometimes you get the thorns."

My mother and I looked at each other and started to laugh. He had just given us the chapter title for which we'd been searching!

The point of this story is that we didn't only collaborate with each other, we collaborated in our complicated lives, with the people around us, with the police officer, with our responsibilities. We used our obligations to inspire new contacts, connections and perspectives. Instead of seeing them as obstacles, we accepted them as opportunities for growth, learning and, yes, also change.

We wove our project into the fabric of our busy lives, our interactions. We seized opportunities for travel and adventure to create this book.

I ask myself, "At each other's throats?" Not even close! This works because we want it to. We already share so much in common, this co-authorship has become an experience that has altered my perception of my mother as a person, her relationship to me, and also my own relation to my daughters.

Change

Jennifer's Voice

I step into the waters of unknown
Steps of caution
Heart pounding quickly,
Loud heart pounding
What I don't know
Can hurt me

Like the snake shedding it's skin
Generating new, different,
Exciting, adventure ahead
Heart pounding vigorously
Water pounding rhythmically
against the rocks

Will I be pounded against the rocks
Heart says try, adventure,
don't know, just feel.
Change comes like the winds
Can't try, just feel.

Straddling the Generations
Interview with Wendy

Wendy and her family live next door to her parents in a city in England. They interact on a daily basis and observe clear boundaries.

What makes your relationship with your mother work?

Love mostly. We know unconditional love and trust. No matter what I do, I know she will never disown me. She may get annoyed with me, but no matter how angry or annoyed we become, we are always there for each other. When my mother is lonely, she knows she can come next door to my house and talk with me for 5 minutes. We don't disappoint each other. Our decisions seem to be right. We argue, and sometimes it gets nasty. But no matter how nasty it can get, we walk away, think about it and then apologize. We listen to what the other has to say. We can tell each other off and then make up.

What obstacles are there when there are obstacles?

The big thing is that I tend to take my dad's opinion over my mom's. My dad can do no wrong in my eyes. I feel sorry for my dad because my mom tends to dominate. I feel he needs my backing. My mom didn't have a lot of love in her upbringing. It makes it difficult for her to share love. You have to please her to get her love. That makes me cross.

You're a very different kind of mother to your daughter than your mother was to you.

I share my love openly with my daughter. My mom probably wanted to do that with me, but it was difficult for her. I know I didn't want my daughter to have a difficult mother as I did. I wanted my daughter to be able to come to me about anything. I love my mom to bits, but I wanted something else for my daughter.

How do you think your mom feels about your relationship with your daughter?

It shocks my mother. She can't understand the intimacy that we share. She sees it works better than what she and I have, but she doesn't understand how to be open. I could never go to my mother about things that went on in my life. She would have been shocked. She's old - fashioned. My daughter can't shock me.

Has your mother's aging process changed her attitudes?

No. She's the same. She tends to look and feel young. Yet, she realizes she can't do what she wants to do. She gets tired and weak. My mother and daughter are not close. My mother is a negative person. She has motivated me to be the opposite of her. My daughter can't relate to her negativity.

"When our knowledge coalesces with our humanity and our humor, it adds up to wisdom."
—Carol Orlock

What We Think

Shura's Voice

When a thoughtful young adult becomes a parent herself, she naturally gives thought to how she expects to mother her child. Willy nilly, her own mother becomes the criterion for judgment. In one way or another, she begins to review her daughterly experiences and make decisions about her behavior as a mother herself.

Does she want to be different from her mother, the role model? In what ways? In what ways will she try to emulate her mother? As her own daughter grows, and as she, the mother, matures, she encounters situations that she had experienced in her own younger days.

How did her mother behave toward her under similar circumstances? And in what ways have the circumstances and the times themselves become altered?

When we are called upon to make decisions, we move from the known to the unknown. The thoughtful mother recalls the critical incidents in her life which inform her present behavior. Our interest in Wendy's response lies in the honest way in which she has been able to make the adaptation from her mother's behavior to a new and different way of mothering. Yet, with her understanding of the power of the mother/daughter bond and the importance of their mutual love, she has found ways to maintain a positive, responsible relationship with her mother. Her insight, confidence and integrity are impressive.

What We Think
Jennifer's Voice

Wendy has been very mindful about her relationship with her mother. She was able to understand herself and her needs. She was then able to complete herself by creating a world in which she attended to those matters that had been emotionally incomplete for her.

She stood on her mother's shoulders and now offers her shoulders to her daughter. In spite of her disappointment in her mother, she offers to both mother and father a part of herself in a caring and responsible adult manner. She says she is there for her mother whenever her mother needs her. Wendy offers her unconditional love.

Wendy seems to live with her integrity intact while she remains fully aware of those parts of her life that had not been completed in her early history.

What Do You Think?

Wendy's story challenges us to find ways to combine honesty of perception with unconditional love. Have you been able to combine these in your relationship? In what ways? What obstacles have you encountered in the process? How did you cope?

Awareness Exercise

Much of the time we are unaware of how we behave in our relationships. The intent of this exercise is to help you become more aware of what you and your mother/daughter do to cope with each other. Using the examples in Wendy's story, write your perceptions of your own interactions.

Honest Perception of your own behavior:
(example: "We get angry, annoyed, argumentative.")

Response:
(example:"Take a step back when ready; tell each other off.")

Obstacle:
(example:"I'm not accepting of her feelings.")

Cope:
(example: "We make up; we let go.")

In Her Own Way

Interview with Samantha

Samantha is a fifty-one-year-old woman—a professional, and a working mother. She lives at a one hour distance from her seventy-six-year-old mother. She shares her maturing understanding of her mother as an aging woman.

What is the nature of your relationship with you mother?

It's moving towards being a caretaker. She's 76 years old and feels more vulnerable, thinking about her impending death.

How do you know this?

She's giving away everything she has. At first she was teary about it. Now it's matter of fact. There are times when she relies on me more and more for making decisions for her. For example, if she wants to buy a TV, she wants me to shop with her. Or, when she was having problems with telemarketers, she told me about it. I told her, "Give me their numbers; I'll take care of it," and she did. She's letting go of some control, yet she's always been very controlling. It's sad, but also welcome. She was never able to say what she needed or to ask for help or to reveal vulnerability. I now feel it's my responsibility to fill in for her. This is more realistic than before.

What was not realistic before?

She always needed to think of herself as perfect. She always had to be right. She had no vulnerabilities from her fears or her childhood. She needed not to need anybody. She tends to close off and be unaware of herself. It is too painful for her. At some earlier points I felt I had to give up on her. Now I feel I can't because I have a responsibility to her. She says to me, "I think about what to do, and then I think what you would say, and that helps me make a decision."

Are you the only child?

My mother's first child was a girl who died at one month old. I have an older sister who was the star of the family. When I came along, there was no more money left to invest in my experiences, so all they let me do was to sit and look out the window and read.

My mother has since cut my sister out of her life. She was tired of dealing with her drama. When my sister was young, she would agree to anything my mother would say or want. My mother saw this as weak and selfish. Now my sister lives in Philadelphia, and I see her as much as I can, but not as much as I'd like to. Sometimes it seems as if my mother will relent and they can start communicating. Then my mother retracts.

I never felt I could be as beautiful as my mother. She was the alpha and the omega, no discussion. I felt she was very powerful. I had to get away from her power. Mom and I never saw eye to eye. She respected my intelligence, but she thought I always had to have the last word. I didn't have the attributes that she considered desirable. My skin was darker than hers. My sister was lighter than me and my mother was fair skinned. I couldn't be my mother's clone. In the sixties and seventies, black people were wrapped up in self-hate. My mother didn't want to affiliate with black people and we were expected not to either. She hated herself for being black. We lived in Harlem and were told not to identify with "those people."

Social relationships were discouraged in general. She did not have many friends either. If she did have a friend and they did one thing that upset her, she would banish them.

She started college in her thirties, when I was in my sophomore year of high school. She went on to get her masters degree after that. In her youth, my mother had been told that her desire to go to college was above her station. She grew up in the south and had limited

528

possibilities. So when she turned seventeen, she got on a bus and went north. She met my father shortly after that. She had borrowed money from her brother to leave home. Recently, she thanked me for all I did for her. I didn't know I did anything for her. She said she knew nothing about the SATs or filling out college applications, and I taught her.

Were you proud of her?

Yes, very, but she had an angry side that was contentious. I respect her, but I can't say that I love her. When I was young, I bought into the idealized "TV family."

What about now, regarding her social life?

The same as when we were young. She doesn't let anyone into her social circle. People are not allowed in her house. She cut herself off from her family. We didn't even have that growing up. Sometimes I think no matter how angry I get at my son, I could never banish him, even if I'd want to. That would make me like my mother. She's not going to change. She's seventy-six. She does behave properly when she's with me, however. I let her know she can't pull that stuff on me that she does to other people.

So, what makes your relationship with her work for you?

I have to set clear boundaries with her. I need to understand and accept that she's not going to change. I acknowledge who she is, accept it and respect it.

How would you like it to be different if you could change it?

The only thing I'd like would be to see her having a better relationship with my sister. But it seems mother is not going to let that happen.

"In my early days I was a sepia Hedy Lamarr. Now I'm black and a woman, singing my own way."
—Lena Horne

What We Think

Shura's Voice

Life experiences can cause a person to make changes. Death, which is part of life, can do the same. Twin elements are combined in this relationship. The first, and most obvious, is Samantha's desire to soften the difficulties of her earlier years. In a sense, she is the prime motivating agent working towards developing a positive relationship with her mother. Somehow, in her own maturational process, Samantha helped herself to become the mother to her own son that she had wished for herself.

Samantha found it important in this interview to cite her mother's early experiences. She understands the suppression of a little black girl's desires for a life that was closed to her. She knows that the climate of her mother's childhood stunted her growth and affected her outlook. Samantha appreciates the effort and courage it took for the seventeen-year-old "to get on a bus and go north."

Now in her mature years, she can accept her mother as she is. Despite the element of neglect in her own child-hood, Samantha now takes responsibility for understanding, supporting and helping her mother. Her childhood idealism of the "TV family" has been replaced by a more realistic view. She also understands that her mother is at a critical point facing her mortality. Samantha is ready to help her mother through it.

We must also acknowledge her mother's altered position. In these later years, Samantha's mother has learned to appreciate her dark-skinned daughter. She acknowledges her own need for a more positive mother/daughter bond.

She has become more willing to accept some help, support and filial devotion.

Both women have matured toward a more fulfilling relationship with each other.

Her mother's rigidity
waned somewhat as she aged.

Samantha used this change
as an opportunity to
strengthen their relationship.

What We Think
Jennifer's Voice

Samantha has allowed her early pain about her mother to teach her about what kind of mother she would like to become—what she wanted to pass on to her son. She also learned about opening her heart toward acceptance of her mother, even though she doesn't approve of her. Perhaps many circumstances of her mother's early years brought on the many fears which prevented her from becoming the person Samantha wished she would be. Samantha's ability to understand this has enabled her to live as the person she herself wants to be.

The relationship works in a limited way because Samantha wants it to. She has created an acceptance in her heart for her mother. If not for Samantha's growth and maturity, there might not be a relationship at all.

What Do You Think?

Have you both developed a more mature relationship, as you both grew older?

Accepting Maturity
Interview with Desiree

Desiree is a fifty-year-old mother of three. She lives at a forty-five-minute drive away from her mother. Her siblings all live in other states. Desiree assumes complete filial responsibility toward her mother.

Tell us about your relationship with your mother, Does it work?

It works in that we have a relationship. We have contact. I do most things a daughter is supposed to do for a mother. She does most things a mother is supposed to do for a daughter.

What are these things?

She comes to graduations and events. I help her with doctor appointments and such.

Is it a close, intimate relationship?

It's not anything like my relationship with my daughters. I think mothers set the rules. I'm more open with my daughters, so we are more intimate. You always yearn for closeness. Either you repeat the pattern (mostly when you are unaware of yourself and your feelings) or you do the opposite (when you are aware). Also, I grew up in a generation that was more open. My mother grew up with a mother who didn't even kiss her. She remained a child because those needs were never met for her. I have accepted my mother, as I got older. Also, I've accepted more of who she is. When I was young, I was angry about those things that she didn't have to give me.

What would your mother say about this question of closeness with you?

I think my mother would say that I have changed. When my father died, my mother expected me to take care of her. When I became a mother myself, I started seeking my mother out. My mother is now a little more aware of the things she says and does. She seems to be more accepting.

Are you the only child?

I have two sisters and brothers. My mother has different relationships with each of her daughters. Her relationships with her daughters are different from those with her sons. In our ethnic culture, daughters are supposed to take care of mothers. Sons are supposed to take care of their wives.

So, what makes your relationship work with your mother?

My acceptance of my mother and my own maturity. It's very hard to be a mother. You can't know that until you are one. It's complicated. There are parts of me that forgive her for the past and understand her. When I was young, I never realized she had tremendous shortcomings as a mother. She doesn't have the intelligence, depth or fortitude. She was hampered by her mother. She was never given an education. She never grew within, to be able to see herself and others. I was able to have an education and grow in that way. She was limited by her emotional problems as well. She wasn't allowed to receive affection or to have experiences with other places and people. She wasn't allowed to jump rope on the street. When she was 5 years old, she suffered from tuberculosis until she was 7 years old. Her parents sent her to a sanitarium. That had a profound effect on her ability to cope with life. That also impacted on her mothering. A part of her was angry that we got to have things she never had. She was resentful.

You've spoken about what you have done to make the relationship work. What has she done?

I think she's gotten old and tired. She used to be much more demanding. Because she's less demanding, there is more guilt involved. She's now 88 years old. I feel bad for her. She lost my father and stepfather and now she lives alone. Her other children live in California. She insists she doesn't want to move or live with anybody.

How does this make you feel?

I feel guilty that I'm not taking care of her. She expects me to take care of her on her terms. There's nothing I can do. I can't take care of her adequately on her terms only. She doesn't drive, so she's stuck in the house. She lives 45 minutes from me. I work, have a family and run a household.

If your mother were here and heard you say this, what would she say?

She'd say, "Is that so much to ask, to drive 45 minutes? Is that such a big deal?" Actually, I have mixed feelings about it. Sometimes I feel guilty and other times I shrug my shoulder and say, "that's her choice." Many years ago, I suggested she go to a senior-citizen community. She didn't want it. She said, "When the time comes, I'll deal with it." She really meant that when the time will come, I'll be the one to deal with it! My mother thinks I'm "fresh." That means I say what I think. So, our relationship works when it's on her terms or when I'm so accepting that I don't care. Life has always been on her terms. I wanted us to have a mutual relationship, not just on her terms. She considers me rebellious.

Was her life really on her terms?

Yes, she did not give in. All of her children took a stance. My brothers stepped out completely. They don't care. My sisters do the same dance I do; we try to please her and then when we can't, we pull back.

What is she like as a grandmother?

She's the way she was with us. She favors my son. She's inappropriate. She says things out of left field. For example, when my daughter was 14 years old, going to the ninth grade dance, my mother said to her, "You look so beautiful, now don't forget, use protection." My daughter had no idea what she was talking about. She was fourteen years old, going to her ninth grade dance! Nevertheless, I'm here in New York, although my siblings are in California, because I wanted to give my kids that example. No matter what, you can find a way to work it out, to make and keep the connection. I started my life in her womb. I need to keep that connection. No matter what limited way, we can do it. My daughters' blood is my blood. My mother's blood is my blood. I need to honor that. There were times in my life when I ran away to avoid the pain of my mother. I realized I still had the pain and no rewards. So I came back.

How do you feel about this interview?

It makes me feel good about myself.

"Our deeds determine us, as much as we determine our deeds."
—George Eliot

What We Think
Jennifer's Voice

Desiree has struggled with her feelings of responsibility toward her mother and devotion to her own mental health. Her rebellious nature pulled her through and protected her from suffering a lifetime of pain through avoidance. Sometimes you find your most fruitful path when you stay with the challenges that face you and working them through by facing their reality. This is what Desiree has done. She remained in New York near her mother. She learned to set limits on her mother's inappropriate behavior, and she faced her own pain to work past it.

On the other side of this type of pain there is often a rainbow. Freedom from pain can offer new and different opportunities for growth that are not available if you avoid, deny, or run away from them. If you try to avoid, deny, or run away from pain, it will follow you.

In real life, wherever you go, there you are. Desiree feels good about herself because she did what she had to do to go forward. She also set the pattern for her children to face their pain and stay true to themselves. The message, "I am here for you unconditionally," works back from where you came from as well as forward to the next generation. This gives her children that much more of a shoulder to stand on for generations to come.

What Do You Think?

What is the most fruitful path through the challenges that face you in your mother/daughter relationship? Have you found freedom from pain? How or why not? What helped you or what were the obstacles?

Her mother behaved
in dysfunctional ways.

Nevertheless, Desiree took the
responsibility for making
the relationship as
functional as possible.

Wings

By Denise Frasca

Songbird on a sill
Sings,
Mother, can I forgive you?

I remember you
sitting on my bed
reading Little Women
weeping for the child
who deserved to hear
many more years
of the songbird on the sill

Songbird on a sill,
Sings,
Mother can I forgive myself,
waiting for you to notice
the wings I grew
the notes I memorized?
Hopeful
for one more crumb
placed upon the sill.

Songbird on a sill,
Sings,
I only wanted to be the songbird
You thought so worth living for.

Annie Finds Her Own Path

Interview with Annie

Annie, the mother of two teenage girls, told us that her relationship with her mother had not worked from the very beginning. Her explanation follows.

What made your relationship with your mother not work?

It's straightforward. My parents both really put my brother first. They thought he was a genius. This was the family myth. I was a hard worker. I spent my life working hard so I could be as good as my big brother. Then, and only then, maybe my mother could love me. It was a "booby trap." I could never work hard enough to make someone fall in love with me.

My mother was hypercritical and I was the wrong match for her. It was a double-edged sword. In some ways we were similar. I have early memories of rejecting my mother. She'd come home from work, take her girdle off and sigh with relief. I'd look at her with disgust and say to myself, "I never want to be like this."

I am like her but I am more delicate than she was. That is partly because of my father and partly due to a severe early trauma. These two ingredients of my young years left me vulnerable, but by nature, I really am more delicate. I became a dancer. That is my saving grace. The way I am most NOT like her is that I am delicate.

I don't think she really loved me. She told me she did, but I never believed her. I raised myself. I brought myself up. It was also my nature to be very independent. When I was three years old I went to a Nursery School. There was a teddy bear for sale at a fundraiser that I really wanted. My parents couldn't afford one. They asked the teachers to tuck it away for me. At the end of the day, they bought it for $3.00. From that point on, I remember seriously feeling I was part of a team. It was me and Smokey. I think I learned that I can't trust people but I can trust things. That's why I became a dancer. I can trust the arts. How's that for an explanation of why it didn't work?

What We Think

Jennifer's Voice

I believe that we humans try to grow towards health. Just as the plant placed in a dark room will seek out the one spot of light, so we try to grow towards the sun.

Clearly, Annie was in a dark room, feeling alone and lonely. She believes nature gave her the tools to be independent and delicate in her life. Sometimes, being connected to our own vulnerability is itself our strength. I believe this is so in Annie's case. Her strong sense of self-awareness and the unadulterated awareness of her family dynamic led her through doors of self salvation.

Unfortunately, she could never achieve something strong and healthy with her mother. She experiences her mother as an unwilling participant in her life.

I wonder in how many other ways her adulthood might have been affected?

"Our only purpose in life is growth. There are no accidents."
—Elizabeth Kubler Ross

Annie had to find her own
ways of trust as she lived
in the shadows of
her mothers criticism.

The gaps between herself
and her mother were
so great that there was no trust!

What Do You Think?

Have you grown in a family where another child was favored? How did you cope with it?

I hear my mother's critical voice following me around wherever I go. Like my credit card, "I don't leave home without it."

Never Too Old to Learn
Interview with Mollie

Mollie is an aging widowed mother whose middle-aged daughter is very attentive to her. Mollie reached out in the relationship to make it work.

What creates the magic between you and your daughter?

I know when to step back. It took me a while to learn to do that. I also had to learn about acceptance. I sometimes make suggestions to her, but I try not to take offense if it's not to her liking. Our relationship is symbiotic. She is a huge support to me and I to her. I know I can count on her in times of need.

How did you learn to do this?

Trial and error. I tend to be dogmatic. I put what I think first. I learned to step back and realize that I am not in control of her life. I need to be an observer instead of what I think of as an agent of action.

When you come to a trouble spot, what do you do?

It's hard for me to confront, regardless with whom I'm interacting. I internalize my feelings. It's not good for me. I know that. When hard times come, I let it pass ninety percent of the time. Then something wonderful will happen and the trouble will fade completely into the background. At this point in my life, given my aging process, what is most important to me is that I know I can count on my daughter to look after me unconditionally.

"That it will never come again is what makes life so sweet."
—Emily Dickinson

What We Think

Shura's Voice

Aging and widowhood intensify the maturational process. In our later years, we are challenged, among other things, to face ourselves and to come to terms with the demands that aging forces upon us.

Mollie has realized these inescapable facts. She recognizes the reality of her aging. She accepts her emotional need for support and love from her daughter. Willingly, she is making some important changes in her attitude and her behavior in order to cope with the current needs of her life.

Mollie's priorities have also shifted. She yields control to achieve acceptance, both for herself and of herself. Her daughter's love takes precedence over being right or wrong. Mollie not only allows these changes, she welcomes them as she realizes they enhance the quality of her later years.

She wanted to maintain
the relationship and
became more flexible as she aged.

She took the initiative to
reach out and adapt
as needed to change.

What We Think

Jennifer's Voice

Mollie seems to have grown a lot. She describes having learned lessons about relationships that have served her well. She learned to be less black and white about what she thought she knew in life. She has become more open to listening. She learned to step back and give space to things she did not like. She learned that what was most important in life were her family relationships. She learned skills that allow her to enjoy the intimacy of these relationships.

It is not easy to let go of a life pattern of thought and behavior. Mollie's need to have her daughter in her life seemed to have motivated great change.

So maybe you can teach an old dog new tricks!

What Do You Think?
Dialogue About Fear

Jennifer: There is an element of fear in every relationship. There is always the potential that you can get hurt.

Shura: There is also the fear that you can hurt the other person.

Jennifer: Fear stifles and numbs. It interferes with our ability to communicate.

Shura: When it seems that a relationship requires some explicit communication about a matter of importance that also carries emotional overtones, it takes great courage to initiate that kind of discussion.

Jennifer: We are not always at our best with words. We often use words that don't express what we really mean.

Shura: Therefore, we sometimes hold back from saying anything at all. We become afraid of our own words. This fear also stifles.

Jennifer: So, we need to develop mindful speech. We need to think about what we mean and how best to say it in the way that the other person can hear it and accept it.

Shura: We must be willing to risk the possibility of the other person's misunderstanding or anger. We must be ready to take it and find a way to clarify our message.

Jennifer: Only then, through such fearless communication, do we have the chance of building a healthy, open, trusting relationship.

Exercise: Face Your Fears

What, if anything, do you fear in your mother/daughter relationship?

How do your fears affect your other emotions?

How do your fears affect your thoughts?

How do your fears affect your behavior?

Do you think your mother (daughter) recognizes or understands that you have these fears?

How do you know?

What would you like to do about this?

What would you like your mother (daughter) to do about this?

Why haven't you taken this important step as yet?

What would motivate you to take it? How can you be helped to take it?

My Mother Is a Fortress
Beatrice's Story

Beatrice struggles to accept the differences between herself and her mother.

My mother is a fortress and her eyes have grown smaller and smaller as she ages. I find that curious. She is the center of her world and I think, in a way, she is swallowing herself—imploding.

As mothers go, she made sure the meals were cooked, house cleaned, clothes washed, and all outward appearances in order. Early on I was treated as if I was a stupid child, one to be seen and not heard. She would dress me up, my hair in ringlets. I remember one specific night while I sat at the table watching her in the kitchen. My thought was that she absolutely hated me.

Not long after that, in pre-adolescence through adolescence, my father began fondling me. My mother has always been so proud of how hard she worked in those days and she did: a full-time job, two children, a husband who wouldn't lift a finger. She would fall asleep on the sofa each night. That's when my father would come to me. But she was proud that she cleaned before collapsing at 7:00 every night. The funny thing is, not only was she sexually abused and physically beaten as a child, my father also abused her. And that's not all. She knew dad was a pedophile. He had been caught with her little ten-year-old sister. I would be angry that she didn't protect me but I really understand that she was incapable of mothering children. She still is.

I was a grown woman when I told her my father had been sexually abusive with me. Her response was, "I can't believe I was married to a man like that." That's when I really got the fact that she couldn't be there for me. Her first response to this horrible news was how it reflected on her. Not what I may have suffered. Not how I coped. Not, "How can I help you now? I'm so sorry I couldn't be there for you back then."

This was when I first realized she was unreachable. After ten years I have broached a kind of compassion for her. I have distance, both figurative and literal. I'm now on the east coast; she's on the west coast. She has her beautiful things—her redecorated show houses, moving to more beautiful houses in different places that will finally make her happy with living. Everything is spotless and new. Everything is in its place, from the hair on her head to the seasonal china she leaves set out on her $10,000 table. Who would not have compassion?

Two years ago I landed in a psychiatric hospital in a complete physical, mental and spiritual breakdown. My mother came out but could not stand to see me that way—so torn up. So she visited me only once.

Now, I am the mother of three beautiful little girls. Like it or not, as they reach puberty, I am able to put into perspective my own abuse history. I feel a fierce love and sense of protection for my girls. We have a beautiful relationship, despite painful as it may be to relive moments with my own mother. Her anger and jealousy. I remember shopping for clothes as a young teenager and my mother grew pouty and disgusted because everything fit me so well and I was a beautiful young girl. She wasn't…in her own mind of course. I realize my girls' beauty both inside and out and sometimes I over identify with them. But I am excited for the lives they're now beginning. To me, any jealousy and anger with them over their positive characteristics feels unnatural.

In a recent road trip conversation with my daughters, we talked about how with each generation we have the opportunity to be better parents than those who came before us. I know the ways in which my mom got it wrong and it's my obligation not to repeat those shortcomings. I'm glad the cycle of child abuse ends with me. I'm glad I have this chance to get it right.

Since going off the drugs that helped me cope with all that had overwhelmed me, I have gained weight. I have come to the point where when I look in the mirror, I see her hands, her arms with fat dimples just above the outer elbows, the extreme hips. On my best days, I'm a cross between a Kachina doll and fertility goddess. On my worst, I am a "scream" in my mother's body.

She struggles to understand
the gaps between herself
and her mother.

Among the gaps are the
problems of her
own emotional barriers.

"Nothing in life is to be feared. It is only to be understood."
—Madame Curie

What We Think

Jennifer's voice

You throw a rock in the water, and there are ripples. Sometimes the ripples last for a long time, even generations afterwards. The result of Beatrice's mother's ignorance, and her inability to mother children has taken its toll on Beatrice's development and life experiences. Simultaneously, it has also given her the inspiration to be a very attentive, loving, kind, creative mother to her children. Sometimes, the very things that don't work for you in your lifetime are corrected and the corrections get passed on to benefit the next generation.

It is also clear that Beatrice has grown and matured a great deal. She is able to have compassion for her mother's ignorance. She also speaks of being appreciative that the child abuse pattern in her family stops with her and that she is able to shift the pattern to a more functional, healthy one. This is also a very good point. Through our awareness and intent to be functional, we can change dysfunctional family patterns.

What We Think
Shura's Voice

Beatrice endured some very difficult times as she struggled to survive the psychological and emotional damages that had been inflicted on her by both parents. Ultimately, she accepted the help of professionals to turn her life around. One may well wonder whence comes this type of strength enabling a young woman to attain the level of health that Beatrice has achieved. One must possess great power and intelligence—a firm grasp for growth and maturation to be able to end such an inter-generational pattern of ugliness.

What Do You Think?

Have you had to struggle to survive psychological or emotional difficulties in your mother/daughter relationship? Have you found ways to change dysfunctional patterns in more positive directions?

"I'm having a good life
because of my mother."

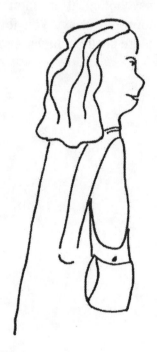

"That's funny! I'm having
a good life in spite of my mother."

You Are What You Eat

A Commentary by Beatrice

I had always pictured my mother as literally stuffing her feelings down her mouth—eating her feelings. Her eyes were literally getting smaller as if she was receding into this mass of stuffed feelings. They were beginning to swallow her!

Creating these drawings was a profound experience for me. While drawing the shape of her body I felt both profound compassion and a gut-wrenching sense of revulsion.

Beatrice's Mother   **Beatrice Herself**

Exercise: You Are What You Eat

We all deal with our emotions in different ways. Some of us smoke them away, some of us drown them in drink, some take pills to escape them, and some of us try to work them off so as to numb them. Some of us eat our emotions, hoping to push them down and not feel them.

All these techniques achieve the same result. We have stored our emotions somewhere within our bodies. In earlier exercises we have suggested ways that tuned us into listening to or "feeling" our physical responses to various situations. This exercise is an opportunity for insight through drawing what you observe in your body.

1. Draw the outline of your body as you think it is. (Don't worry about whether it is realistic or not.)
2. Using the models on the preceding page as guides, try to identify your emotions and where you store them in your body.
3. Draw another outline representing your mother or daughter and do the same for her.
4. Compare the similarities and/or differences, as you may perceive them.

The Roses and the Thorns
Felicia's Story

Felicia describes the extremes of pleasure and pain that she experienced with her mother

For many years, my mother is an enigma to me. When I speak or write about her, I am puzzled about how to tell anyone about her. It took a long time for me to come to terms with the choices she made in her life. For example, she was an excellent student in her youth. She graduated as valedictorian from a very prestigious and scholarly high school. She was admitted into college, but she quit school to get married and join my father in his chosen career, which didn't include college. He was quite successful in his career and she helped him a great deal.

My father was less successful as a parent than he was in his career. He started to beat me up when I was age thirteen and a half and continued to do so until I was seventeen and a half. That was the last time. Because of his abuse, I moved out of his home. My mother had seemed to think it was okay for him to do this. Not until the last time when he was beating my head into the floor did she finally tell him, "That's enough—stop!" That image has remained with me throughout my life. It has taken me a lifetime to cope with that memory. However, now I, a mature woman in my sixties, am able to reverse the situation in my imagination. Now, as I recall those days, I am beating him severely.

I know that my mother became terribly sad that she had stuck with him, and wished that she hadn't. She was incredibly loyal to him and felt very protective toward him even when he did those terrible things.

She would tell me this in a moment, weep from the depths of her being and go on with her life. I never knew what to do.

I always wondered why she didn't get herself a job outside the house. Maybe she felt that she didn't want just any job. She was very smart, but never wanted to go back to school. She did love her house. She loved her garden. She loved entertaining. It was not just a matter of lacking self-confidence. Mom could do any damn thing she set her mind to. She read more books in a year than I've probably read in my lifetime. She read on every conceivable subject and was very knowledgeable about my father's field of work as well. She herself was a well-known and respected member of our community. People of all ages came to her for her warmth, her help and her friendship.

My mother was not one to delve deeply into the psychological reasons that might motivate people to certain kinds of behavior. She tended to take people at their face value. This was always very interesting to me because she herself was very discerning about the people she chose for her friends. Also, the books she read often delved deeply into peoples lives and behavior. Yet, she would tell me to "quit picking about everything."

I know that she was always angry with my dad over how he treated his kids, and also at how he treated her. She was in a rage at him for a very long time. It makes me weep just to say this. Yet, I also had a very volatile relationship with her myself, partly because I was so upset that she had remained with him all her life. All I could ever do was to be there for her when he mistreated her, as he often did!

She is dead now and I'm glad she is somewhere in peace. She seemed to have made many unfortunate choices, but the incredible thing about my mother was her phenomenal emotional strength, and her great joy in life despite all her suffering. She was rich within herself, and when she laughed it was the most wonderful thing. She believed that life was not a bowl of cherries and that one took the bad with the good.

Despite the oft-times very painful relationship I had with my mother, and feelings of disappointment in what she felt about me, when she died I felt I had gotten everything I needed from her to continue with my life; a deep sense of strength, an uncompromising sense of being able to stand up for what I believed in, much as she did, and a love for my children, gardening and life. She did love us. Unfortunately, after she died, their joint will revealed that my share of the inheritance was to be placed into a trust fund because my father was sure I would blow it all.

Money was always a source of contention between my parents. So, in the end, she gave in to him once again. Of her three children, I, the eldest and only daughter, had my money put into a trust fund. ROSES AND THORNS!

Felicia was finally able to go
beyond the pain and
damage of the early abuse.

Despite her abusive father,
she seems to be at
peace with her mother.

What We Think

Jennifer: Felicia's experiences, with an abusive father and a mother who couldn't seem to do anything about it, had to be very damaging in her growth and development.

Shura: They colored her whole life. As she says, not until she was very mature was she able to find the strength to go beyond the experience of abuse.

Jennifer: When she was able to put it together, she found the strength to reach a deep understanding of herself. She still has some unanswered questions about her mother's motives, but she does understand her as a woman.

Shura: Felicia's story is one of extremes. We see that life and human relationships are never either roses or thorns. Life is a combination of pain and pleasure.

Jennifer: Roses grow with thorns.

What Do You Think?

Have you had to overcome any controversy with your mother? If so, what lessons have you learned? What changes have you had to make within yourself to overcome those hurdles? Have you come to peace with her? If not, what needs to be resolved at this time in order to do so?

Speaking Without Speaking
Interview with Kristy

Kristy is a thirty-two-year-old woman who grew up in Hawaii with a close knit family of Japanese descent. Her mother, age fifty-nine, and her grandmother, age ninety-two, both still live in Hawaii. Kristy has married a man who derives from another culture and they have relocated in California. Kristy's life in Hawaii was small town living with both sides of her extended family living within eight miles of her house. She describes the relationships among the women in her family village.

What influence did your grandmother have in your home when you were growing up?

I'm closer with my maternal grandmother because my mother went back to work after I was born, and Grandma took care of me. She was always included in our family vacations, and we spent a lot of time together, so she was a great influence on me.

How did she help shape who you are?

I come from a Japanese culture. My mother's mother was first generation Hawaiian. We were brought up with her family's friends and community. Our identity lay in our last name. Everyone referred to us by our family name. That shaped my behavior in public. My behavior represented my family. My grandmother will be ninety-two years old in September and she is very strong willed.

In the Japanese culture, women are not supposed to be vocal. Much of the communication that gets passed on is not verbal. My mother and grandmother would communicate in Japanese. I don't speak Japanese, but I always knew when they were speaking about me. Much of the teaching was indirect. Guilt and obligation are two powerful dynamics in the Asian culture. Even though communication was indirect and non-verbal, I understood what there was to understand. It's interesting, you just know what there is specifically to know. I suppose you do a lot of guessing. I always knew specifically what I did wrong. At the same time, we were close and involved in each other's day-to-day lives.

How do your mother and grandmother get along?

They respect each other very much. They interact a lot out of obligation. My mother is the oldest girl. A great deal of responsibility falls on her shoulders. Family gatherings are at her house. They talk a lot and they are very close, but still much is unspoken.

How do they work out their problems between them?

Many things are not dealt with at all, they are just pushed aside, denied, and eventually they dissolve. Then if the issue should arise again, they might deal with it. For example, one time my grandmother wanted to go out for ice cream, but there was no time. Over a period of eight years, she brought up to them that they did not validate her and they had dismissed her desire for ice cream. I'm different from them in that way. I don't like things festering inside of me. But my family is still generous and kindhearted.

What do you think makes your relationships work?

It's changed over time. There are times when I felt it was obligation that made it work. But we depend very much on each other and we all talk several times a day. We respect each other. There is a lot of caring for each other.

My mother's role and my grandmother's role are changing now that my grandmother is older. Three years ago, she gave up her driver's license. So now my mother needs to drive my grandmother around. My mother doesn't like having this job. She has just retired and was looking forward to her freedom. My grandmother doesn't like it either. She doesn't want to be dependent. They are both learning to adjust and juggle things around to make it work.

My parents are buying property adjacent to my grandmother's and they are building a house there for themselves. I come from a family of coffee farmers. They all work hard and this is an important value they have passed on to us. My grandmother still gets out there and harvests. She also works in a nursing home. She volunteers. She says the people there are too young for her to be friends with and she misses her friends who are now deceased.

"As a traveler who has once been from home is wiser than he who has never left his own doorstep, so a knowledge of one other culture should sharpen our ability to scrutinize more steadily, to appreciate lovingly, our own."
—*Margaret Mead*

She had two major gaps to
bridge, the cultural and
the generational ones.

She finds ways to allow the
differences in cultures
and ages to enrich her life.

What We Think

Jennifer's Voice

Kristy has a rich heritage which to this day lives itself out in it's own adaptation to the American culture. As she describes it, her mother and grandmother seem to regard age as incidental.

Grandmother still continues to live her life as she always has lived it. She harvests coffee and she volunteers in an old age home. She even regards the folks there as being too young for her to consider as peers.

Mother's lifestyle is designed to enable Grandmother to be as independent as possible. There seems to be no limit to mother's willingness to make adaptations in her own life to include and consider Grandmother's needs. For example, mother and father are building a new home next to Grandmother's current land.

Kristy has these relationships as her role model. At this point, she is able to blend the values that she treasures from her childhood and culture with other and newer values. She herself grew up to marry a man from an Eastern European culture. Their cultures and values have now merged and adaptations of this new family pattern are in their hands.

As our world gets smaller through computer technology and increased opportunities for communication and travel, more people will be experiencing such possibilities to meet the demands of their lives in this changing world. We are all connected and our cultural differences will remain important but will separate us less and less. Hopefully, we will learn to enjoy our commonalities and to celebrate our differences.

What Do You Think?

Kristy's life is enriched through its inter-generational and multi-cultural dimensions. Do you experience either of these in your family relationships? In what ways is your life enriched? Do you find it a burden? How do you cope?

Earth Mother

Interview with Antoinette

Antoinette is an 82-year-old mother and grandmother who maintains important relationships with her grown sons and daughters. She describes these relationships.

What are the ingredients of your relationship with your daughters? What makes it work?

I think a big part of it is being interested in what they are each doing, what they are interested in, even if they are far away. I have three daughters; two live at some distance, one lives near me. We are inseparable. She needs me more than the others. The others are married and have families. She is divorced and alone. She doesn't have her own family. She goes to school just now, I don't see her that much. So we talk on the phone a lot. She tells me everything. We get together, although not as often as I'd like.

How is it that you get along so well?

Through the years, you acquire ways of getting along. I have always listened. I listen to everything. When they want to talk, I listen.

They are my priority, always have been. I drop everything when they want me. You get that through the years, this closeness. It doesn't start when they are forty years old, you know. My daughters-in-law are also very good to me. I'm good to them.

People treat you the way you treat them. You must overlook the unpleasant things. I live by, "If you can't say anything nice, don't say anything at all." I don't hold grudges. I overlook and look beyond.

If people are not pleasant, I don't want to lower myself to their level. I want to be who I am even when someone is nasty to me.

When my daughters are upset, I try to advise them according to what I would do. I tell them what I think, but I try not to hurt them.

You seem to have been the one to encourage them

When my kids were afraid and hesitant I'd encourage them to go and do. I think it is important to move—and to move on. Even now, I sit and move my arms. I encourage my children to follow who they are and to do whatever they want to do. I see each daughter for who she is. I try to do the same for myself. When my daughter was married, I felt free to travel and do the things I prefer to do. When I felt that I was needed at home, I stayed at home. When I go to visit one of my children, I keep in touch with the others by phone. I call my daughter who is alone every day because we have this strong connection.

What responsibility do they have in their relationship with you?

They have to be able to accept what I'm giving. If they don't accept it, it's awfully hard. I hand out a lot. I try again. Then, often, they have to take.

Do they offer you anything?

They encourage me, too. "Mom, you have to do this or that." There is a give-and-take in our relationship. I take what I can get. They have a lot to do with what I do. They encourage me back.

We share emotions and love. They feel for me. It's not about giving money or things. It's about love and emotions.

What We Think

Shura: Antoinette seems like an eighty-two-year-old Mother Earth. She's a very caring and nurturing woman.

Jennifer: It seems that Antoinette's secret to success lies in her respect for other people's boundaries.

Shura: Yes, and this respect, I think was extended to her children even when they were younger. She allows people to be themselves.

Jennifer: Allowing people to be themselves is very important in any relationship.

Shura: Even when she has an opinion different from that of her daughters, she has the patience to wait and allow them time to consider her point of view without intruding.

Jennifer: I always become conflicted in a relationship when I see someone I care about being "herself," but in so doing, behaving in a self-destructive way. I want to respect her freedom to "be herself," but I feel a responsibility to point out what I observe.

Shura: Antoinette has the confidence in her daughters that they will consider carefully what she says. They may not do what she advises, but they are in some way influenced by her viewpoint.

Jennifer: It takes years to build such a relationship based on respect, trust, and mutual understanding.

Shura: And don't forget love. Unconditional love which may not be unconditional acceptance but is the basis for a strong and respectful relationship.

"God couldn't be everywhere, and therefore he made mothers."
—Jewish Proverb

What Do You Think?

Do you allow yourself to be who you are? Do you recognize your mother/daughter for the person she is? In what ways do you express this recognition?

Every Snowflake Is Different
Letter from Charlotte

Charlotte is an eighty-year-old mother of three adult daughters (and two sons). She writes from her own experience about her relationship with her adult daughters.

Just as when they were young, each of "the girls" is a unique individual—each having her own personality, her own strengths and her own trigger points. I have learned, over the years, how to relate to each of them and what pushes each one's buttons. Not only do I feel that I have a loving, trusting relationship with each of my daughters, but they have similar relationships with each other.

My daughters reached their formative years during the sixties, when many families around us were experiencing troubles with their children. I believe it may have been because we were a closely-knit family with a loving relationship with our extended families, that we, my husband and I, were able to convey positive values to our children. Because we were a relatively large family and a very active family, the children always had responsibilities to keep the household running smoothly. Our household was filled with people, fun, laughter, learning, and, yes, even disagreements. When situations would get out of hand or if topics arose that would need discussion, we would call a family counsel where we could talk things out and where everyone's opinions would be respected.

The forties and the fifties, when I came of age, had been different times with different roles for women. Typically, the most acceptable positions for women were teaching and social work. In my case, after graduating from Teachers College, getting married and having a family, there was no question that I would be a stay-at-home mom. My grown daughters, on the other hand, have chosen other professions and have been working women—some combining jobs with raising their respective families. I am appreciative of their life styles and I have confidence in their decisions about conducting their own lives. I am cognizant of the changing roles for women and of my daughters' ability to fit into this milieu.

I have attempted never to compare one daughter with another and have always tried not to impose my values upon them—except by virtue of their observations of the way I live my own life. Instinctively, I seemed to know just what might cause unnecessary friction in our interactions and I attempted to avoid these subjects. I still remain sensitive to their trigger points. Sometimes, I do wonder whether that means that I don't have an intimate relationship with my daughters, but I don't really think that is the case. We are always able to discuss, with honesty and respect for one another, whatever problems or situations that may arise.

When I think back to my own relationship with my mother and my mother-in-law, it is with fondness and love. As they grew older, I was always protective toward them. Now I sense that my daughters have similar feelings towards me. As for the future, I hope I will be able to continue my independent way of life. Inasmuch as we have mutual respect for each other, I would not choose to live with any of my daughters. I assume that, being the independent woman that each one of them is, they would understand and agree with my opinion.

In conclusion, I feel fortunate to have had the privilege of being the mother of these three most outstanding women who are a credit not only to our family, but also to society.

They have been able to
bridge the inter-generational
gap, with unconditional
love, and mutual respect.

Her strong boundaries enable
her to see the individual
uniqueness of each daughter.

What We Think
Shura's Voice

In a seemingly matter-of-fact way, Charlotte offers an insightful review of her experiences as the mother of mature women. Yet there is nothing matter-of-fact in her feelings of love and admiration for all her daughters.

From her account, family relationships have been developed in accord with an accepted and shared value system. Family life and individual behavior have been practiced according to the fundamentals of these values. Charlotte recognizes the social changes that have motivated her daughters to live their adult lives somewhat differently from the way she has lived hers. However, it seems that she has kept up with these changes to the point where she can accept the differences and maintain the wholesome, loving relationships that she built with them from their childhood.

What Do You Think?

Do you find it possible to treat each member of the family as a unique individual? Have you yourself received such treatment? Have you experienced broad social changes that affected the family structure and its internal relationships? In what ways? How did you cope?

Harmony
Mother/Daughter Interviews

Kay, the eighty-seven-year-old mother of Mary Kay lives with her daughter, son-in-law and family. Mary Kay and her husband work full time. Their two children are still in need of parenting, guidance and care. The three adults share responsibilities and duties. Kay looks after the children when Mary Kay is at work. The children enjoy their grandma's presence as an active participant in family life. We were fortunate in being able to interview both mother and daughter. We begin with Kay.

What do you think makes it work between you and your daughter?

I don't know that it's any one thing. We are considerate of each other and we love each other. I think I'm still her mother, a mother. It isn't like I want to tell them what to do, but I still give my true opinion. Sometimes it's what she wants to hear and sometimes it isn't. But we respect each other's opinion.

What happens when you get angry at each other?

Yes we get angry sometimes, but ten minutes later, we don't remember we were angry. I think it's healthy and good to get on each other's nerves once in a while. It's not often. It's never anything serious. I know her well and I know how to read her cues.

What's the hardest part of living together?

I feel guilty about my son-in-law having to live with his mother-in-law. I feel sorry for him. He's very nice and we get along, but he has had a mother-in-law living with him for fifteen years. You hear mother-in-law jokes. It was hard for me to move in as an in-law, but I wanted to take care of my grandchildren.

For me, it's also hard that I don't have any peers. I'm interested in politics, not crafts. I miss my peers. So, I keep myself busy all day.

It's a real gift you have given them and everyone involved wins.

I love them. I said to my daughter, "I'll never stop being your mother." My daughter is a working mother and also a stay-at-home mother. When she comes home, she does everything a stay-at-home mother does. I fill in the chores so she doesn't have to focus on that. She can just focus on her children. I'm needed. Moving keeps us going, so I can't sit. It also helps me financially to live with them and I love Berkeley. I love being able to help my daughter, but I do feel guilty about my son-in-law.

Interview with Mary Kay

Mary Kay is Kay's daughter

What is the nature of your relationship with your mother?

I would describe it as close. I genuinely like my mother as a person. She's warm. I like who she is. She is fun with a great sense of humor— at least she laughs at all my jokes.

I know that you live with your mother. How did that come about?

My father died when I was in law school. My mother never wanted to live in Fresno, California. They had moved there from Pittsburgh. My father always wanted to live in California. When my father died, I finished law school in Washington, D.C. and decided to return to the Bay area where I had gone to college. My mother loved the Bay area. I got pregnant, but I still wanted to work. My mother was alone, so she came up to the Bay area to live with us and help us raise my daughter. My mother is a first generation Italian-American and the oldest of ten. She spent a lot of time raising children. She helped my sister raise my niece. I trusted her, more than anyone else, to help us.

What makes it work for each of you?

My mother is happy to be in a place she loves. Berkeley is a good place for someone who is politically liberal like her. She can walk everywhere. All my friends love my mother because she is vibrant and interesting and genuinely warm.

The hardest thing for her is that she has no peers. My mother has outlived everyone she's very close to. It's very hard for her as she loses people in her life. She misses her circle of friends.

It sounds like you welcome having her in your life because you like each other.

My children are growing up with a second mother in the house. I think it makes a difference. They see the good and the bad. Their other grandparents live in New York and my children don't know them as well. I see people who live far from their own families adopting friends as families because those friends live closer to them. I feel very lucky that my children are getting to know my mother in this way. My husband and I are both lawyers and our hours are difficult to control. My mother enables us to work the long hours that are often required of us.

She has her own bedroom and bathroom, so she has her privacy. She allows us to pursue our careers fully. We are also freer socially. We know my mother is there for the children, so we are able to go out.

How do you work out the trouble spots?

The idea of "repression" just doesn't happen in my family. My mother is Italian, my father was Irish. Growing up, our house was alive with heated discussions. You tell the person what you think. You yell at them sometimes and then it's over. It's probably harder for my husband because it's not in his blood. But for me, if tension is out there, it's out there and then it's over. No grudges, no bottling up, no one harbors anything. We say what we think, but we are not mean about it. I think a lot of this chemistry is personality matching. A lot of people don't want a parent in the house because they don't want the parent to tell them what to do. I welcome it. I trust my mother's judgment and if we disagree, we discuss it, and sometimes I do what she wants me to and sometimes I won't. For example, if one of my daughters acts inappropriately, my mother may disagree with how I handle it, but we try to respect each other's point of view and judgment. Later, we will often see the other's viewpoint and tell each other so.

So, if we disagree at first, often one of us will consider the other's viewpoint and eventually come around. We respect each other and each other's opinions. I know there is no one who will ever love me as unconditionally as she does. If I really want to know the truth, I always ask my mother. I appreciate her being there for my family and me.

What would your mother say is the most difficult part of your arrangement?

The worst part for her is not having peers and not having her own place. It's always easier for my mother to give than to take. What she is doing is a labor of love. At eighty-five, things are getting harder for her. She is generous and wants to feel useful. She likes to see that she is needed in the house. It makes her feel good. She often tells me, "I don't know what I would have done if I didn't have you." That sentiment is mutual.

What We Think

This seems to be a win-win situation. Kay and Mary Kay have worked out a pattern of living and a system of mutual support. Each has identified her own needs as well as those of the other.

Kay needs to live in a situation where she can continue to feel useful and where she is not isolated. At this point in her life, she has selected these needs as her priorities over some of her earlier activities, such as her political interests. Mary Kay, a working mother, needs help in her role as family homemaker. She needs time with her children and opportunities to nurture her mid-life relationship with her husband. Her mother's help allows her the freedom to accomplish both tasks without being bogged down by a list of "to do's."

Both women realize that by combining their skills, extending their sensitivities toward others, and meeting mutual family needs they are making their relationship work in a healthy way.

This team has found graceful
ways to bridge all the gaps
that might possibly exist.

They have found all the
treasures of a three
generation household.

What Do You Think?

This living arrangement is somewhat unusual in today's culture. What do you think of it? What obstacles or pitfalls might be there for you, if you were living in such a mother/daughter situation?

Brief Encounters: What Makes It Work?

These brief interviews with mature daughters yielded the following replies.

Linda

Linda, a forty-something-year-old daughter of a seventy-five-year-old mother, says that the lovely magic between herself and her mother comes from the mutual patience and understanding they have with each other. Linda says that she picks up on her mother's mood and knows how to sculpt her conversations with her mother around them. If she feels her mother needs to have more space, she cuts the conversation short. She feels it is very important to acknowledge and respect each other's feelings and then to honor them.

Linda is always encouraging her mother's independence and enabling her to act on it. For example, her mother is now participating in Tai Chai sessions. Linda is delighted and listens to her mother's stories about this. She also has taught her mother to develop what she calls a "no-bullshit zone." She explains this saying that she encourages her mother to be assertive about her boundaries and especially not to accept bad treatment from other people.

She and her mother speak every day on the phone openly and honestly. She feels that it is key to their relationship that both she and her mother share the loving sentiment of wanting it to work. So they make it work.

What We Think

Linda is able to view her mother as a separate person and to recognize her needs as an older woman. She encourages her mother to enjoy new experiences, to maintain her self-esteem, and to be assertive. She believes that her mother is equally aware of Linda's maturity and boundaries. Describing their mutual patience, understanding, and sensitivity toward each other is a clue that both women are mindful of each other as mature women. Each contributes toward making their relationship friendly and loving.

What Do You Think?

Have you experienced a similar, balanced relationship? What were your skills in achieving it?

Kathy

Kathy is a fifty-year-old daughter whose mother was mentally ill. She describes how difficult it was to grow up with mother so afflicted. As a child, she did not understand that her mother's inconsistency and rejecting nature were driven by her mental illness. At the time, Kathy thought that these were expressions of her mother not caring about her. As she matured, she grew to understand that consistency in action is a most important expression of love. As a result, she values dependability and reliability.

What We Think

Kathy had to experience her own maturity before she understood the nature of her mother's mental illness and its impact upon behavior. The child cannot see or understand what she will perceive and understand later, as an adult. In the meantime, she is hurt by the behavior of what seems like an uncaring mother. Kathy translated her adult understanding into positive behavior toward her own children.

What Do You Think?

How do you have express your mother/daughter relationship? Through patience? Encouragement? Listening? Finding common ground? Developing hindsight or insight?

Have you found it necessary or possible, at your point in life, to understand difficult or puzzling behavior of your mother/daughter? How did you or do you cope with such behavior?

Leila

Leila is a 50-year-old woman living on the West Coast. Her mother raised her alone after having been abandoned by her biological father. Mother was left very bitter about the situation and blamed Leila for father's behavior. Leila grew up never knowing a father, only an angry, self-involved mother. Leila was never good enough, pretty enough, kind enough—for her mother. This taught her to feel bad about herself and be image conscious, always falling short of her mother's expectations of her. Leila also received confusing messages from her mother about what love is. If she were a "good girl" and pleased mother, mother would show her affection. There was no room for Leila in Leila's world, only her mother. Therefore, she matured without understanding about self-love. She has difficulty accepting love from any partner. Her conflict has been knowing that her mother taught her some self-destructive life skills, but not knowing with what to replace them. She is struggling to release herself from her self destructive conditioning, which keeps her connected to her mother's way. In her maturity, she is learning to replace these ways with self-acceptance. As a result, she is more able to accept her mother for who she is and not get too wrapped up in her own reactions to her mother's anger.

What We Think

Leila is struggling to find her way free from her conditioning. It's as if her mother had given her a compass that did not accurately mark North from South. Leila needs a new compass and struggles with her sense of betrayal. This is a lifelong struggle. She needs to be free of that good girl who actually sabotages her adult needs at this time of life. Leila is bravely facing herself as she is, learning to accept what she is learning about herself (even if she doesn't like it) with the goal of allowing for love in her life. The psychologist, Maslow suggests that humans experience a pyramid of needs. As each need is met, the person is able to move onto the next level of psychological development. At the base of that pyramid are the survival needs—food, clothing, and shelter. Above these lies Safety and beyond Safety stands Love. If Leila grows up with a mother on whom she relies for basic needs—but who cannot be relied on for love, how is she to feel safe?

What Do You Think?

Do you feel safe with your mother's love? Do you feel stunted at any point of your development? If so, how?

Ali

Ali is a first generation American woman of a Philippine family. She grew up in this family that lived in accord with the Asian culture where women are subservient and emotions are ignored. Her mother was of that generation of Philippine women that accepted this view and its practices. Mother was the target for her father's loud, abusive outbursts and remained quiet and accepting of his behavior. Their interaction depressed Ali on many levels. Growing up with a mother who conformed to this environment clashed with Ali's own self image as a woman.

Ali always knew she was different from the other women in her family. She was a non-conformist artist in a family of conformists, a family that neither appreciated nor accepted her world-view. Ali felt invisible and misunderstood by her family. She felt invalidated by her mother, her role model.

Ali needed to grow and to understand that she and her mother are women who are products of different cultures, different personality styles, different values, and different priorities. She needed to make room for both in her world. She needed to come to terms with her own disappointment at her mother's passivity. She also needs to accept herself as a person who aspires to be her own woman, independent, outspoken, and maybe even a bit outrageous!

What We Think

Part of the maturation process involves breaking away from what you have experienced as a child and what you have learned as part of your family group. As you grow, you begin to evaluate these experiences in light of your development. You then have an opportunity to become your own person. Sometimes this person you have become is similar to your role models; sometimes she is very different. When she is different, it is often difficult for her to dare to be different. However, people whose courage allowed them to be different and "to make a difference" have achieved some of the most important events in history. Ali needs to continue being brave and daring if she is to go through life being true to herself. This is an honorable quest.

What Do You Think?

Do you feel that you are similar to your family, your role models? Do you have the same values? Do you have different values that suggest that you are not at all like your family of origin? In what ways are you different? Can you bridge the gap and still maintain your integrity?

A Special Birthday

Harriet Richards

Daughter to Mother on a Special Birthday

Dear Mom,

I wanted you to know how I feel about you because today we are celebrating a special birthday. Almost every child praises her mother, extols her virtues, and thinks her mother is the absolute best. That is certainly true of you. I am one lucky daughter.

From the time I was a little girl, I can remember you being the center of our family. When there was a problem, or a crisis, you were the one to turn to. You always knew what to do and we knew we could count on you to come through for us. Even if you were busy preparing dinner or getting coverage for the staff at the nursing home, you found time to help me with my homework or give me advice, (not that I always took it)!

I don't know how you managed to be there for everyone, but you were.

My childhood and later years are filled with many wonderful memories of you—teaching me how to bake cookies, helping me to learn how to ride a bike, going shopping with me for my Prom dress, planning a wedding for me, and helping when Allison and Brian were infants. I remember all those Saturdays that we went shopping and had lunch together. Those were special times for me. As your daughter, I cherish the special times we have spent together. I would not be the person I am today without your love and support. You have always been there cheering me on. I hope that you will continue to do so, and that we may share many more birthdays together.

People say that a daughter is a gift. Today, I want you to know that having you for my mother is an even greater gift!

Love always,
Harriet

What We Think
Shura's Voice

Having discussed, in earlier chapters, so many diverse stories describing problematic mother/daughter situations, it seems almost simplistic to offer this letter from Harriet to her mother Faye in this final chapter.

Yet, it is completely heart warming to read these straightforward words written for a special occasion but extending through a lifetime of their important relationship. This note seems to epitomize the wish of every daughter and every mother to be able to present their relationship in such an acceptable and loving way.

What does it "take" to achieve the sharing of such seemingly mundane activities? We see beyond the cookies and the shopping; we recognize that they symbolize intimacy and love. We understand, of course, that this is exactly what we have been exploring throughout these chapters.

And, as Harriet writes, the mother and daughter who experience these events are the "lucky" ones.

What Do You Think?

Have you ever written a similar message to your mother/daughter? Are you among the "lucky ones?"

An Evening to Remember:
A Mother/Daughter Tale
Preface: Shura's Voice

One misty winter evening, I cabbed with my friend Dorothy down to the New York Public Library for the Performing Arts at Lincoln Center. She was to join her daughter Wendy there. Mother and daughter were there to read selected letters from a new book by Claudia Gitelman. This book, entitled, *Transatlantic Currents in Dance Modernism: Mary Wigman's Letters to Hanya Holm.* is about two famous women who had been important in the twentieth century modern-dance world. Mary Wigman was the leader of the German dance of expression (known as Ausdrukstanz) and Hanya Holm was a celebrated Broadway choreographer and prominent in American modern dance. Mary Wigman had been Hanya Holm's teacher and employer. As they worked on different continents, they maintained their significant friendship through their 164 letters that are reproduced in the book.

When we arrived at the theatre, I took my seat in the audience and Dorothy went backstage to meet her daughter. The next time I saw her, they were both seated on the small stage which featured a large photo of the book cover. Dorothy, tall, erect, and elegant was sitting beside Wendy who looked very interesting, scholarly yet informal.

The audience included listeners of three generations. Some were elders who had known or worked with Hanya Holm or Mary Wigman. Later, in the discussion that followed the readings, they shared their memories. There were also people of Wendy's age who had taught, choreographed or written for the dance world. Finally, there were young dancers and students of dance, who had come to listen, to learn, and to enjoy these memories.

Claudia Gitelman, author of the book, chaired the evening. She explained its background, described the two famous dancers, and also introduced the mother/daughter duo who would read the letters.

Dorothy, a woman in her eighties, had been a dancer in her youthful days. A creative and dynamic person, she had founded the New Milford School of Dance and the Perron Dance Workshop. She had been Wendy's first dance teacher and had imbued her with the love of the art. Wendy, her oldest daughter, the editor-in-chief of Dance Magazine, has been a dancer, performer, choreographer, teacher, and writer all her life.

It was utterly thrilling to see and hear them together on the stage sharing their common interest in this unique program. It was so appropriate for them to be reading the letters of this earlier dance/duo who had been in a quasi mother/daughter relationship themselves.

Wendy Describes the Evening

She writes, "Claudia Gitelman asked me to participate in a reading of her book of letters from dance pioneer Mary Wigman. I pulled my mother into it because the letters span five decades and I thought it would be good to have an older woman read the older letters while keeping the continuity of one person—or at least one family—but also because my mother was the first person who told me about Mary Wigman. My mother, in daily conversation, mentioned a lot of names of famous dancers—Diana Adams, Tanaquil Le Clerq, Jillana—whom I learned about much later. Mom had her dance school in our basement for almost four years—the Milford School of Creative Dance—and she always taught with a drum. I found out many years later that it was called a Wigman Drum. The sound of that drum is what gave me the sure sense of rhythm that helped me become a dancer.

"My mother had recently done a terrific job, reading in a play at the Williams Residence (a senior residence run by the Salvation Army where my mother lives), so I recommended her to Claudia.

"When the three of us got together at my mother's room in the Williams Residence for a rehearsal, we all read aloud for each other.

My mother not only read clearly and with great expression, but had that extra something that makes a story warm and exciting—that extra something she had when she read to my two brothers and me every night while we were growing up (me lying on her belly and Tommy and Reed at either side)—that something that eventually pulled me and all my siblings into literature and theatre.

"Sitting there with Claudia, I was so impressed with her reading that I was thinking, 'She's a star!' She had so much charisma—but maybe I was imagining it.

"Claudia, utterly delighted with the performance, said to my mother just what I was thinking, 'You're the star of this show.' So she had picked up on what I had been feeling! The vitality, the perfect theatrical timing, the subtly modulated knowledge of when to speed up or quiet down—when to hold back so the listener feels the suspense—or when to soup it up by infusing the words with a haughty or humble tone. And when we were doing the reading at the Library, all those qualities enlarged on the meaning of the letters and brought Mary Wigman to life."

Dorothy Adds Her Poignant Note to Her Daughter's Description.

She writes, "It was the only time that I could remember that Wendy and I performed together. I guess one can call it a performance since there was an audience and it took place in the New York Public Library for the Performing Arts at Lincoln Center, no less! Our readings went well.

"During the question and answer period, I deferred to Wendy and Claudia (our director) since I've been out of the dance field for forty years.

"The experience of sharing a stage with my Wenditchka was heartwarming and unforgettable. I know I didn't embarrass her."

Post Script, Shura's Voice

The entire audience was obviously affected by the warmth and emotion that pervaded the meeting. In the discussion that followed, many voiced questions and comments—shared information and memories. The mutual emotions of nostalgia and exhilaration were palpable, combining to weld this audience into a group, unified around a common interest.

The enthusiastic spirit of the evening was clearly expressed when the formalities ended. Many members of the audience thronged to the dais to continue their informal dialogue with the speakers. They reminisced eagerly, sharing stories and ideas along with their memories. The passion and excitement of this experience will linger long in the memories of those who attended. It was, indeed, an evening to remember!

What We Think
Jennifer's Voice

I love that Wendy included her mother in this project. It seems like a natural flow for Dorothy, the mother/dancer to be the one to represent mother/dancer in this particular theatrical piece. They certainly offer an inspiring example for possibilities of other mother/daughter projects. Speaking for myself, I have found this book-writing project with my mother to be an important growth experience for myself and for my relationship with my mother.

What Do You Think?

What interests do you share as mother/daughter? Can you see yourself doing a project together? What type of project would be appropriate for you? (It might be a one-time thing like baking a cake together, planning a party, or something more extensive.)

Musings

A Dialogue About Hurt, Pain, and Forgiveness

Shura: In any relationship there is a possibility of inflicting pain or being hurt.

Jennifer: If we come to the table accepting as a given that sometimes we experience pain or cause others to be hurt, it doesn't become quite the source of great suffering as it may otherwise be.

Shura: When there is great love, the flip side is the possibility of deep pain.

Jennifer: When there is great love, there is also a greater possibility of acceptance of the pain.

Shura: The experience of pain and hurt becomes a process. When you come through it, there is a possibility for achieving an even deeper level of unconditional love: but also the possibility of a complete break in the relationship.

Jennifer: Pain is intrinsic to love.

Shura: Therefore, love can accept pain.

Jennifer: That thought brings us to the concept of forgiveness.

Shura: People talk about forgiveness. I wonder where the word comes from. The Webster dictionary says it means, "to give up resentment of or claim to requital."

Jennifer: So forgiveness is a "letting go of."

Shura: Yes, I think so. I don't like to use that word. It implies a power situation.

Jennifer: I agree. When I forgive you it implies that I have the power to forgive you for any wrongdoing.

Shura: The idea of one person being in a position of power over another person is not helpful for a healthy relationship. It can actually be destructive.

Jennifer: People seek forgiveness when something goes wrong, or doesn't feel right. However, for the relationship to regain equilibrium, the process should not involve one person having power or authority over the other.

Shura: It is more important for both to focus on the desire to maintain the relationship.

Jennifer: So when people talk about forgiveness, it is really about looking for ways to come to terms with or to get over the bad feelings, the pain and hurt, that have developed.

Shura: The goal is "repair" rather than "requital;" that's why the term "forgiveness" does not seem appropriate.

Some Concluding Thoughts
About Forgiveness

The forgiveness process has altered the balance of a relationship. It has put one person in power over another.

There are many subtle complexities in the dimensions of the forgiveness process.

One must consider the feelings of the person doing the forgiving, but also the feelings of the person being forgiven.

The person who has been hurt is compensating for that hurt by assuming the power and the right to forgive.

Perhaps, we only think we are "forgiving" the other person; perhaps we are actually coming to terms with ourselves about the cause(s) of the pain or hurt that has been inflicted.

Untitled

By Denise Frasca

I am not afraid
Whether I walk this way
Alone or with your welcomed shoulder
Brushing against mine
I am not afraid
To forge a path
Or rediscover one that was
Abandoned long ago
I am not afraid
Of your sins or my own
I am not afraid of bad decisions
Or new places
Or wrong turns
Or dark spaces
I am not afraid
Because I know
I know
How to forgive

Exercise: "What Works and What Doesn't Work?"

Think about your mother/daughter relationship. Consider her and yourself as two mature women sharing an important part of their lives. Do you want to make any changes? If so:

What part of your interaction, your feelings, your behavior in this relationship would you...

Keep? How? What would you change?

Discard? How? What would you substitute?

What would you like your mother/daughter to keep?

What would you like her to discard?

What do you understand about your relationship?

What don't you understand about your relationship?

What other changes would you make to improve your relationship?

What other changes would you like her to make to improve the relationship?

Guideposts for Thought

1. If you want it "to work" you have to work at it.
2. What works is not the same for every one.
3. Family culture and communication patterns can differ widely within the different generations of the same family
4. Different people in this relationship may be satisfied with different patterns of behavior and communication.
5. Key to a positive relationship is a shared understanding of what would be considered acceptable by both mother and daughter.
6. Understanding and acceptance breed acceptance and understanding.
7. If a change in the relationship is needed or desired by either or both, at least one member of the dyad must initiate it.
8. It is important to realize that the relationship may not always work and may not work always.
9. Fear and pain are inherent in human relationships. It is necessary to understand and accept this concept in order to maintain a relationship.
10. Forgiveness is an equalizer that can deepen and firm the relationship.

Afterword

During the two years of writing this book, we had occasion to communicate with many women within the age groups we are writing about. Every woman was interested in the topic, had something to tell us about it, and wanted to read the book. Not everyone, however, was willing to contribute. For some, the experiences that they were recalling were too complex, too personal and often too painful! Some felt that they couldn't do justice to the essence of the relationship. Others could not bring themselves to share their experiences in public. Several women actually wrote a story, and, after thinking it through, decided to withdraw it.

Even those who withdrew their stories told us that they had found the writing worthwhile. They had been stirred to a reconsideration of earlier thoughts and feelings. This response—emotional, intellectual, and psychological—is precisely the purpose of this book. We hope that readers will be challenged to probe more deeply into the diverse contours, convolutions, and ins and outs of their own relationships.

The mother/daughter relationship is the core and beginning of all future relationships that a person will develop. This book knowingly leaves many dimensions unexplored. We refrained from even attempting to examine each topic to its deserved depth. Each chapter could be a book in itself. Our efforts were focused on our primary agenda—to stir the reader to consideration of her own experiences, emotions, and ideas as a result of reading those presented by other women.

We are aware of the omission of many important considerations in the lives of mothers and daughters. A most common comment was that we had not included the fathers, husbands, sons, and brothers. There is no question that their men are important figures in the lives of the women. However, the stories in this book remain focused on the women.

Another omission is that we have only hinted at the impact of such complexities as social policy, cultural mores, poverty and war. Also, we have certainly not examined the effects of such pathological circumstances as long term debilitating chronic diseases, mental illness, or neurological conditions such as Alzheimer's disease and others. This book has offered neither the information nor the viewpoints to be found in the myriad of professional texts.

Instead, we have presented some universal concepts of change and maturation, unconditional love, caring, filial and maternal responsibility, and the commonalities of the human condition which make life both interesting and challenging to everyone.

Finally, we have refrained from any judgments or suggestions that we have the answers or the recipe for a "better way. We believe strongly that these stories of women's experiences will help the reader find her own way through the demands of her own needs and her own life journey. We certainly hope so.

—Jennifer and Shura

Printed in the United States
77621LV00003B/49-99